◆ GRADES 5-1.
(YOUNGER CHILDREN MAY

TRUTHQUEST
HISTORY

MIDDLE AGES

(500-1400)

BY MICHELLE MILLER

To my dear friend, Gina Snyder, and her family,
who brought me into homeschooling
and helped me grow through the 'dark night of the soul.'

And to Kambi Scott and Brad Shepler,
who launched me into the middle years of my life
with their humble ministry
that led me to meet the Lord in a deeper way than I had known before.

Thank you, Courtney Bowman Norris, for the proofing and the incredible help!

TruthQuest History guides are not affiliated with the TruthQuest Inductive Study Bible.

Scripture taken from THE MESSAGE.
Copyright by Eugene Peterson, 1993, 1994, 1995
Used by permission of NavPress Publishing Group.

Other Scripture taken from the KJV, NASB, and NIV.
The following information is required for NIV usage:
all Scripture taken from the HOLY BIBLE, NEW INTERNATIONAL
VERSION. Copyright © 1973, 1978, 1984 International Bible Society.
Used by permission of Zondervan Bible Publishers.

ISBN 0-9752908-2-7
Printed in the United States of America

ThinkWrite, L.L.C.
PO Box 2128
Traverse City, MI 49685-2128
info@TruthQuestHistory.com

www.TruthQuestHistory.com

We'd love to have you join us on an online discussion group. Simply send an email to:
HIStoryQuesters-subscribe@YahooGroups.com

Notes for Dad & Mom:

"How does one 'do' TruthQuest History?
Isn't it just a lot of words and booklists?
It looks too easy.
Are my kids just supposed to read?
Aren't they going to 'do' something?
Where are the activities and the daily lesson plans?
How will I know if they're learning anything?"

Good questions! They show your spirit of excellence. But you're about to leave *regular history* behind.

" Regular history. What do you mean by that?
History is history! It's the people and events of the past.
It's the story of mankind! "

Is it? Where did you get that definition?

" Are you crazy?! I went to school. I sat through many a history class.
That's what we studied!"

Ah, but this is where I must challenge you, as I've been challenged. We only *think* that's what history is, because that's what was in our history books. So, we were learning not only the history they taught us, but also the *definition of history* they taught us. As Christian adults, though, we must hold every definition up to His blazing light. Is history indeed the story of mankind? Could the secular minds that birthed our history textbooks also have had a secular definition of history itself? Is it possible?

" Okay, okay! You yak a lot. Just let me think."

Gladly. That's just what I hope you'll do. I hope you think about history in a brand new way, for it is *not* first the story of mankind, but of the One who *made* mankind! Yes, the Lord God Creator initiated all life and, of course, the laws that govern life. He towers over all human existence. Thankfully, He chose to make us in His image; He chose to make our humanness special by giving us free choice. In other words, we have the privilege of deciding how we will *respond* to His preeminence!

God's initiation and *our response*...that's history. To the degree that we choose to believe and obey truth, to that degree our lives are blessed, our nations free and healthy, our science beneficial, our laws wise, our businesses prospering, and our art glorious. Each of these spheres of life cannot be understood without grasping the spiritual issues at their base. Again I say, *now that's history!*

" *Then that means...er, that means the opposite is true!* "

You hit the nail on the head! For a couple hundred years now, western civilization has put God on the sidelines of life, so that most history is taught as the story of mankind, as if people were the 'prime force' of the universe, as if they were the makers of themselves and of truth. How presumptuous! But there's more! After Darwin, little reason was seen to learn about the past; folks believed they were moving–on their own power–toward a perfect future. Since then, history has become a dull, meaningless 'obligation.' (No wonder it was so boring!) It should be a *personal* encounter with the King of the Universe, the Maker of our souls! It should be one of the most inspiring, personal, real, and intimate topics because it hooks us up with the truths that make life work! And our practical-minded boys *especially* need to know that history is about *right now*...about truth and power and law and right and good government...and all the other things for which this world is secretly hungering. Now *that's* something into which kids can pour their energies and ambitions!

" *I admit that my history classes were dull and meaningless,*
but I never wanted to admit that to my kids. "

Well, isn't it good to know all that's behind you?! Because history *is different* than what you were taught, you can teach history in a *different way* than you were taught. You won't need the artificial motivations of 'questions at the end of the chapter' and 'multiple-choice tests.' Why? Because you're not giving your kids dead material! Their eyes won't glaze over! Real truth is a spark that lights its own fire! All you have to do is convey truth to your kids in the way the Bible often does: through story. Hence, the copious booklists in this guide, and the happy fact that your children's 'history time' will be spent basking in great reading. Since all your children can learn together, they will play it, eat it, dream it, and talk it. Besides, as Jeremy Jackson put it: *history is philosophy* [beliefs] *teaching by example*. All these great books give lots of great examples. But...

" *What do you mean 'but?' That was sounding good!* "

All that good reading will still be mere humanistic fluff unless your kids have first been 'primed' to look for the deep spiritual issues at work in the lives of all those people and events they're reading about. Otherwise, your child will just be impressed by the human heroics. Ooh, more humanism, even though well-meant! That's where this guide's commentary comes in (the emboldened text). You'll see that a paragraph or two introduces each new topic. It does that 'priming' for you, and incrementally and subtly weaves together the deepest issues of this era of history. By the end of the guide, the veil will lift. History will be truly connected. The key importance of God and of beliefs will be seen, and the consequences of truth and untruth will be personally grasped by your children. If you, Mama, can just read the emboldened text too, you'll find yourself much better able to lead–and enjoy–vivid and profound conversations with your kids on some of the most important topics in life...and isn't that why we're homeschooling?! (It isn't absolutely necessary, but it's great if you can!) To help your kids think deeply, *ThinkWrite* exercises focus their seeking and synthesizing. (Sample answers are provided for you in Appendix 1.)

" *OK. So what about Day One. Tell me how I should plan each week.* "

Well, that's up to you. But you mustn't panic! Remember, this history is a new kind of history. You'll see that it takes on a life of it's own. You'll gather the little kids on the couch to read aloud to them, or you'll have kids sprawled around (or sitting in an orderly row) as each is absorbed in their books. At dinner time or while driving to piano lessons you'll have the most fascinating conversations, guaranteed! Older students can more deeply research special topics. Yes, this can be enough. It's that simple.

But you may want more, as befits your style. You can arrange special bi-weekly or monthly evenings where you gather as a family, or with other families, to give oral reports, put on skits, show off projects, and eat 'historical' food. You can all talk about what you've learned. Believe me! Your mother-in-law will be thunderstruck by the good, deep stuff flowing out of your child's heart! You can make notebooks, do narrations, or create timelines. You can draw, paint, sculpt, or build Lego towers. You can 'publish' a newspaper reporting on 'breaking news' and mail it to friends and family. (Many ideas are shared on our online discussion loop.) Or, you can do none of the above. You can simply immerse in and discuss great living books (as listed in this guide).

You'll be spending a great deal of time in this era, and the learning (both factual and ideological) will be quite impressive. You won't need any tests to show that your kids are learning; they'll be living what they learn, playing what they learn, talking what they learn, and praying what they learn!

As for overall planning, it's good to jot down a general plan. How many years do you have left with your students? How many historical eras do you need to cover? (There is a *TruthQuest History* guide for each era, after the Old Testament epoch.) If you have plenty of time, you can 'play' this guide by ear (knowing that the content of this guide has been carefully planned) and go at the rate of interest in your students, allowing time for greater or lesser depth as you feel led...*or* you can divide the number of units in this guide by the number of months you have available, and then see to it that you get through them in a timely fashion. Either way is fine.

You know what's best because you're the one who is seeking God for His plan for your family! He certainly doesn't have a one-size-fits-all-plan for His children. He has made each one uniquely, and has a unique plan for their lives; how and what they learn is part of that plan! Assuredly, I don't know what that plan is, so what right do I have to schedule your day?! Heaven forbid! (Literally!)

Enough said.

Let me just close, then, with a few 'housekeeping' details:

1.) Be assertive! Feel free to skip topics as you deem best. I've even mentioned some that can be omitted. Why do I include them at all? Because each child is unique. He may need to know something others do not. I've included as much as possible. Executive decisions are yours!

2.) All worrying about acquiring listed books is hereby outlawed! You can see that I've listed oodles of books...so you have as many choices as possible! Certainly, you're *not* supposed to read each book on each topic. It's a smorgasbord; enjoy all the delicious options! And, your library will have even more choices! But don't try to be such a 'good mother' that you bore your kids to tears by reading a million books on each topic! Wondering which books to select?

Probably, the newer the book, the more *post*-Christian is its outlook, but there *are* new books which are very good, especially in the picture book section.

3.) Books which were known or deemed to be *in-print* at the time of this writing are marked with an asterisk. (*) The asterisk does *not* mean it is a 'preferred' book, as is often assumed.

4.) We will often refer to a handful of books which provide a connected, narrative overview of Greek history for the sake of families who like to follow history through such a 'spine' book. However, if you feel spine books 'steal the thunder' of topic-specific books, you needn't worry. You can *definitely* use this *TruthQuest History* guide *without* reading the spine books because *TruthQuest History* is not the type of curriculum that leads you through a required set of books; instead, it helps you use whatever is at hand. If you decide to use one of these overview books, please know that references to these books are distinguished in the booklists by appearing *before* a dashed line. (--------) These books are:

> *Story of the World: Volume 2*, by Susan Wise Bauer   Gr. 3-6
>   Many classical-method families read this aloud to younger students.
> *Greenleaf's *Famous Men of the Middle Ages*   Gr. 3-7
> *An Island Story*, by H.E. Marshall   Gr. 3-8
> *Story of the Middle Ages*, by Christine Miller & H.A. Guerber   Gr. 4-8
> *The Middle Ages*, by Dorothy Mills (rare, but good)   Gr. 6-12
> *Dark Ages*, by Isaac Asimov   Gr. 8-12

5.) What happens if you can't find a book on a topic? Be creative! Use an encyclopedia or some other general resource. Hey, when you decide to use 'living books' (to learn through real literature), you're automatically committed to using whatever you can find. That's true no matter which curriculum guide you choose. See why I list so many books here? I'm trying to increase your chances of finding gems. A **copyrighted** list of books cited in this guide is also included in Appendix 2. It may **not** be copied for others, but you may make a copy to keep in your purse during book hunts!

6.) Don't forget you're the boss! You decide which topics, books, and films are appropriate for your family. I would have to live a thousand years to read all the books in this guide, so you know I've not personally read every book listed here. I have selected those from more reliable authors, publishers, or periods. Remember, the grade levels marked on the booklists denote estimated independent reading, *not recommended* reading, level. Only you, the parent, know best!

7.) Some kids have favorite book series, so the series names are in parentheses in the listings.

8.) Searches through your library's database will usually work *only* if you do *not* use a book's subtitle. So why did I include them in the booklists? They give a glimpse of the book's content. But few library databases include subtitles, so don't nullify your searches by including them.

9.) One last thing...enjoy!

Table of Contents

TruthQuest
History

Middle Ages
(500-1400)

TruthQuest History

☉

Middle Ages

1🍀 The Great Chessboard

Ah, the Middle Ages! Dashing knights and damsels in distress! Mighty castles and towering cathedrals! Prancing chargers and rustling gowns! Hmm. Were the Middle Ages really that colorful? And, hey, what do they mean by *Middle Ages* anyway? Middle of what?

Good questions! That mind of yours is working already! Well, the whole period from the fall of Rome (around the year 500) to the Renaissance and Reformation (around the year 1400) is known as the Middle Ages. That's a lot of years! Almost a whole millennium!

Anyway, the Middle Ages–the medieval period–got its name from later historians who were a mite humanistic. To them, the medieval centuries were merely dead space between two exciting chapters in history– the classical Greek and Roman period *before*, and the Renaissance's revival of classical Greek and Roman values *after*. These historians thought *real* history was about man learning to rule himself as the Greeks, Romans, and later Renaissance people had striven to do, while the Middle Ages was a 'backward' time when people were religious, seeing God over and in all.

So, were these historians right? It's a question worth asking–and answering– since folks around you believe them today. Are people repressed when God is a very

real part of their lives? Or, are folks better off with *God*less beliefs (they had many pagan gods), as the Greeks and Romans held? Was life easy and free for the pagan barbarians who moved into Europe at the falling of Rome? More good questions! Let's find out!

We'll begin, then, by unveiling the first half (500-1000) of the Middle Ages, the half-millennium more specifically known as the Dark Ages. Hmm. *Dark* Ages? They don't sound very good, do they?! Why were they *dark?* What was it like to live then? If these centuries were so dim, where was the hand of God? Is it even fair to call these years 'dark?' That's what we're here to explore!

Our exploration will fail, though, unless we have the most important tool–a grasp of the deepest beliefs of the previous civilization, which in this case is the Roman Empire. You *TruthQuest History* regulars are not surprised to hear me say that! You know it is people's beliefs about the two great questions of life (*Who is God?* and *Who, then, is mankind?*) which impact the rest of life: government, war, art, business, science, literature, and everything else! So, these effects are long-lasting! In fact, the beliefs not only affect the current civilization, but the following ones as well! That's why I call them the *Big 2 Beliefs*.

These beliefs are big for another reason too. They show the power of God's truth, for if what we believe is true, good things

1

happen. If what we believe is false, well... you can guess! So, do you see the big picture? You'd better, for in *TruthQuest History* you'll not be memorizing meaningless facts about people who lived centuries ago. How silly! Instead, you will explore profound truths which empower today and tomorrow!

So, to dig into the heart–the good, the bad, and the ugly–of the medieval 'Dark' Ages, we must begin by quickly recapping the *Big 2 Beliefs* of Rome.

Even if you didn't study with us before, you know about the mighty Roman Empire. It was all about power...human power. Why, statues of caesars were actually worshiped, so you can see they made a god of human authority. That was, simply put, Rome's *Big Belief #1.* They thought that by their power, by doing what seemed good to their orderly minds, they could manage the world. That's called *humanism*, by the way, and it simply means humans are trying to take the role of God.

Want proof? Get a load of this birthday greeting composed not for the birth of Jesus Christ, but for the caesar (Augustus) ruling at the time:

> *This day has changed the earth. The providence which rules over all has filled this man with such gifts for the salvation of the world as to make him the savior for us and for coming generations. Of wars he will make an end....It is impossible that one greater than he can ever appear. The birthday of God has brought to the world glad tidings.*[1]

Makes your flesh crawl, doesn't it?! But aren't we already seeing into the deep, dark

---

[1] Norman Langford, *Fire Upon the Earth* (Philadelphia: Westminster, 1950) 10.

heart of history? Didn't the very first people–Adam and Eve–choose to "be like God" by deciding themselves what seemed good? Didn't they think their plan for life would work out great?

You had better not, for one itty-bitty second, think I'm only talking 'church-stuff' for this is the pulsing center of life. You'll feel it throbbing all through the Middle Ages, because it was a time of epic battle, not just between kings and knights, though there was plenty of that. The *real* struggle which fueled the others was the age-old question: who is in charge? God or man?

Keep your eyes peeled, and pray hard for wisdom, because that's just the question we want to answer about the Middle Ages. Of course, the medieval period was not a blank slate. Coming into it, as we've said, were the two competing beliefs held by the Romans: the authority of God as understood by Christians, and the human authority of the Roman government. That massive, fierce, rich, orderly bureaucracy was their pride and joy. It stretched over most of the 'known' world and captured in its net each individual in the realm. "All roads led to Rome," and so did everything else! The Roman Empire had total control centered in its capital. Indeed, the very name of their great empire was the name of that capital city: Rome. Can you think of other empires named after cities?

Of course, there's a word for this–there always is!–*centralization*. It meant more than just having a capital city though. The essence is that no one in a local setting could be trusted with much oversight, let alone the masses themselves. No, the top guy in the capital had to control everything. He even decided–since he was the god of

⟨ Centralization ⟩

Rome—who lived and who died. And there you have Rome's *Big Belief #2.* Humans were valuable only if the government said so. Others were utterly dispensable, even for the mere sake of 'sport,' as in the gladiator 'games.' You know the Roman love of bloodshed and vulgarity is mind-numbing to us. But that's about the quickest way to show you (in this brief overview) how a pagan becomes a sort of humanist, who then becomes a barbarian.

Yes, the mighty Roman Empire smugly thought it would rule the world forever...but it collapsed into humiliating dust, thus beginning the 'Dark' Ages of the medieval era, during which hordes of even more barbaric invaders from the north and east swarmed over the high-falutin' remains of Roman civilization, wreaking their special brand of havoc. Here's the question, though. Were the incoming barbarians having a heyday because they were so strong...or because Rome's *Big 2 Beliefs*—which placed divine power in the hands of one human—made the empire weak?

But, hey! There was another *Big Belief #1* coming out of Rome and into the Middle Ages. The mighty church knew the Lord's goodness and overarching power! They knew He is in charge of governments and people! He is the one Who initiates life and truth! He is the one Who came to die and rise again! He is thus the *centerpiece of civilization!*[2] We are given the privilege of deciding how to respond, and it is a high privilege! We have that authority in our own lives.

While we're talking about authority, ponder this:

The church, you see, is not peripheral to the world; the world is peripheral to the church. The church is Christ's own body, in which he speaks and acts, by which he fills everything with his presence (Eph. 1:22, *Message*[3]).

Yes, all during the time of the Roman Empire, the church—in which God vests some of His authority—was growing and growing and growing! At first, Roman onlookers thought the church was merely a beleaguered minority, but it was soon the official religion of the Roman Empire! As you know, 'official' status brought earthly power to the church and many changes—some good and some not so good, as you'll see.

Here's the irony: with all its authority, the Roman Empire thought it would wipe out Christianity as easily as it would swat a pesky gnat. But in the end, the great Roman Empire collapsed, and all that was left standing was the church! Nero and Diocletian (strong Roman caesars) would not have believed it!

You're ready now to get a grip on the prelude to the Middle Ages—say, around the year 400. It will help to think of Europe's map as a giant chessboard. But you must not forget something *terribly* important! Chess pieces have only the power given to them by the maker of the game! Do you get my drift? We're going to talk a lot about *real* kings and queens and bishops and knights and castles and pawns...but it is the Maker of it all who has the highest power!

---

[2] I heard this phrase in a taped sermon played at a church service; alas, I do not know whom to credit.

[3] I know the *Message* is a highly paraphrased rendition of the Bible so it only has certain merits, but the wording of this verse powerfully and effectively conveys an important truth to young people. Feel free to cross-reference literal translations as well.

Our chessboard looks pretty funny right now. No kings are standing; in the year 400, the mighty Roman Empire is dying. Most of the other pieces are knocked over too. There is no real civilization and no order. Barbarian chieftains are grasping squares of Roman territory.

Think there's no real leader on the board then? Look again! You're just too accustomed to thinking of kings and queens as power-holders. Do you see? There *is* one chess piece still standing: the bishop! Yes, he represents the great church. And during the latter years of the Roman Empire, the church, as we said, was becoming stronger and stronger!

Think of it! With the collapsing of Rome's leadership (which was barbaric enough) and the volatile realms of the more-barbaric invaders, the church would have an incredible opportunity to serve and guide Europe during the Dark Ages. Not only could she spread the life-changing gospel, but she could teach the nations (soon to be forged from barbarian holdings) the godly truth about human worth, law, family life, government, business, justice, science, etc. As you know, obedience to God's principles is always the path to lasting freedom and blessing for people *and* nations!

But unlike a Hollywood movie, you cannot label the white-hats and black-hats as easily as you may first think. It is people's *Big 2 Beliefs* that reveal what they *really* think and what they will then do. So, that's what you must watch (start *ThinkWrite 1: Investigation Supreme*), because as people–even the white hats–come to power in the Middle Ages, there would be even more temptation to prideful ideas and self-serving goals. We *all* struggle with this! Of course, this is not to say people shouldn't have leadership–God ordained it! But it must be very carefully and very humbly held, or else... Well, you'll see!

ThinkWrite 1:
Investigation Supreme!

Throughout your study of the Middle Ages you must carefully watch the *Big 2 Beliefs* of the secular rulers and the church leaders.

That means you're looking for two things: Based on their actions, who do you think was their real authority? God or themselves? How did they treat others based on that view of authority?

To help you sort this out, try to nail down the *Big 2 Beliefs* of a pagan, a barbarian, a humanist, and a Christian. How similar are these? Can one claim to be a Christian, and still be one of the above? Can people be pagans or barbarians now?

At the end of this guide, please wrap up your insights. They'll be rich!

Saddle up your steed; we're off!

2✍ A Cast of Thousands: The Barbarians Onstage

We begin our study of the Dark Ages (the first part of the Middle Ages) with a look at the newcomers to the stage, the latest pieces on the chessboard: the barbarian invaders. (You may have met some of the barbarians when studying in the Rome guide with us, but we'll probe more deeply this time since they overlap both periods.) Actually, you're going to hang with *two* sets of barbarians...and you thought history would be dull!

First, there were the 'local' barbarians–the wild Celts and Teutons who had not been conquered by Rome. They lived beyond the Empire's northern borders. And then there were the 'long distance' barbarians–the Goths, the Vandals (both originally Germanic), and the Huns (especially fierce warriors from Asia). They were now sweeping in from further north and east. That's a lot of barbarians, don't you think?!

What happened? Well, it's an interesting story! The Romans–who were hardly neighborly–had been fighting the nearby Teutonic and Celtic barbarians right along, always trying to conquer them. Of course, these local barbarians were glad to return the favor. They made daring forays into Roman territory whenever their lack of farming made them hungry for food and land.[4] These glimpses of Roman civilization didn't seem to tempt them; the barbarians remained utterly uncivilized and held a strong sense of independence. Life got easier for

> ### ThinkWrite 2: "Shuffling the deck!"
>
> Begin a map showing the shuffling of the European people groups. There was a lot of movement! It shaped western history and the development of modern European nations, that's all!
>
> I'll be specific. Map the basic movements and/or locations of general groups (Celts and Teutons) and specific tribes (Britons, Picts, Scots, Franks, Vikings, Angles, Saxons, Jutes, Vandals, Visigoths, Ostrogoths, and Huns). You'll be working on this during the next several sections of this guide.
>
> Don't their very names sound intimidating?! That's because we still use some of their names for certain descriptive words. Need I say more?

them anyway, because as Rome weakened during the 200s and 300s, she slowed her conquests. By the 400s, the great Empire was even sucking in her borders so she had less to defend, thereby yielding rich Roman lands to the neighbor barbarians. Right about then, the 'long distance' barbarians made their move.

What were the flabby, corrupt Romans to do? The great military power of the ages was now too sickly to even defend itself. Time to hire out. The local barbarians–who had been enemies of Rome for centuries–were now paid to protect her from the long distance baddies! Do you see? Rome had–in one stroke–dissolved her border with the local barbarians. They were now partners against worse barbarians. You can bet a real blending began to occur. The Teutons, especially, moved into Roman society, intermarried, settled down, and injected their locally-oriented ideas into ever-centralized Roman thought.

---

[4] Isaac Asimov, *The Dark Ages* (Boston: Houghton Mifflin, 1968) 3.

So get this picture in your mind: the further-out barbarians were pressing deeper into Europe, ever Rome-ward. The squeeze was on, and people (ancestors to most of us) were getting shuffled! It was a time of great stirring after centuries of fairly static Roman rule. Interesting! Wouldn't you like to be a mouse in the corner when heavenly decisions were made regarding all these things...not that I know what those decisions were, mind you!

Yes, there was a step backward from the previous Greek and Roman achievements in engineering, architecture, science, and math. The barbarians foolishly pulled down important aqueducts and took pleasure in destroying important buildings, libraries, and artworks since these things were not of value to them. Roman homes had often been of good stone, and the wealthiest even had a sort of central heat and water supply; but the barbarians–great and small–lived in tents and huts, foraging for wild roots and shooting what wild game was at hand. The barbarian men plied only war and dice (hardly constructive activities) not law and engineering, as had the Romans.

Anyway, you'll want to keep your eye out for the chief barbarian players just prior to AD 500 (whom you may have met when studying the fall of Rome): Alaric the Visigoth, Genseric/Gaiseric the Vandal, Attila the Hun, Clovis the Frank, and Theodoric the Ostrogoth. They will also be mentioned later, so don't worry if you don't find a lot of information right now. Just watch for their names. (Begin *ThinkWrite 2* as you study the barbarians.)

2a♣ General resources

You probably won't be surprised to discover that few books are written for youths on the topic of barbarian invaders! Don't worry; just use whatever is handy or check an encyclopedia!

Oops, I try not to talk so much at one time, but we better get a little 'housekeeping' done before we start. You may be one of the families who *elects* to study history through the use of "spine" books–historical overview books which provide continuity of coverage. For your ease, I'll follow a few spines throughout this guide, giving you several choices. The various chapters in these spines will be cited gradually as we work our way through the medieval era. To make it easier to spot the spines, they are listed first in each booklist *before* a dashed line (--------).

However, it is not (usually) *necessary* to use spine books. Indeed, some families prefer the topic-specific books listed *after* the dashed line in each booklist. So, you can be selective. For example, you can use a spine book all the time, or only when your library doesn't have a topic-specific book. Keep in mind, though, that spine books are sometimes the only known books addressing certain topics. These spines are great books, so don't be afraid of them. You may want to use them, you may not. Just see how it goes. In other words, don't worry!

Now, let's dig in!

Story of the World: Volume 2, by Susan Wise Bauer, Ch. 1   Gr. 3-6
  Classical-method families like to read this aloud to their grammar-age students.

*Greenleaf's *Famous Men of the Middle Ages*, Ch. I-IV   Gr. 3-7

Story of the Middle Ages, by Christine Miller & H.A. Guerber, Ch. XVI-XX   Gr. 4-8
  Earlier chapters of this book (I-XV) are actually set during the Roman era. It would be
  very wise to catch up on those if you haven't covered that material previously.

Middle Ages, by Dorothy Mills, Ch. I and Ch. V, Pt. 1   Gr. 6-12

Dark Ages, by Isaac Asimov, Ch. 1 & 2   Gr. 8-12

Child's History of the World, by V.M. Hillyer, Ch. 39-40   Gr. 1-4
  Most families enjoy this book as a parental read-aloud for young students, thus the
  grade recommendation is not for independent reading, as is usual in this guide.

Birthdays of Freedom: Vol. 2, by Genevieve Foster, pp. 5-6   Gr. 2-5
  Some recent scholars doubt the accuracy of the Teuton/German emphasis on
  democratic government, but it's a strong possibility!

The Barbarians, by Odile Bombarde (Young Discovery Library)   Gr. 2-6

First Book of the Barbarian Invaders, by Donald Sobol (First Book)   Gr. 3-8
  Mr. Sobol is the author of the beloved 'Encyclopedia Brown' books.

Middle Ages: Cultural Atlas for Young People, by Mike Corbishley, pp. 12-15   Gr. 3-8
  This is probably in most public libraries.

The Barbarians, by Richard Suskind   Gr. 5-12
  This book contains an excellent map.

The Invaders of Rome, by Bern Keating   Gr. 5-12

The Celts of Northern Europe, by Kathryn Hinds   Gr. 7-12
  We'll meet the Celts again later in books that focus more on their British ties, but this
  book focuses on the race as a whole which was spread widely over Europe.

Dark Age Warrior, by Ewart Oakeshott   Gr. 8-12
  I've heard this is amazingly detailed and offers excellent drawings.

2b♣ Attila the Hun

First Book of the Barbarian Invaders, by Donald Sobol, pp. 45-49 (First Book)   Gr. 3-8
  This entire book was cited above, but these pages refer to Attila in particular.

The Invaders of Rome, by Bern Keating, Ch. 9   Gr. 5-12
     This entire book was cited above, but this chapter refers to Attila in particular.

Attila, by Stephen Vardy (World Leaders Past and Present)   Gr. 7-12

Attila the Hun, by Robert Webb (Masters of Infamy)   Gr. 7-12

Fiction/Historical Fiction

*The White Stag, by Kate Seredy   Gr. 4-10
     This stirring and dramatic story relates the Hun legend of Attila's rise to power. (It may make dark Hun religious elements seem real to some readers because the book is so powerfully written; parents should use discretion.)

3✿ Heart of a Barbarian

We need to understand these barbarians because their bloodlines and beliefs contributed to what would become the nations of Europe: Germany, France, England, Spain, Italy, Hungary, the Scandinavian countries, etc.

You're probably saying, "Hey! We just studied those guys in the last section! Why are you bringing them up again?" You'd have a good point *if* the purpose of learning was to cram a bunch of meaningless facts about dead people into your brain, an accomplishment that is too often temporary anyway. The Bible says that knowledge (alone) puffs up. We're after wisdom!

We want always to be focused on truth, and analyzing the deepest beliefs of people while measuring them against God's laws teaches us a lot about the power of His truth...and what happens when it is denied or ignored.

> *ThinkWrite 3:*
> *"What'chya believe?"*
>
> After you've gotten a taste of the Teutons' belief system, write a paragraph describing it. Be on the lookout for their beliefs about personal freedom. Give your hypothesis about what type of behavior you might see from people who held these beliefs. At the end, see if you're right!! You'll need this for your *Investigation Supreme* too.

That's why we need to take a <u>short</u> dip into the *Big 2 Beliefs* of the barbarians by checking their spiritual values as revealed in their religious stories/myths. We'll use the Teutons as a sample. We'll then know who they believed to be God, and what they made life like for people. Now, that's worth learning for it will help us better know and love God's truth ourselves, as well as helping us avoid the mistakes of the past! (Do *ThinkWrite 3* while studying this topic.)

[<u>Mandatory note for parents</u>: I've listed some resources below, but because you need to consider your children's spiritual maturity before beginning this topic, *the grade recommendations in this section refer to reading level, not appropriateness!* The goal is to see the Teutons' *Big Belief #1* in their religion's dark nature and their *Big Belief #2* in the basing of human value on strength. You may feel your children already grasped these concepts in the reading they just completed; that's fine. Others may want the insight which comes from reading a couple Teutonic myths (their religious stories), but I would strongly encourage you to sample only a chapter or two instead of reading these entire books, because even with our analytical purpose here, you must be very careful about pagan religious input. Furthermore, unlike Greek myths, the Teuton legends contributed little to our current literature and culture, thereby eliminating yet another reason to delve deeply into Teutonic mythology. Whenever learning mythology, remember that Satan is a counterfeiter, but we can always see the surpassing purity of God's truth above all!]

3a✤ General resources

*Greenleaf's *Famous Men of the Middle Ages*, Intro I   Gr. 3-7

Dark Ages, by Isaac Asimov, Ch. 1 & 2   Gr. 8-12
> These chapters were also cited in the previous section on barbarians.

Child's History of the World, by V.M. Hillyer, Ch. 39   Gr. 1-4
> This chapter was also cited in the previous section on barbarians.

Gods and Goddesses of the Ancient Norse, by Leonard Everett Fisher   Gr. 2-6
> This offers 'snapshots' of the various deities; it may not focus as much on their 'stories.'

First Book of the Barbarian Invaders, by Donald Sobol, pp. 16-27 (First Books)   Gr. 3-8
> This book has a helpful section on Germanic beliefs without going into details of the mythology. It also shows the rugged nature of their lifestyles and the value they placed on the lives of men, women, and children...which all tie with their beliefs. Good option!

Adventures with the Heroes, by Catharine Sellew   Gr. 4-9

Children of Odin, by Padraic Colum   Gr. 5-12
> I think this is being republished as: *Nordic Gods and Heroes.*

Legends of the North, by Olivia Coolidge   Gr. 5-12

Tales of the Norse Gods, by Barbara Leonie Picard   Unknown

For another peek at barbarian beliefs, you can read the famous *Beowulf*. It just happens to be the oldest extant tale in a modern European language, so it appears in most literature textbooks. It was probably written some time during the eighth century (700s), and is the story of an Anglo-Saxon warrior who battles monsters and Northmen (Vikings). The authors of *Invitation to the Classics*—a Christian analysis of literature—feel it reveals the conflict between the barbarian way of life and the incoming ideas of Christianity.[5] You'll find many versions of *Beowulf,* including retold versions for young students. I've mentioned some, but not all, below.

[<u>Mandatory note for parents</u>: I sincerely hope you can read the first couple paragraphs in the short article about *Beowulf* in the aforementioned *Invitation to the Classics* because it will otherwise be much harder to understand the deeper meaning of the book. Considering the story's gruesomeness (which aptly shows barbarian values), it's nice to probe for something of greater value. If all this sounds off-putting or if you have younger students, don't worry! Your study of the Middle Ages will not be disabled if you skip *Beowulf!* Be at peace! And don't forget, because of the nature of this story, the grade recommendations below refer only to reading level, not appropriateness! *You'll need to be the judge of that!*]

Story of the World: Volume 2, by Susan Wise Bauer, Ch. 2c   Gr. 3-6
    Classical-method families like to read this aloud to their grammar-age students.

Be a Wolf! by Brad Strickland (Adventures of Wishbone)   Gr. 3-6

Heroic Deeds of Beowulf, by Gladys Schmitt (Legacy)   Gr. 4-8
    This is a highly adapted version, so it may be more acceptable for younger readers.

Beowulf the Warrior, adapted by Ian Serraillier   Gr. 6-12
    A translation intended for older youth.

Invitation to the Classics, by Louise Cowan & Os Guinness, pp. 85-88   Gr. 8-12

Beowulf, adapted by Rosemary Sutcliff   Gr. 9-12
    A translation intended for older youth.

Beowulf, by various translators   Gr. 10-12
    Invitation to the Classics cites the translation by Charles Kennedy as the most poetic, but you can feel free to use whatever version is available.

Favorite Medieval Tales   Osborne, Mary Pope

---

[5] Louise Cowan and Os Guinness, *Invitation to the Classics* (Grand Rapids, MI: Baker Books, 1998) 85-88.

? DVD Beowulf + the Anglo-Saxons

4 • The Angles and Saxons Come for a Visit

Okay. You have a pretty good idea about who these barbarians were. Let's see what they were up to in Britain, for starters. You may recall the native people of Britain (called *Britons* by the Romans and considered by them to be barbarians) had been chafing under Roman rule for about 400 years. When Rome had to face Attila the Hun in Gaul[6] and itself began to fall, she recalled her troops from Britain in the early 400s and took many of the best native fighters with her. Surprisingly, this left Britain in a tough spot. The feisty, even-more-barbaric Pict and Scot tribes–living north of the protective walls the Romans had built after giving up defeating them–soon realized there were no longer any Roman soldiers on the other side! Ah, Britain was ripe for their picking and they swept in, destroying and pillaging. H.E. Marshall puts it this way:

> *During nearly all the time that the Romans remained in Britain, the Britons fought with them and rebelled against them. But, strange to say, hardly had the Romans gone away than the Britons wanted them to come back....So in despair they sent a letter to the Roman Emperor, asking for help. This letter was so sad, that it was called "The groans of the Britons." "Come and help us," it said, "for the barbarians drive us into the sea, and the sea drives us back again to the barbarians. So those of us who are not killed in battle are drowned, and soon there will be none of us left at all."*[7]

But the Romans were too busy losing their own battles. The Britons were on their own (in 410, officially), and good leadership was hard to come by. A man named Vortigern had an idea. He thought he'd invite the Saxons (actually, the intermingled Angles, Jutes, and Saxons who lived in the lands we now know as Germany)[8] to come to a little Pict-chasing party. They came by the shiploads under their captains, Hengest[9] and Horsa.

There was a problem. The Picts, Scots, and Celtic Welsh (Cymbri) were eventually beaten back, and the Anglo-Saxons began to notice Britain was a mighty fine place. Quite simply, they didn't want the party to end. Besides, the Huns were pressing on their continental homeland, making their decision to stay a whole lot easier.[10]

---

[6] Christine Miller and H.A. Guerber, *Story of the Middle Ages* (Ft. Collins, CO: Nothing New Press, 2002) 66.

[7] H.E. Marshall, *An Island Story* (New York: Frederick A. Stokes, 1920) 31-32.

[8] There is confusion about the ethnic and linguistic roots of the tribes living in what we now think of as Germany. It seems Teutonic tribes ousted or absorbed earlier Celtic tribes, so there is no clear way of knowing to what degree the Germanic tribes were Teutonic or Celtic or both! We know the Bible refers to people movements as a result of the flood and the Tower of Babel. The word *Teutonic* is often deemed synonymous with *Germanic*, especially since the Romans called the people of the German area *Teutones*, as Mr. Asimov explains in the first pages of his *Dark Ages*. Bill Cooper may have more on this in his book **After the Flood*, if you desire further input.

[9] Sometimes spelled *Hengist.*

[10] Bern Keating, *Invaders of Rome* (New York: G.P. Putnam's Sons, 1966) 99.

You can imagine the Britons had not planned to trade one invasion for another, and they were unhappy that the Angles and Saxons were more pagan. Yes, Christianity had begun to spring up in Britain during Roman rule there, as you learned in the last guide, though it was not yet widespread. The awful Druid religion still held many Britons in its grip, as well as Scots, Picts, and Cymbri. Well, the Britons expressed their opinion about the Anglo-Saxons' overlong stay at sword-point.

What was the Anglo-Saxon response? They simply invited more relatives–boatloads of them–to join the party! So much did they move in and settle down that Britain would eventually be known as Angle-land...*England!* By the year 600, their domination was complete[11] and the surviving Celts were hiding out in rugged Wales and Cornwall, losing their Romanized ways and their use of Latin, resuscitating their Celtic languages (now Welsh and Cornish), and too-often lapsing back into Druidism after having known Christianity.[12] Of course, there would be mighty Celtic resistance and Christian commitment, especially under a particular hero you've heard about all your life. We'll meet him in a bit. (Heh, heh...is the suspense getting to you?!) In the meantime, though, the various Angle and Saxon chieftains carved out separate 'kingdoms' for themselves: the small realm of the southern Saxons (Sussex), the eastern Saxons (Essex), the western Saxons (Wessex), and there was also East Anglia. These are still the names for key regions of England today! Get the picture?

> The Anglo-Saxon burial ship found at Sutton Hoo reveals much about their culture. You may find books on this topic at your library, or if you're in London you can look at the actual artifacts in the British Museum! Talk about a field trip!

✗ *Story of the World: Volume 2*, by Susan Wise Bauer, Ch. 2a-b	Gr. 3-6
Island Story, by H.E. Marshall, Ch. VIII-X	Gr. 3-8
Story of the Middle Ages, by Christine Miller & H.A. Guerber, Ch. XXVII	Gr. 4-8
The Middle Ages, by Dorothy Mills, Ch. VII, Pt. 1a	Gr. 6-12
Birthdays of Freedom: Vol 2, by Genevieve Foster, p. 7	Gr. 2-5
Looking at History, by R.J. Unstead, pp. 42-49	Gr. 2-5
Saxon Villages, by Robin Place (Beginning History)	Gr. 2-5
The Anglo-Saxons, by Peter Chrisp (Look into the Past)	Gr. 4-12

---

[11] R.J. Unstead, *The Story of Britain* (London: Adam and Charles Black, 1969) 33.

[12] Keating 100.

Saxon Britain, by Tony Triggs	Gr. 4-12
The Invaders of Rome, by Bern Keating, Ch. 6	Gr. 5-12
Story of Britain, by R.J. Unstead, pp. 32-33	Gr. 5-12
Green Blades Rising: The Anglo-Saxons, by Kevin Crossley-Holland	Gr. 9-12
The Anglo-Saxons, by Roger Coote (Look into the Past)	Unknown

Activities

**Anglo-Saxon Helmet* (British Museum Cut-Out Model)	Various

Fiction/Historical Fiction

Hengest's Tale, by Gillian Paton Walsh Legend of Saxon-Jute invader.	Gr. 6-12
Dawn Wind, by Rosemary Sutcliff British boy survives Battle of Aquae Sulis.	Gr. 7-12
**Lantern Bearers*, by Rosemary Sutcliff	Gr. 7-12

This much-praised novel is also listed in *TruthQuest History: Ancient Rome* because it deals with the end of Roman rule in Britain. But it also covers Vortigern and the coming Anglo-Saxons, so if not read earlier, you may want to enjoy it now.

5♣ Mighty King Arthur

So who was the famous British hero I mentioned earlier? The one you've heard mentioned all your life? You're about to meet him! King Arthur!! Arthur was probably a real Briton (Celt) who lived during the 500s and whose exploits–however great they may actually have been–have been told and retold until they've achieved legendary status! There is reason to believe he was a true Christian. One thing's certain: he was fighting the Anglo-Saxon invasion with every fiber of his being, even if no one else was helping him! I better not tell

> *ThinkWrite 4:*
> *"Yeah, King Arthur!"*
>
> What lessons can you learn from looking at the life of King Arthur?

his story, but let you discover it yourself! I'll list only a sampling of books; you'll find plenty at your library. Be careful, though, to avoid those which are darkly mystical; you'll find the darker books tend to focus more on a supposed magician named Merlin than on King Arthur himself. (Do *ThinkWrite 4* after learning about King Arthur.)

5a ❧ General resources

Island Story, by H.E. Marshall, Ch. XI-XIII   Gr. 3-8

Story of the Middle Ages, by Christine Miller & H.A. Guerber, Ch. XXVIII   Gr. 4-8

The Sword in the Stone, by Grace Maccarone   Gr. K-2

Arthur and the Sword, by Robert Sabuda   Gr. 2-6
    This striking book is illustrated so that each page looks like stained glass.

The Story of Young King Arthur, by Clifton Fadiman (Legacy)   Gr. 2-6

King Arthur and His Knights, by Mary Robinson (Landmark)   Gr. 3-8

The Sword of King Arthur, by Jay Williams   Gr. 4-8

The Boy's King Arthur, edited by Sidney Lanier   Gr. 6-12
    Gorgeous illustrations by N.C. Wyeth enhance Lanier's slight editing of Sir Thomas
    Malory's epic rendition of Arthur's story. This is in many libraries.

King Arthur, by Don Nardo   Gr. 6-12
    This book opens with a chapter analyzing the historical evidence regarding Arthur.

Brother to Galahad, by Gwendolyn Bowers   Gr. 7-12

Sir Gawain and the Green Knight, by J.R.R. Tolkien   Gr. 7-12
    Ordeal of an Arthurian knight shows honesty and faithfulness.

Trilogy: *Sword and the Circle; *Light Beyond the Forest; *Road to Camlann*   Gr. 7-12
        all by Rosemary Sutcliff
    The rise, quest, and end of King Arthur. Sutcliff is a knowledgeable and highly-reputed
    author, though a few of her books are dark. I've not read this trilogy.

Pendragon Cycle: *Taliesin; *Merlin; *Arthur; *Pendragon; *Grail*   Gr. 9-12
        by Stephen Lawhead
    Novelized story of King Arthur, with King Arthur's Christian character emphasized.

Story of King Arthur and His Knights, by Howard Pyle   Gr. 9-12
    Classic version of the King Arthur legend for older students and adults. Three shorter
    excerpts have also been published: *Story of the Champions of the Round Table*, *Story of Sir
    Launcelot and His Champions*, and *Story of the Grail and the Passing of Arthur*.

Idylls of the King, by Alfred, Lord Tennyson   Gr. 11-12
    Classic poetry based on Malory's tales about Arthur.

Le Morte D'Arthur, by Sir Thomas Malory   Gr. 11-12
    Malory produced his epic tale of Arthur in the 1400s!

Activities

King Arthur Coloring Book (Dover)   Various

Audio/Video

King Arthur and His Knights, told by Jim Weiss   Various

5b✦ Related stories

Sword in the Tree, by Clyde Robert Bulla   Gr. 1-5
    Don't miss this story of a brave young boy during the Arthurian era. It has
    singlehandedly launched several children I know (especially boys) into a love of reading.

Page Boy for King Arthur and *Squire for King Arthur,* by Eugenia Stone   Gr. 2-7
    Both these stories are tender and much enjoyed.

Melor: King Arthur's Page, by Catherine Owens Peare   Gr. 5-12

A Connecticut Yankee in King Arthur's Court, by Mark Twain   Gr. 7-12
    Classic, humorous, insightful tale of 'modern' man transported back in time to Britain.
    It's not really about King Arthur, but there are important points made about slavery and
    medieval life in this wonderful, witty book.

5c✦ Celts

Life in Celtic Times, by A.G. Smith & William Kaufman   Various
    This is a Dover coloring book; the captions give some info.

Everyday Life of a Celtic Farmer, by Giovanni Caselli   Gr. 3-8
    This is actually set during the Roman occupation, but still gives info on Celtic life.

Step Into the Celtic World, by Fiona Macdonald   Gr. 6-10

6✿ Clovis and the Franks

We'll get back to England soon, but you must catch up with events on the continent. You didn't think folks there were just twiddling their thumbs, did you? Certainly not! The Romans were going out of business, and the local Teutonic barbarians, such as the Franks, were in a hurry to set up shop for themselves. Hadn't they been invited to help Rome defend her borders? Hadn't they begun to move into Roman territory, seizing nice little hills and dales, with nary a word from the weak Roman rulers? They had a good thing going...and they kept going! In 486, a Frankish leader named Clovis had the guts to attack the Roman garrison at Soissons! Victory went to the Franks, and the surrounding land would one day be known as *France*. Franks. France. Franks. France. Get it?

Now, Clovis was married. Isn't that sweet?! No, I'm not getting mushy on you. I'm trying to tell you that his wife, a lady by the name of Clotilda, was a Christian...and she soon won her husband to the faith, though he seems to have had some respect for the infant church previously.[13] I can't have you thinking, though, that ambitious Clovis became an upstanding Christian gentleman overnight...or ever. He continued his cruel, usurping ways, and there is great doubt regarding his supposed conversion: was it sincere or was it politically motivated to gain the support of the budding church?[14] This question would rage in the lives of many barbarian lords who claimed to become Christians...and who then forced their subjects to convert or be slaughtered. Hardly what Jesus had in mind when He spoke the Great Commission!

There's even more to this intriguing issue, but we'll save it for our next section. Right now, let's simply meet Clovis and the Franks who would begin forging France...keeping in mind the words of Ms. Mills:

The two great powers of the medieval Europe were to be France and the Papacy, and it was the work of Clovis that first brought them into alliance.[15]

Actually, it is Clotilda who should receive the credit here. Indeed, she was eventually sainted.[16]

---

[13] Donald Sobol, *The First Book of the Barbarian Invaders* (New York: Franklin Watts, 1962) 55.

[14] Asimov 55-56.

[15] Dorothy Mills, *The Middle Ages* (New York: G.P. Putnam's Sons, 1935) 61.

[16] Asimov 63.

7❧ Spain and Italy...and Their Unwelcome Guests

As we continue our quick tour of the remains of the Roman Empire, we see that the Vandals had moved through what is now Spain and had settled in North Africa, vandalizing (yes, that's where the term was coined) along the way and later terrorizing the Mediterranean with their pirate ships. It is said that:

> they crossed to Africa, pillaging, ravaging, burning, destroying wherever they went. "Where are we going next?" a Vandal once asked his chief. "Wherever there is a people with whom God is angry," was the answer.[17]

Now, I *hardly* think Mr. Vandal was flawlessly in tune with God's will, but it is an interesting comment. One thing's certain, the Old Testament says God sometimes stirred armies against nations as tools of His justice. But He often had to chastise these same armies for going too far, being too cruel, and seizing the action as their own. That's another whole topic!

Anyway, the Vandals' nasty rule was short-lived because the emperor of the surviving Eastern Roman Empire based in Constantinople (the Roman Empire had been split into eastern and western halves before its fall) tried to shut down their piracy and the Muslims soon swept in, as you'll find out further on.

---

[17] Mills 11.

It was the Visigoths (the western Goths) who settled down in Spain for a longer stay. You'll later see what happened when the Visigoths and local residents were forced to live together for a century or two.

In Italy itself–home of Rome, hub of the crumbling Empire–it seems every barbarian with as much as a pea-shooter tramped through, not content until they had put the 'Eternal City' of Rome underfoot. Often, the locals were glad to see them, being happily rid of the crushing taxes which had long supported the hideously luxurious life of the caesars.[18] In the end, it was the Ostrogoths (the eastern Goths) who held sway in Italy under their ruler Theodoric the Great. Sadly, Italy would be ripped by warring factions for many centuries to come. Of all the western European lands, she would be slowest to recuperate from her own excesses, her own Roman Empire.

Story of the Middle Ages, by Christine Miller & H.A. Guerber, Ch. XX	Gr. 4-8
Dark Ages, by Isaac Asimov, pp. 61-67	Gr. 8-12

First Book of the Barbarian Invaders, by Donald Sobol, pp. 34-44, 50-53	Gr. 3-8
The Barbarians, by Richard Suskind, portions of Ch. III	Gr. 5-12
The Invaders of Rome, by Bern Keating, Ch. 8	Gr. 5-12

8⚫ Justinian Has His Say

Did you remember? The Roman Empire had been split into eastern and western halves not long before its fall. Well, I should be more accurate. It was really only the western half that fell, but since that was the portion based in the city of Rome itself and because it ruled what we think of as Europe (while the eastern half was based in Constantinople/Byzantium and ruled mostly Asian and African provinces), the fall of the western half is considered by Europeans as the main 'fall of Rome.'

We really should pop over to Byzantium and check out what would eventually be called the Byzantine Empire. It would serve civilization as an important repository of Greek and Roman knowledge while Europe was under the unlearned and destructive barbarians. It also kept invading Asians out of Europe by 'standing guard' at one of the entrances, as Mr. Asimov points out repeatedly in his *Dark Ages*.

---

[18] Keating 110.

18

Did you know there had been some disagreements between the bishops of Rome and Constantinople over the years? Eventually, the church leaders of Constantinople would develop the Orthodox Church, headed by a 'patriarch' (while the Rome-based part of the church would still be called *catholic* and be led by a pope). Many nations in the world still have Orthodox-based churches (*e.g.* Russian Orthodox).

Let's take a moment to talk about Byzantine art too, for not only was it a crowning achievement of Byzantine culture (especially its mosaics, in my opinion), but this style would eventually spread to western Europe as well. Mr. Schaeffer, an important Christian thinker, describes it:

> *Byzantine art became characterized by formalized, stylized, symbolic mosaics and icons. In one way there was something good here—in that the artists made their mosaics and icons as a witness to the observer. Many of those who made these did so with devotion, and they were looking for more spiritual values. These were pluses. The minuses were that in the portrayal of their concept of spirituality they set aside nature and the importance of humanity in people....*

> *This art had a real beauty, but increasingly only religious themes were given importance, and people were depicted not as real people but as symbols. This came to its climax in the ninth, tenth, and eleventh centuries. The portrayal of nature was largely abandoned, and even more unhappily, the living, human element was removed. This, we should stress once more, was in contrast to the early Christian catacomb paintings in which, though simply portrayed, real people lived in a real world which God had made.*[19]

Schaeffer's comments bring us to a key issue of the 'Dark' Ages, but we will discuss it later. (More suspense!)

For now, you can bet the eastern emperors were hoping to oust the barbarians in Europe and reunite the old Roman Empire under their headship. They each wanted to resuscitate the glory of Rome, but only one was very successful–Justinian , who reigned from 527-565. He made the eastern empire solid (not without some tyranny) and that was no small accomplishment considering its location! He's also noted for building a great cathedral called Hagia Sophia. Furthermore, he found Belisarius, an extremely talented, young general...and the Ostrogoth hold on Italy was suddenly in jeopardy!

8a❧ Justinian

Story of the World: Volume 2, by Susan Wise Bauer, Ch. 4	Gr. 3-6
*Greenleaf's *Famous Men of the Middle Ages*, Ch. VI	Gr. 3-7
Story of the Middle Ages, by Christine Miller & H.A. Guerber, Ch. XXI	Gr. 4-8
Middle Ages, by Dorothy Mills, Ch. III	Gr. 6-12

---

[19] Francis Schaeffer, *How Should We Then Live?* (Old Tappan, NJ: Fleming H. Revell, 1976) 31.

Dark Ages, by Isaac Asimov, pp. 67-85　　　　　　　　　　　　Gr. 8-12
　　　These pages discuss both Justinian and related events.

Child's History of the World, by V.M. Hillyer, Ch. 41　　　　Gr. 1-4

Birthdays of Freedom: Vol. 1, by Genevieve Foster, pp. 53-54　　Gr. 2-6

Middle Ages: Cultural Atlas for Young People, by Corbishley, pp. 16-17, 26-27　　Gr. 3-8

The Fall of Constantinople, by Bernadine Kielty, Ch. 3-5 (Landmark)　　Gr. 4-12
　　　I've been told this is one of the drier Landmarks, alas, but only three chapters are cited.

Justinian the Great, by Thomas Fitzgerald (Immortals of History)　　Gr. 8-12

Constantinople: The Forgotten Empire, by Isaac Asimov　　　　Unknown
　　　Asimov wrote an entire book on Byzantine history. Just thought you'd like to know;
　　　few would have time to read it fully, though.

Fiction/Historical Fiction

Dancing Bear, by Peter Dickinson　　　　　　　　　　　　Gr. 5-12
　　　A story of Constantinople in the 600s when being attacked by the Huns. I've only read
　　　the beginning, which does move rather slowly, but I've seen it on recommended lists.

The Iron Charm, by Joanne Williamson　　　　　　　　　　Gr. 6-12
　　　An enslaved Roman meets Justinian, King Arthur, etc. Some of Williamson's other
　　　books are so good they're being reprinted, so this one may be a gem too.

Byzantium, by Stephen Lawhead　　　　　　　　　　　　Gr. 9-12
　　　Rich, powerful, insightful Christian adventure tale of the general era. (Includes elements
　　　for mature readers only.)

Excellent!

8b♣ Theodora

Justinian's wife, Theodora, is reputed to have undergone a very dramatic conversion to Christianity. I'm sorry I can't provide you with titles of any particular books about her. The only thing I recall reading was an article in *Christian History* magazine, and I don't even know the date of the issue. You could check at www.ChristianityToday.com, and then click on the *Christian History* hotlink, if you want to pursue this further.

8c♣ Belisarius

Belisarius, by Glanville Downey　　　　　　　　　　　　Gr. 8-12

8d🕮 Byzantine history

If you have time and need to cover the full sweep of Byzantine history....

The Byzantines, by Thomas Chubb	Gr. 4-12
Constantinople: The Forgotten Empire, by Isaac Asimov	Unknown

8e🕮 Byzantine art & architecture

To view Byzantine art, you can probably check almost any book on art history. Just get a good look at it so you can understand its mood. To see Byzantine architecture, you need look no further than Justinian's *Hagia Sophia.*

Child's History of Art, by Hillyer & Huey (*Architecture* section, Ch. 10) **OR,** *Young People's Story of Architecture: 3,000BC-Gothic*, by Hillyer & Huey, pp. 90-99	Gr. 2-8
*Building Big, by David Macaulay, pp. 136-139	Gr. 5-12
*Architecture, by Neil Stevenson, pp. 46-47 *(DK Annotated Guides)*	Gr. 7-12
Buildings of Byzantium, by Helen & Richard Leacroft	Gr. 7-12

9🕮 The Church Bursts Forth!

It's time. It's *high* time! We've been giving you a chance to become familiar with the players on the chessboard, but you haven't yet met the strongest. Step back. Take another long look at the chessboard of Europe at AD 500. Do you see one king overall? No. One queen? No. Look instead at the piece just beside the king and queen: the bishop. Take a *long* look, for you must get something in your skull. It's already in your heart, but needs to be in your brain too!

You've been studying history for a while now in your school career, probably focusing on ancient history (before Jesus Christ was born and before the church came into existence). You may not, then, have been fully aware of a chief avenue of God's work in history:

> *The church, you see, is not peripheral to the world; the world is peripheral to the church. The church is Christ's own body, in which he speaks and acts, by which he fills everything with his presence* (Eph. 1:22, *Message*).

Our study of the 'Dark' Ages, then, gives you a great opportunity. Why? With no movie-star king to dazzle your eyes, you'll not be fooled into thinking people are the movers and shakers of history. You'll be able to see the Lord working through His church to fill the land with His own presence and truths (which alone yield yearned-for change). This is an *intensely* important point because you don't have anything to offer this world if you don't realize the positive power of your knowledge of Christ. The world tells us to keep our beliefs to ourselves, but an understanding of God is actually a gift the whole world needs!

First, let's look at the church *prior* to the fall of the Roman Empire. I heartily applaud the first Christians for remaining faithful and active in the face of horrible persecution. They loved their neighbors, were good workers, gave generously, spoke out bravely, and even forgave those who tortured them. Amazing! No wonder the church of the New Testament spread throughout the Roman Empire to the point it was called *catholic*...the Latin (Roman) word for *universal!* (We think of the word *catholic* with a capital *C* which denotes something specific, as you'll later see, but now we're using the word as it was originally used: the simple adjective for *universal.*)

These early churches were very local and intimate. Leadership was drawn from the members themselves.[20] The apostles traveled to various churches, exhorting them. They also sent letters, some of which were divinely-inspired and thus became part of the Bible. Over time, though, the church began to develop a Roman-Empire-like structure: bishops were set in important political cities and given authority over local churches in a designated area.[21] We must ask: was this God's specific direction (though I can think of no scriptures saying regional church leaders should be established in cities of political significance to Roman caesars) or was it simply because folks grew up in the centralized mindset?

Why do I raise the question? *Not* to stir up denominational arguments, certainly! My reason is *positive:* because the church is so impactful, we must always check its thinking–its *Big 2 Beliefs.* We'll do the same throughout our study of history, including our own age!

So, particulars of church organization is not our focus. But we *do* need to know if the church was unwittingly *baptizing*[22] the world's thinking rather than *revolutionizing* it, because it's a crucial issue of history! Sadly, the former happens all too often, which we can understand because it's happening with *us!* The ideas of our own culture seep in effortlessly. We don't even realize we've embraced specific ideas; it *seems* we're merely observing what is obvious and normal; we don't sense a need to check the ideas with God's Word. Often, it isn't until we study history that we realize we've swallowed time-specific and location-specific beliefs, thinking they were God's timeless truths! So, we're not picking on the church, we're seeing its significance!

We can see why centralizing 'made sense' to the church of the later 300s. Christianity had just been made the 'official' religion of the Roman Empire, and pagans were suddenly joining. While reaching pagans is the goal, it brought a tidal wave of darkened thinking. Potent heresies (false teachings) sprang up; bishops felt it was their job to monitor the beliefs of local churches.[23] You saw in *TruthQuest History: Ancient Rome* that God used disciples such as Augustine and Ambrose to expose heresy and teach truth.

---

[20] Jeremy Jackson, *No Other Foundation: The Church Through Twenty Centuries* (Westchester, IL: Cornerstone Books 1980) 49.

[21] Mills 16.

[22] This concept of 'baptizing' worldly thought comes from Jackson 122.

[23] Jackson 52.

We just said the Roman Empire declared Christianity to be the official religion of the Empire. Well, this had another historical effect as well: in one second, the church was given worldly authority and wealth. While great good came from this, as you'll see, it also became increasingly difficult for the church's top leaders (as it would have been for any of us) to maintain single-minded devotion to building the kingdom of God. In other words, it was even harder for the church not to baptize Roman thinking...because that same thinking had endorsed the church. You know how it is: we look favorably on those 'smart' enough to look favorably on us! Anyway, we've got a double-edged sword here!

Intriguingly, just a few years after the church had been made official, the Roman Empire fell apart. Barbarians and chaos were everywhere, and folks were looking for leadership and order. Where could it be found? Only in the church![24] Remember? The church had organized along the lines of the empire, and it was able to step into the void fairly quickly. Think! Who faced Genseric the Vandal at the gates of Rome when he was poised to attack? Was it an emperor? A general? A senator? No, it was Bishop Leo! Who went to face Attila the Hun as he swooped into Italy? Bishop Leo![25]

I do declare! What an opportunity for the church! How was this golden opportunity handled?! That is a mighty good question! We'll watch and see. And I have a question of my own: how would different styles of church organization have ministered differently in this breach? How differently would Europe have developed? But we'll stick here to what *did* happen, remembering God is in charge.

> During the fourth and fifth centuries, as the Empire began to fall before the Germanic invaders, the Church grew more powerful, especially in Rome, for as the civil government became more and more incapable of keeping order, the Church gradually began to take its place. The Roman rulers were weak and incompetent, but the Bishops of Rome of this period were statesmen as well as churchmen. When the [Roman] emperor and his court went to Constantinople [capital of the Eastern Roman Empire], the Bishop was the most important man left in Rome, and he gradually assumed a position of great power and responsibility. In 445 a decree was passed which declared that the Bishop of Rome had supremacy over the whole Church, and for more than a thousand years this supremacy was never seriously questioned on the continent of western Europe.[26]

Local priests were often called *papa*, but Bishop Leo of Rome was now seen as *the* papa (*pope*[27] in English, and *papacy* is the word for his office) because the people of Rome and Europe were grateful for his leadership, and because it was thought that Peter—upon whom Christ said He'd build His church—was the first Bishop of Rome. Are you getting this?! The pope—not a king or emperor—would be the most powerful man in Europe throughout the Middle Ages!

---

[24] Jackson 82.

[25] Asimov 41, 65 and Sobol 44, 48.

[26] Mills 17.

[27] Asimov 64.

Just one more thing and then I'll stop, and this will knock another hole in the idea that religion is only private! Do you remember we talked earlier about heresy? Well, we must mention a particular one–Arianism–because it affected Europe's politics. Arians–like the Visigoths, Ostrogoths, and Vandals–said Jesus Christ was important, but not the divine Son of God. (The missionary who converted them to Christianity was an Arian named Ulfilas.) This naturally created tension in the many European regions where they were ruling over orthodox (non-heretical) catholics. Where's the political impact? All over western Europe–wherever there was spiritual unity, as in Clovis and Clothilda's orthodox Frankland[28]–the previous residents and new barbarian invaders started to intermarry, work together, and develop their own language as a blend of Latin and the barbarian tongue. In other words, they were forging what would become the nations of Europe. But lands with Arian rulers–Italy, Spain, areas of eastern Europe, and northern Africa–had a harder time merging as nations.[29] They remained tense. So which do you think was the most powerful medieval nation, and which do you think were the weakest? Yup. Religion matters. The *Big 2 Beliefs* are big.

Okay, I'm done talking. (Hey, you don't have to look *that* excited!) Instead, I want you to meet some great folks of the church.

9a☙ General resources

Story of the World: Volume 2, by Susan Wise Bauer, Ch. 3   Gr. 3-6

Middle Ages, by Dorothy Mills, Ch. II, Pt. 1-2   Gr. 6-12

Dark Ages, by Isaac Asimov, pp. 85-91   Gr. 8-12
    This section includes information on both Gregory and Benedict.

Island Story, by H.E. Marshall, Ch. XIV   Gr. 3-8

Fire Upon the Earth, by Norman Langford, Ch.6   Gr. 4-8
    We cite this book throughout *TruthQuest History* because it tells the history of the church in an easy-to-read style for young/middle students and is readily available on the used-book market. We do *not* endorse the last chapter.

No Other Foundation: The Church Through..., by Jeremy Jackson, Ch. 6   Gr. 11-12
    This book is too difficult for virtually all students, but it's so worthwhile that I must mention it just in case....

---

[28] Asimov 64.

[29] Sorry, I cannot locate the source of this comment, though I've checked the books used for research.

9b✤ Monasteries and monks

We'll touch on this important topic throughout this guide; related resources will be mentioned later.

Meet Benedict, who developed one of the first strong monasteries in the west; gradually there would be many more. These monasteries–homes for monks–were oases of light during the 'Dark' Ages. They alone offered ministry to the needy and kept learning alive (for example, they fostered the educational ideas of Boethius and Cassiodorus, the latter being instrumental in setting monks to copying manuscripts.)[30] The monasteries even had an economic impact, for they were often shining examples of productivity: creating magnificent handmade manuscripts, fruitful gardens, herbal medicines, and more! Sadly, over time, some monks became too far removed from the people who needed them (a snare we all face). Some even became lazy and greedy, living off the peasants instead of helping them, but that was not the heart of Benedict or most of the first monks who tried hard to serve God and man.

Story of the Middle Ages, by Christine Miller & H.A. Guerber, Ch. L   Gr. 4-8

Illuminations, by Jonathan Hunt   Gr. 1-5
    A lovely book showing illuminated manuscripts. Recently in-print; check your library!

Medieval Monastery, by Fiona Macdonald (Inside Story)   Gr. 4-12
    This interesting cut-away book was recently in-print and is probably still at your library.

Life in a Medieval Abbey, by Tony McAleavy   Unknown

Activities

Illuminated Alphabet Coloring Book   Various

Medieval Alphabet to Illuminate (Bellerophon)   Various

9c✤ St. Benedict

Greenleaf's Famous Men of the Middle Ages, Ch. VII   Gr. 3-7

Child's History of the World, by V.M. Hillyer, Ch. 42   Gr. 1-4

The Holy Twins, by Kathleen Norris   Gr. 2-4
    Easy, fictionalized biography of Benedict and his twin sister, Scholastica.

---

[30] Jackson 79 and Asimov 49-50.

St. Benedict, by Mary Fabyan Windeatt (Vision)   Gr. 4-12
      This is in a distinctively Catholic series.

9d🍀 Irish monks

Ireland proved to be a strong Christian outpost and was dotted with monasteries, many of them laboriously producing wonderful illustrated manuscripts.[31] On another note, some think Brendan, an Irish monk, may have made a journey to the New World around 590, which would be almost 900 years *before* Columbus!

Middle Ages, by Dorothy Mills, Ch. II, Pt. 3a   Gr. 6-12

**Brendan the Navigator*, by Jean Fritz   Gr. 3-7
      This book includes fanciful, legendary elements.

Fiction/Historical Fiction

The Emerald Sea, by Sandy Dengler (Heroes of the Misty Isle)   Gr. 5-12
      Another in a Christian series of novels; this one finds fictional kids having adventures with Brendan. Check your church's library, or that of a neighboring church.

9e🍀 Columba of Scotland

Columba left Ireland for Scotland in 563, establishing a monastery on the isle of Iona and then reaching out to the Picts.

The Man Who Loved Books, by Jean Fritz   Gr. 1-6

Beggars, Beasts and Easter Fire, by Carol Greene, Ch. 4   Gr. 2-8
      This colorful book gives the facts and legends of great Christians. It was recently inprint and may still be in your church library.

**Across a Dark & Wild Sea*, by Don Brown   Gr. 3-6
      I've not seen this, but have read it is very lyrical.

Fire Upon the Earth, by Norman Langford, Ch. 7   Gr. 4-8

The Story of Britain, by R.J. Unstead, pp. 34-35   Gr. 5-12

---

[31] Mills 23-24.

Fiction/Historical Fiction

King of the Stars, by Sandy Dengler (Heroes of the Misty Isle)   Gr. 5-12
> One in a series of Christian novels; this one is about Columba. It was recently in-print and is probably in the library of your church or another in town.

Fields of Bannockburn, by Donna Fletcher Crow   Gr. 8-12
> This interesting "novel of Christian Scotland" devotes its first section to Columba. It was recently in-print and could be in the library of your church or another in town.

Isle of Glory, by Jane Oliver   Gr. 10-12

9f✺ Gregory the Great (Pope, 590-604)

Pope Gregory felt a great burden to reach the pagan barbarians. He sent missionaries across Europe, including the Augustine you'll meet below (not the earlier church writer by the same name). Indeed, Ireland–where St. Patrick had worked so hard–and England had become such Christian strongholds that monks, such as Boniface, were sent to preach to the barbarians on the mainland! Gregory was also concerned about ignorance of many new priests and the blurry blend of Christianity and paganism in many new converts (to ease transition, some local church leaders 'reassigned' barbarian holidays and gods to new Christian holidays and saints),[32] so he beefed up the church's structure. The striking sounds of Gregorian chant are attributed to him. 'Take a listen!'

*Greenleaf's *Famous Men of the Middle Ages*, Ch. VII   Gr. 3-7

Story of the Middle Ages, by Christine Miller & H.A. Guerber, Ch. XXX   Gr. 4-8

Birthdays of Freedom: Vol. 2, by Genevieve Foster, p. 9   Gr. 2-5

Gregory the Great, by George Sanderlin (Vision)   Gr. 4-12
> This is in a distinctively Catholic series.

Trial and Triumph, by Richard Hannula, Ch. 8   Gr. 5-12

9g✺ Augustine

Augustine (not the earlier theologian of the same name) arrived in England at the behest of Pope Gregory to preach to the pagan Anglo-Saxons around 597.

---

[32] Jackson 81-82.

Story of the Middle Ages, by Miller & Güerber, Ch. XXIX, XXXI   Gr. 4-8
    Chapter XXXI covers Christian writers after Augustine, including Bede the Venerable.
    Bede's *Ecclesiastical History of the English People* is in-print if mature students care to read
    it! Bede is also covered in: *Heroes and Saints*, by R.J. Unstead, Ch. 6, Gr. 3-9.

Middle Ages, by Dorothy Mills, Ch. II, Pt. 3b   Gr. 6-12

Birthdays of Freedom: Vol. 2, by Genevieve Foster, p. 10   Gr. 2-5

Looking at History, by R.J. Unstead, pp. 50-52   Gr. 2-5

Augustine Came to Kent, by Barbara Willard   Gr. 4-12
    This is an excellent novelized telling of the events.

Story of Britain, by R.J. Unstead, pp. 35-37 (Augustine) and 46-47 (Bede)   Gr. 5-12

9h☙ Paulinius, St. Aidan, St. Cuthbert, St. Hilda, and a Queen impact English kingdoms

**It was Aidan who founded the famous Lindisfarne Monastery on an island donated by
the Christian king. From it would come one of the most famous illustrated manuscripts
of the Middle Ages: the Lindisfarne Gospels.**

Beggars, Beasts and Easter Fire, by Carol Greene, Ch. 5   Gr. 2-8
    This colorful book shows both the known facts and legends regarding the lives of great
    Christians. It was recently in-print and may still be in your church library.

Heroes and Saints, by R.J. Unstead, Ch. 4-5   Gr. 3-9

The Story of Britain, by R.J. Unstead, pp. 38-45   Gr. 5-12

9i☙ Boniface

Middle Ages, by Dorothy Mills, Ch. II, Pt. 3d   Gr. 6-12

Beggars, Beasts and Easter Fire, by Carol Greene, Ch. 6   Gr. 2-8
    This colorful book shows both the known facts and legends regarding the lives of great
    Christians. It was recently in-print and may still be in your church library.

The Story of Britain, by R.J. Unstead, p. 48   Gr. 5-12

Trial and Triumph: Stories from Church History, by Richard Hannula, Ch. 9   Gr. 5-12

10🍀 Meanwhile, Back on the Ranch

Let's take a quick visit back to the home of the Franks (or France, as it would later be called), as well as Visigothic Spain.

The death of a Frankish king was a disaster, but not because he had been a teddy bear. Hardly! It was because Frankish custom split a king's land among his sons. These sons—do I sense a little ungratefulness here?—then fought to the death to get their brothers' shares! Things got mighty messy! But one situation tops them all: two Frankish kings each married a Visigothic princess of Spain because each king wanted the neighboring Visigoths to support their wars.[33] But the two princesses were sisters! Whoo-whee! A *terrific* feud was set off! A famous story—one of few barbarian epics left to history—was told of it: the *Nibelungenlied*.

Of Clovis's descendants (Merovingian dynasty), there was one later standout: Good King Dagobert. He died in either 638 or 639; it's thought he first built a real church on the burial site of St. Denis, patron saint of France. After him, you see Frankland enter a horrible time. Mr. Asimov says it powerfully:

> *...the feud of* [Queens] *Brunehilde and Fredegund, and the long and ferocious civil wars it had inspired, ruined the Frankish realm as the wars of Justinian had ruined Italy.*
>
> *The peasant population, harried by contending armies, could barely feed themselves. Very little food was left over for the cities and what there was could scarcely be transported into town as the old Roman roads fell into disrepair and were scarcely usable.*
>
> *The land fell into a kind of village economy, in which each little tract was forced to be as self-sufficient as possible, and the city population dropped to not more than three percent of the whole. The aqueducts were broken down too, and as the supply of reasonably clean water diminished and life grew more miserable, disease flourished.*
>
> *So the darkness grew deeper.*[34]

Of course, you remember from your study of ancient Rome that Emperor Diocletian had already jerked Europe toward this desperate, isolated, self-sufficiency when the late Roman economy collapsed due to centuries of 'bread and circuses,' corruption, idleness, extravagance, and the stopped inflow of wealth and slaves when the Roman army was too weak to campaign. Desperate and unaware of God's principles, Diocletian used force to tie folks to their father's trade or one plot of land for life!

---

[33] Asimov 92-93.

[34] Asimov 97.

This forced tying of people to land would later be called *feudalism*. We'll explore it further in this guide, for it was a *huge* factor in the Middle Ages and entails things such as knights and castles! For now, just be aware of the forces shattering Europe and setting most everyone to scratching one field for all their impoverished days.

Let's move to Visigothic Spain. Under some strong rulers, including the father of the two warring queens, the Visigoths gained control of all Spain—even seizing remote Basque enclaves and land earlier won by Justinian. There were still complications aplenty: the Visigoths were the last ones clinging to the Arian heresy. A new Frankish bride changed all that, though! It did result in a religious war between her father-in-law (Visigoth king) and her husband (Visigoth prince). In the end, Spain converted to orthodox catholic faith. Asimov comments:

> *The disappearance of Arianism in Spain was different from the disappearance elsewhere. In Spain, it seemed to leave a heritage of guilt among the rulers....*
>
> *The Visigoths...had been Arians for two centuries....It seemed as though the now-Catholic Visigoths had to do penance for the sins of their heretic ancestors and be more Catholic than the Catholics. The extremism they developed remained, somehow, a Spanish heritage right down into modern times....*
>
> *Once the Visigothic kingdom went Catholic, however, the kings had to prove their orthodoxy by taking stern action against non-Catholics. This might have meant the Arians, but they had all vanished as conversion spread. That left the Jews. The later Visigothic kings therefore initiated a policy of brutal anti-Semitism which has stained Christian Europe ever since.*
>
> *Again, apparently as a consequence of guilt, the king and the aristocracy [which remained Visigothic for a century and a quarter after the conversion) became remarkably subservient to the Catholic clergy, who were of Roman Catholic descent. Spanish churchmen insisted on crowning the Visigothic kings and presenting the crown as a gift of the Church, which could be withdrawn at any time.*[35]

Interesting, huh?

10a❧ The Franks and Visigothic Spain

Story of the Middle Ages, by Miller & Guerber, Ch. XXXII-XXXIIIa   Gr. 4-8

Dark Ages, by Isaac Asimov, pp. 91-103   Gr. 8-12

---

[35] Asimov 100.

For further probing of the Teutonic heart and mind, students can read their great epic, the *Nibelungenlied*. (*Nibelung* is another name for *Burgundian*, a southern Frank.)[36] This tale is adventurous, but not essential. Naturally, it includes Teutonic mythology, so if you read it, use it as an opportunity to see their *Big 2 Beliefs* (don't forget that's your goal in your *Investigation Supreme!*) There are many editions of the original and there are many adapted versions for younger students (see below). Just select one that fits your student, if you decide to pursue this.

*Greenleaf's *Famous Men of the Middle Ages*, Intro II	Gr. 3-7	

Sword of Siegfried, by Katharine Scherman (Legacy)	Gr. 3-6	
Treasure of Siegfried, by E.M. Almedingen	Gr. 5-12	
The Story of Siegfried, by James Baldwin	Gr. 8-12	
Nibelungenlied	Gr. 10-12	

> Want to explore opera? Wagner wrote an opera based on the *Nibelungenlied*. Story versions of the opera were written by Robert Lawrence and Clyde Robert Bulla.

11✦ A New Force: *Islam!*

It's time to take a *big* trip...to Arabia! There lived Mohammed/Muhammed (570-632), who founded a powerful religion called *Islam*, which means *submission*. Those who submit to Islam are called *Muslims/Moslems*, and they do submit! So, how did Islam begin?

I'll let someone else explain:

> *Muhammed spent most of his time in solitary meditation. He began to have many disturbing visions.*

> *Thus, the* Quran, *sacred book of the Muslims, is the "reciting" of revelations given to Muhammed. Over a period of 22 years, Muhammed reported many other revelations. Encouraged by his wife, he began to preach in the streets and marketplaces of Mecca [Mohammed's home town]. Muhammed never claimed to be divine, bust insisted that Allah [the god of Islam] had called him to be a prophet....He was met with bitter opposition....Muhammed was forced to flee to...a friendlier city....This flight, called the* hegira, *marks the beginning of Islam [622]. Soon the Meccans organized an army to destroy Muhammed and his followers. The fighting ended in 630 with Islam forces triumphant....He destroyed every idol in the Kaaba, the main temple, except the Black Stone, a sacred meteorite enshrined there. Muhammed then declared the Kaaba to be the most holy shrine in Islam. Since that time it has been the spot toward which all devout Muslims direct their prayers.*

---

[36] Asimov 96.

During the next two years, Muhammed strengthened his position as the leading prophet and ruler of Arabia. He united the tribes into a vast army to conquer the world for Allah. His death in 632 did not lessen the fervor of his followers. They carried their faith across Asia, Africa, even into Europe—and to this day the growth of Islam has not ended.

Muslims believe in four God-inspired books: the Torah of Moses...the Zabur (Psalms of David), the Injil (Gospel) of Jesus, and the Quran. But the Quran is Allah's final word to mankind, so it supersedes and overrules all previous writings.

The Quran lists 28 prophets of Allah. These include Adam, Noah, Abraham, Moses, David, Jonah, and Jesus. Of course, to the Muslim, the last and greatest prophet is Muhammed.

The Quran denies that Jesus is the Son of God....The Quran...places Him in rank far below Muhammed. Surah 4:171 says that "Jesus...was only a messenger of Allah...Far is it removed from His transcendent majesty that He should have a son."

The Quran says that Christ never really died on the cross. "They slew him not nor crucified, but it appeared so unto them" (Surah 4:157). ...Surah 4:111 declares that man must take care of his own sins.[37]

Islam's impact was not only spiritual, but was also political. As Islam spread to the Arab descendants of Ishmael—often by conquest, not conversion[38]—it merged formerly isolated nomads and townspeople into a unified force. They launched further conquests, converted more and more people to Islam, and attacked Christian lands. A major campaign—lasting many centuries—was begun! They fanned out across Africa and Europe and Asia: "a seemingly irresistible advance that...stretched virtually unchallenged from southern Frank-land and Spain across North Africa and on through Persia into the grasslands and deserts of central Asia as far as the borders of China itself."[39]

Sadly, many of the areas which became Islamic had formerly been Christian strongholds, such as Antioch and Alexandria. These cities were hotbeds of theological debate, though, which seems to have created a discord and overemphasis on intellectualism which may have made it easier for people to convert to Islam.[40] Also, in North Africa, for example, the native Berbers equated Christianity with the uninvited rule first of Rome and then of Constantinople, so invading, nomadic Arabians with a new religion *seemed* to be more desirable than their current masters.[41] Of course, that makes me wonder how meaningful and vital was the Christianity of

---

[37] Fritz Ridenour, *So What's the Difference?* (Glendale, CA: GL Regal Books, 1967) 65-71.

[38] Miller 87.

[39] Samuel Hugh Moffett, *A History of Christianity in Asia: Volume 1* (San Francisco: HarperCollins, 1992) 297.

[40] Jackson 47.

[41] Asimov 113.

both the Byzantines and the North Africans, if it could so easily be overthrown merely for political considerations. But then, whenever the church fails to live powerfully in God, decay begins all around. (Remember our theme verse?)

A point is often made of the cultural supremacy of the Arabs, as compared with that of medieval Europe. While there were many advances in Arabia (as you'll see in your readings below), you should keep in mind that this statement is often intended to make Christianity seem backward or repressive. Keep in mind, though, that medieval Europe had suddenly been overrun by races which had been barbarians for centuries, and it was no small task to move them forward in cultural development. What should be noted, then, is how much the barbarians *did* change under Christianity.

Aha, one other point is intensely intriguing:

> *It was from the Nestorians* [a Christian sect in Asia] *that the Arabs learned much of the Greek science and learning they were later to pass on to Europe, which, overrun by barbarian invasions, was losing much of its ancient Greek heritage.*[42]

Islam was, and is, a potent force in world events. Indeed, Islam's teachings on the afterlife,[43] as well as its positions on Judaism and Christianity, have stirred up many 'intense' followers, and though it is not politically correct to say so, this 'intensity' has led to violence throughout history. Of course, those claiming to be Christians have initiated plenty of violence too, but there is a *huge* difference between a religion's sacred book calling for violence (as with Islam)... and mere members of a religion calling for violence (as with Christianity).

11a❧ General overview
Some of these books do more than just casually describe Islam; they are pro-Islam. Parents, be cautious!

Story of the World: Volume 2, by Susan Wise Bauer, Ch. 6-7	Gr. 3-6
Greenleaf's Famous Men of the Middle Ages, Ch. VIII	Gr. 3-7
Story of the Middle Ages, by Miller & Guerber, Ch. XXXIV	Gr. 4-8
Middle Ages, by Dorothy Mills, Ch. IV	Gr. 6-12
Dark Ages, by Isaac Asimov, pp. 103-105	Gr. 8-12

Child's History of the World, by V.M. Hillyer, Ch. 43 & 44	Gr. 1-4
Birthdays of Freedom: Vol. 2, by Genevieve Foster, pp. 11-12	Gr. 2-5

---

[42] Moffett 297.

[43] Asimov 104.

The Silk Route, by John Major   Gr. 2-6
    Get a glimpse of life in the Near and Far East—areas coming under Arabic domain—
    around the year 700, by looking at this very good book. Actually, all ages enjoy it!

What Will You See Inside a Mosque, by Aisha Khan   Gr. 3-6
    Provides an overview of the Islamic faith and their mosques.

Atlas of Islam: People, Daily Life and Traditions, by Neil Morris   Gr. 3-12

Fire Upon the Earth, by Norman Langford, pp. 73-76   Gr. 4-8

Muhammed, by Demi   Gr. 4-8
    This book is very beautiful but one reviewer noted its talk of Islam's toleration of other
    religions without honestly mentioning its opposition to Judaism and Christianity.

The Arabs, by Harry Ellis   Gr. 4-10
    Story of Mohammed and the Islamic Empire which resulted.

Qur'an and Islam, by Anita Ganeri   Gr. 4-10

The Buildings of Early Islam, by Helen & Richard Leacroft   Gr. 5-12
    This book presents Islamic architecture and many famous mosques.

Islam, by Philip Wilkinson & Batul Salazar (Eyewitness)   Gr. 5-12

The Moors, by Gerald Hawting   Gr. 5-12

Sword of the Prophet, by Robert Goldston   Gr. 8-12
    This offers a history if Islam from its inception to modern times.

11b ❧ In-depth study

Because of ministry burden, the 9-11 attacks, or events in Israel and Iraq, some families may want to study Islam more deeply. Here are a few of the many new resources being produced to meet this need.

The Dark Side of Islam, by R.C. Sproul & Abdul Saleeb   Gr. 9-12

Light in the Shadow, by Ravi Zacharias   Gr. 10-12
    Answers questions about Islam in the era following the 9-11 attacks.

Blood of the Moon, by George Grant   Gr. 11-12
    Tells of Islam and its struggle against western civilization.

Unveiling Islam, by Ergun & Emir Caner   Gr. 11-12
    Two formerly Islamic brothers, now Christians, reveal the truth of Islam.

12🙞 A Case of Bad Timing: More Frankish Chaos with the 'Mayors of the Palace'

Apparently, we're all slow to learn two things: selfishly grasping for control is hard on those nearby, and it makes us oblivious to danger. Case in point? How about the death throes of the Merovingian Dynasty, which saw kings busy either eating, drinking, and making merry (when at home) or killing their brothers (when on the war front). These kings were called the "do-nothings" (*rois fainéants*), which isn't a very good reputation if you're in the legacy-making business.[44] The chaos and ineptitude became so great that the little clerks left at the 'palace' to keep up on paperwork soon were running the kingdom! They were called *major domo* (in Spanish) or *mayor of the palace* (in English). What a windfall for them...except soon the 'mayors of the palace' were fighting amongst themselves and the budding nobility. These nobles had been ordered by earlier kings to rule outlying areas, but many of them longed (and finagled) to rule their assigned areas as king independently.[45] The mayors, meanwhile, wanted to be bigger mayors of bigger palaces. A couple mayors named Pepin were unusually successful. The latter Pepin would have a very famous son, but we'll meet him later.

I hope you're noticing something important: as the kings and mayors spent the lifeblood of their kingdoms in civil war, their governments became ineffective. What does this show about their *Big 2 Beliefs?* While they claimed to be Christians, did they have Christian beliefs, or were they still quite barbarian at heart? What does God say government *should* be? Romans 13:3b-4 makes it clear: government is to punish evildoers and reward the doers of good. This results in nations where people are safe and at liberty to pursue greater culture, inventiveness, and prosperity. Good government– government which is doing what God calls it to do, and no more or less–is a gift from God. Without it, nations are either in tyranny or chaos...or both. That was just the situation with the Franks and Visigoths, and at a very bad time too–not that there's ever a good time–because a new onslaught of massive proportions was about to befall them!

Story of the Middle Ages, by Christine Miller & H.A. Guerber, Ch. XXXIIIb   Gr. 4-8

Dark Ages, by Isaac Asimov, pp. 106-113   Gr. 8-12

13🙞 Islam on the March: Moorish Spain

As with the Franks, the Visigoths in Spain selfishly fought amongst themselves to see who would be king next, rather than putting the needs of the people first. Ironically, in the end, the

---

[44] Mills 61.

[45] Asimov 107.

answer to which Visigoth noble would be king was...*none of them*. Why? Because at some point in some civil war, one faction had the *seemingly* brilliant idea to invite the Islamic armies in North Africa–how strong could these mere tribal folks really be?–to help them overthrow a rival faction. I'm sure it was thought the newly-converted Muslims of Mauritania (the area across from Spain on the North African coast giving these folks the name *Moors* in English) would simply take their 'paychecks' and go home when the job was done. But the Muslims didn't want to leave and they had been grossly underestimated. They simply became Spain's new rulers for the next several centuries! The era of Moorish Spain had begun. Their famous building of later years, the *Alhambra*, shows their distinct architectural influence; we'll visit it later. Eventually, much Arabic influence would be felt, including increased toleration for the Jews, oddly enough. (Note: You can refer to the fuller list of general Islamic history books cited when Islam was first introduced. There are few youth books on Moorish Spain in particular, so don't worry if you can't find anything, but I'm guessing any encyclopedia would have some info.)

Story of the World: Volume 2, by Susan Wise Bauer, Ch. 12	Gr. 3-6
Dark Ages, by Asimov, pp. 113-117	Gr. 8-12

Birthdays of Freedom: Vol. 2, by Genevieve Foster, pp. 13-14	Gr. 2-5
The Moors, by Gerald Hawting Just cover the pertinent sections.	Gr. 5-12

14 ❧ Islam Reaches Deeper: Charles Martel and the Battle of Poitiers/Tours

Yes, in Spain the Muslims (called Moors or Saracens) had a foothold in Europe. But why, they wondered, should they have only a foothold when much of Europe was snared in selfish, ridiculous conflict over which feisty noble, mayor, or puppet-king should rule? They didn't debate too long, then, about marching down the Pyrenees Mountains into Frankland (or Gaul, if we use its old Roman name). They could then sweep into the open area of Europe! Would her Christian cultures (infant as they were in most of Europe) be annihilated as they had been in North Africa, as well as the Near and Middle East? Mr. Asimov says:

> *Was it not time for Christian Europe to bury its local feuds and stand shoulder to shoulder against the Moslem menace? Unfortunately, the Europe of 712 could not possibly have done so. It was too far gone in disintegration. Communications were so battered, transportation so nearly impossible, all sense of unity so lost, that a pinch at the nerve endings in the Pyrenees simply could not be felt in the Alps, three hundred miles away.*[46]

What happened? Does the nickname of the next Frank on the scene–Charles "The Hammer" Martel, son of the most recent Pepin–give you a clue?! And what of his 'heavy cavalry' (designed to face the Moors on their swift Arabian horses) which would be the progenitor of the

---

[46] Asimov 125.

medieval knight now pictured so romantically? Do make note that Charles looked to the church—which now owned one-third of all Frankish lands—to help pay for this cavalry.[47] Make further note of the great Battle of Poitiers (or Tours, as some think) of 732 which cooled Moorish ambitions for a while. Lastly, be aware that in 717 and 718, a massive Arab army was striking at Constantinople itself but somehow this important Christian capital held. The Arabic defeat would exhaust the Islamic spread which—at over 5,000 miles in width—was getting hard to handle.[48]

Story of the World: Volume 2, by Susan Wise Bauer, Ch. 13a	Gr. 3-6
*Greenleaf's *Famous Men of the Middle Ages*, Ch. IX	Gr. 3-7
Story of the Middle Ages, by Christine Miller & H.A. Guerber, Ch. XXXV	Gr. 4-8
Middle Ages, by Dorothy Mills, Ch. V, Pt. 3	Gr. 6-12
Dark Ages, by Isaac Asimov, pp. 117-128	Gr. 8-12
Middle Ages: Cultural Atlas for Young People, by Mike Corbishley, pp. 20-21	Gr. 3-8
Hammer of Gaul, by Shane Miller (Credo Books) The Credo series is distinctly Catholic.	Gr. 6-12

15❧ Pepin the Short...and Church Power!

I hope you didn't think we had run out of Pepins, for Charles Martel's great victory continued development of the Frankish kingdom under a dynasty named for him: the Carolingian. (*Charles* is *Carolus* in Latin.) The next strong leader after Charles was his son, Pepin the Short. This Pepin ruled from 741-768.

Just then, Rome was invaded by barbarian Lombards. The Byzantines—who always considered themselves fellow Romans—had offered to protect the pope, but they were 'otherwise engaged.' That's a nice way of saying they had their hands full of Muslim attacks just then. Besides, the pope and the Byzantine patriarch were embroiled in a conflict over the use of icons (religious images). This argument contributed to the full split which eventually came between the western church and the Eastern Orthodox Church.

---

[47] Asimov 120.

[48] Asimov 121-122 and 115 (reference to 5,000 miles).

The pope looked the opposite direction to Pepin of the Franks. Now it just happened that Pepin was glad of the pope's notice. You see, Pepin's forefathers had scraped together a realm out of what had been only tribal bands, thereby forging what would eventually become various nations, but Pepin was still only mayor for a puppet Merovingian king. That just wouldn't do! Pepin was king in fact, and wanted to be king in full! He felt the pope had the authority to make such a declaration...which shows Europe's respect for the position! Are you getting this? The pope was becoming a kingmaker! He who makes kings has more power than kings.

So, Pepin gathered an army and set off to rout the Lombards for the pope. He dispatched the invaders and gave the pope some of their land. This *Donation of Pepin* would not only play a role in later history, but would impact right away! Why? No sooner had the pope added kingmaking to his spiritual role than he was suddenly made an actual king, for he directly governed and benefitted financially from the residents of the Papal States given him by Pepin![49]

You can bet the pope quickly declared the Merovingian dynasty ended, and made Pepin king by title. Picture the new element at Pepin's coronation! It was not only Pepin's nobles who crowned him, but the Frankish priests too–maybe even St. Boniface himself.[50] These church officials said he ruled "by the grace of God."

> *In other words, Pepin had acknowledged the right of the Pope to say who was a legitimate sovereign and who was not. Once acknowledged, such a right was hard to withdraw and there were yet to be centuries of dispute in later European history over just this point.*[51]

Get it? The church was telling the secular rulers that God was the ultimate ruler. His authority was greater than the barbarians' human authority (*Big Belief #1*), which came only from brute strength and clever skill at war. Great! I'm soooo glad the church was saying this...but would they live it too? The pope and many other top church officials ruled lands directly. Would *they* remember God's higher authority (*Big Belief #1*) and their God-mandated role of service to mankind (*Big Belief #2*)? Or would they instead be tempted to use church power to increase their own political and financial power now that they had a foot in all three worlds?

You can bet the up-and-coming kinglets were watching the 'spiritual kings' to see just how *real* this Christianity was. If the popes ruled like there was indeed a higher God.... If they didn't.... Well, I'll let you fill in the blanks! So be watching! You're at the precipice of a mighty point in history! Don't snooze through it! Sit up! Wake up! Think! Watch!

You and I also live in nations which claim to be Christian, but have little understanding of God's truth. Since neither individuals nor nations can be solid or free without this truth, our yieldedness to Christ's work in and through us has greater impact on humankind than anything

---

[49] Asimov 136.

[50] Asimov 149.

[51] Asimov 132.

38

else we do. We can't get away from our position in Christ as part of His body. Even if we're doing *nothing*, that lack is powerfully affecting our world. So don't get judgmental as you watch those who came before you, because we face the same question! Are we the caring advocates and sources of truth we should be? Either way, our lives have effect. What is it?

Greenleaf's Famous Men of the Middle Ages, Ch. IX	Gr. 3-7
Story of the Middle Ages, by Miller & Guerber Ch. XXXVI	Gr. 4-8
Dark Ages, by Isaac Asimov, pp. 128-140	Gr. 8-12
Middle Ages: Cultural Atlas for Young People, pp. 20-21 by Mike Corbishley	Gr. 3-8

> *Candle at Dusk* Gr. 9-12
> by E.M. Almedingen
>
> This is a fictional story set in Frank lands during the general time period we've been discussing.

16 Roll Out the Red Carpet for a 'Star' of the Dark Ages: Charlemagne

Pepin, as you know, had actually become a king, so his son did likewise (768). Now, this son happens to be one of the most famous men of history! He was named Charles for his grandfather (Charles Martel), but you know him by his French name—Charlemagne—wherein the French word for 'great' actually *became one* with 'Charles'—a unique honor![52]

Don't think this guy is famous? Well, how do you answer when asked how tall you are? Four feet? Five feet? Six feet? Whose foot do you think was the standard for that measurement? Yup. Charlemagne's, or so it is said.[53]

Charlemagne, a human thunderbolt, made quick work of the Lombards (with whom Pepin had tangled). He was now king of the Franks and Lombards, and the papacy was again free of the Lombard threat. A friendship sprang up between the pope and Charlemagne, though there were also subtle power struggles, especially relating to the title of *Roman Emperor*, as you'll see. Nonetheless, a certain curtain had come down:

> *All were gone now of those tribes that had ripped the Western [Roman] Empire apart since the time of Alaric. Gone were the Visigoths, the Vandals, the Sueves, the Alemanni, the Ostrogoths, the Lombards. All had vanished from the pages of history—all but the Franks. They alone had survived.*[54]

---

[52] Asimov 142.

[53] Miller & Guerber 97 and Asimov 141.

[54] Asimov 145.

The Franks weren't just surviving, though! Under Charlemagne, they were thriving! They decided to 'thrive some more' by annexing the lands held by fellow (German) barbarians further to the east: the Bavarians, Thuringians, Frisians, and Saxons. (You geography buffs will recognize these names in sections of modern Germany!) Of course, the Franks no longer considered themselves barbarians compared to the tribes still in huts shaded by dark German forests. St. Boniface had found success in Christianizing the first three tribes we mentioned. They quickly adopted Frankish customs. This made the remaining tribe–the doggedly pagan Saxons who sometimes offered human sacrifices[55]–resist Christianity even more. To them it meant accepting not only a new religion but a new king and culture as well, something in which they were not remotely interested. (You can see, even this early, what happens when missionaries tie cultural specifics with the supra-cultural gospel.) Charlemagne's response: convert them at swordpoint. It makes me wonder what understanding of God's truth Charlemagne really had, his famed devoutness notwithstanding.

Because they shared enemies, Charlemagne developed a friendship with the caliph of Baghdad, Haroun al-Rashid. He ruled the huge Islamic Empire (now in its Abbasid dynasty) and was the idealized subject of the famous *Arabian Nights* stories.[56] You may have heard stories of the gifts exchanged between Haroun and Charlemagne, including an elephant which astounded the Franks!

Before we close our discussion of Charlemagne, we must address one more topic. He was aware that Frankland was more backward than its neighbors–Spain, England, Italy, and Byzantium[57]–but think of what the earlier Franks had been! Remember, the Teutonic men had done nothing but make war and play dice! Productivity and learning had *not* been one of their hallmarks. Even the new Franks still were not interested in reading or writing; it was done only by priests (our word *clerk* comes from *cleric* for this very reason)[58] who were usually from the original Roman families of the area. Conquering the Romans had made the Franks (foolishly) believe the sword was mightier than the pen.[59] Charlemagne, however, pushed himself to learn and sent away for a top-notch scholar since there was no local talent in that regard; Alcuin of York (a British gentleman) took the job.[60] Together, Charlemagne and Alcuin built a school which would admit boys–even of ignoble birth–who showed promise![61]

---

[55] Miller & Guerber 91-92.

[56] Asimov 153.

[57] Asimov 164.

[58] Asimov 165.

[59] Asimov 164.

[60] For more information on Alcuin, see: *Heroes and Saints*, by R.J. Unstead, Ch. 7, Gr. 3-9.

[61] Jennifer Westwood, *Stories of Charlemagne* (New York: S.G. Phillips, 1972) 9.

Charlemagne was well known for his support of the church, and he encouraged priests to become better educated by providing improved monastic schools.[62] He also worked at organizing his lands and providing better laws. In fact, he sent out inspectors to see that all was well, established town markets, and set uniform weights and measures; these changes helped his people work together much better.[63] Altogether, his impact–the *Carolingian Renaissance*–was the brightest light in the Dark Ages of the Franks, and that was no small accomplishment! Even centuries after his death, he was fodder for dramatic medieval songs (*chansons-de-geste*) which admittedly were sometimes more romantic than accurate.

ThinkWrite 5: "Charlemagne–how great was he?"

What kind of man was Charlemagne? What about the contradictions in his life? What was the significance of the pope crowning him and his Roman title? What was his impact on history?

Well, let's meet the man! (Do *ThinkWrite 5* after you've studied Charlemagne.)

16a❧ Charlemagne

Story of the World: Volume 2, by Susan Wise Bauer, Ch. 13b	Gr. 3-6
Greenleaf's Famous Men of the Middle Ages, Ch. X	Gr. 3-7
Story of the Middle Ages, by C. Miller & H.A. Guerber, Ch. XXXVII-XXXIX	Gr. 4-8
Middle Ages, by Dorothy Mills, Ch. V, Pt. 4	Gr. 6-12
Dark Ages, by Isaac Asimov, Ch. 7 and pp. 172-175	Gr. 8-12
Child's History of the World, by V.M. Hillyer, Ch. 45	Gr. 1-4
Birthdays of Freedom: Vol. 2, by Genevieve Foster, pp. 15-16	Gr. 2-5
A Book of Heroes, by Dorothy Heiderstadt, pp. 29-37	Gr. 3-6
Middle Ages: Cultural Atlas for Young People, by Mike Corbishley, pp. 20-21	Gr. 3-8

Most students should know more about Charlemagne than is covered in this book.

Fire Upon the Earth, by Norman Langford, pp. 76f-79   Gr. 4-8
Church history during Charlemagne's reign.

---

[62] Mills 77.

[63] Miller & Guerber 96.

Son of Charlemagne, by Barbara Willard   Gr. 4-10
   Charlemagne's life through the eyes of his son. This book is in the format of a novel,
   but is so historical and so interesting that I'm going to list it here, where there is less
   chance of anyone missing it.

Charlemagne and the Early Middle Ages, by Miriam Greenblatt   Gr. 5-12
   I've not seen this book. An online reviewer said the final section includes letters,
   poems, and *spells*, so be warned about that.

Trial and Triumph: Stories from Church History, by Richard Hannula, Ch. 10   Gr. 5-12

The Importance of Charlemagne, by Timothy Biel   Gr. 6-12
   Online reviewers claimed this book was interesting. It was recently in-print.

The World in the Time of Charlemagne, by Fiona Macdonald   Gr. 6-12

Charlemagne, by Manuel Komroff (Messner)   Gr. 7-12

Charlemagne, by Susan Banfield (World Leaders Past and Present)   Gr. 8-12
   One reviewer said this book is poorly written and hard to follow.

Charlemagne: Monarch of the Middle Ages, by M. Stearns (Immortals of History) Gr. 9-12

Holy Roman Empire and Charlemagne in World History, by Jeff Sypeck   Gr. 10-12

The Life of Charlemagne, by Einhard   Gr. 11-12
   This biography was written by Charlemagne's own secretary!

Fiction/Historical Fiction

Marvellous Blue Mouse, by Christopher Manson   Gr. 1-4
   I hope you can find this don't-miss book for the younger set. What did one of
   Charlemagne's inspectors find?

Two Travelers, by Christopher Manson   Gr. 1-4
   Another don't-miss book from Manson. It is probably still at many public libraries, and
   is based loosely on the true story of a servant delivering to Charlemagne a gift elephant
   from Haroun al-Rashid.

The Emperor's Arrow, by Burke Boyce   Gr. 1-6
   Legend of a boy who helps Charlemagne.

Baghdad Mission, by Sidney Rosen   Gr. 3-9
> Boy taken to Baghdad tries to return to Charlemagne. Rosen's books are usually very interesting, especially to boys; I've not read this one.

Little Dusty Foot, by Marian Magoon   Gr. 4-10
> Boy fleeing from Saxon raids travels far with a caravan. This book is hard to find.

Charlemagne and the Twelve Peers of France, by Alfred J. Church   Gr. 5-10
> These tales are based on the later-written *chansons-de-geste* ('songs of deeds') which reflect the ideas of their age (1100s and 1200s) on Charlemagne and current events...and became the beloved, romantic ballads of traveling medieval singers. This book is a rare antique, but I mention it anyway since some folks don't want to miss children's books by Mr. Church.

For Charlemagne! by F. Emerson Andrews   Gr. 5-10
> Story of a young student and soldier.

**Stories of Charlemagne*, by Jennifer Westwood   Gr. 7-12
> These tales are based on the later-written *chansons-de-geste* ('songs of deeds') which reflect the ideas of their age (1100s and 1200s) on Charlemagne and current events...and became the beloved, romantic tales told by traveling medieval singers.

16b✸ Roland, Charlemagne's knight

Roland–probably a real knight and governor under Charlemagne–was immortalized in one of the later tales (*chansons-de-geste*) written about the battles of Charlemagne. In the story, he bravely gives his life in a battle with the Moors/Saracens at Roncesvalles. Charlemagne really did fight a battle there, and was attacked from the rear, but that attack came from the Christian Basques who wanted to maintain their independence! However, the Crusades were raging at the time of the song's actual writing so a Saracen enemy was deemed more suitable.[64] Some consider the story of Roland to be "the greatest poem of the early Middle Ages."[65] Furthermore, "the ideals of [medieval] chivalry which developed later owed their beginnings to Charlemagne, for whatever may have been some of his deeds, he handed down traditions of both knighthood and kingship...."[66]

---

[64] Westwood 13.

[65] Mills 68.

[66] Mills 68.

The Song of Roland, by Eleanor Clark (Legacy)	Gr. 2-8
The Horn of Roland, by Jay Williams	Gr. 3-10
The Ivory Horn, by Ian Serraillier	Gr. 5-12
The Story of Roland, by James Baldwin Classic version with gorgeous illustrations.	Gr. 6-12
The Song of Roland, by Robert & Marguerite Goldston	Gr. 9-12
The Song of Roland, by Dorothy Sayers	Gr. 9-12

16c❧ Haroun al-Rashid, Caliph

*Greenleaf's *Famous Men of the Middle Ages*, Ch. XI   Gr. 3-7

Child's History of the World, by V.M. Hillyer, Ch. 45   Gr. 1-4

Birthdays of Freedom: Vol. 2, by Genevieve Foster, p. 14b   Gr. 2-5

> The stories of the *Arabian Nights* were collected during Haroun's reign. If you'd like to read some, there are many versions for various ages.

Fiction/Historical Fiction

Two Travelers, by Christopher Manson   Gr. 1-4
> I hope you can find this don't-miss book! It is probably still at many public libraries, and is based loosely on the true story of a servant bringing to Charlemagne a gift elephant from Haroun al-Rashid. (This book was also listed under *Charlemagne*.)

17❧ Chaos Propels Europe to Feudalism...on the Eve of *Another* Invasion!

Charlemagne's empire crumbled almost instantly after his death, and the next 150 years of history show the petty rulers of the area locked in endless warfare as they vied for the crumbs. So, rather than one realm under a strong king like Charlemagne, there were mini-lands under various kings, dukes, and counts. We'll never know if this might actually have been a decent situation, because these same kings, dukes, and counts did not govern, they grasped. Sadly, they probably claimed to be Christians the entire time their continual wars killed and maimed people, and ruined farms and towns. What does that say about their *Big 2 Beliefs?* Did they really think they would be answering to a higher God for their treatment of others? Or, like barbarian pagans, did they justify their own selfish and base desires? I'm thinking it's the latter, because the rural folk, for example, were reduced to making a living (if they lived at all) by growing a few veggies...which were too often trampled by war horses or eaten by raiding soldiers.

There was chaos in eastern Europe too. The Slavic people there had been squashed by wave after wave of overlords. They had no real history of their own until Rostislav built a Moravian kingdom. It was extremely short-lived, though, because the Magyars (Ugrians) of Ukraine invaded, eventually settling in what we call Hungary (*Ugrian land*, with the *U* being changed to *Hun* apparently to signify that the area had also been home base for the Huns during their European stint); the Hungarians still refer to themselves as Magyars.[67] You'll want to know it was Rostislav who asked the Byzantines (rather than the catholic pope) to send missionaries so his people could become Christians without being 'Frankified.' Two were sent: Cyril and Methodius.[68] These two would eventually convert many Slavic peoples to the Eastern Orthodox Church and develop for them a written alphabet. Indeed, the Russian alphabet of today (the original Russian rulers based in Kiev were largely Slavs) is still called the Cyrillic alphabet. Finally, a group of Bulgurs made a little dominion in the area which is now Romania.[69]

As you've seen, the 'Dark' Ages were dark in western Europe too. (Spain was still under Moorish-Islamic rule, so it was out of this main picture.) Let's check Italy:

Italy had split into several dukedoms, which quarreled among themselves, each trying to dominate the Papacy. The various attempts at domination canceled each other out and left the Papacy at the mercy of the Roman aristocracy. As Popes and Franks alike sank into weakness, it fell to the Byzantines in the south [they still held some land on the end of Italy's boot] to control the Moslems. Fortunately for Rome, the Byzantine Empire was entering another period of relative strength. Its holdings in southern Italy expanded and the Moslem menace was held somewhat in check....[70]

Moreover, the Popes of that time were no longer of the heroic mold. They could easily and rapidly be made and unmade by the decadent and corrupt Roman aristocracy and after being made could be forced into anything. [It] is sometimes called "night of the Papacy."[71]

📖 Feudalism

Heads up! You must see something! All this chaos forced the common people–who hadn't the luxury of stone walls, weapons, or horses–to look to the strongest neighborhood lord for protection, though they practically had to sell themselves into perpetual slavery to get it. What was this called? *Feudalism.* It was a system wherein individuals yielded control of themselves and their lands to a lord who would protect them. They were now *serfs* who were tied to that land and could not leave it. These serfs were required to give to the lord a certain amount of their harvest; they

---

[67] Asimov 214.

[68] Asimov 206.

[69] Asimov 152.

[70] Asimov 211.

[71] Asimov 213.

could keep whatever–if any–was left. Together the lords and serfs made a self-contained community, living off what they could grow and build. While that could have been rather cozy, few lords treated their serfs well. The serfs were obligated to submit, or give homage, to the lord, and they had to soldier when the lord gave the call to arms. Lords provided knights and fortifications (usually built by the serfs) for protection; they also gave homage and troops to higher lords. The highest lords could thus field relatively large armies. There were often confusing overlaps in the various layers, but you'll see all that when you find out more yourself.

The church became intricately involved in feudalism, not only because it was an intimate part of each community but because–through various means–the church had soon come to own one-fourth of the land of Europe as feudal estates! Don't you think it was harder for the church to confront the problems of feudalism when it was getting rich off the system? In other words, had the church *baptized* feudalism? What could folks think if they were as beleaguered by the church as they were by a secular lord?!

This talk of feudalism brings us, once again, to a question of governments. Was the centralized system of Charlemagne better? He at least had the power to fend off enemies and quell selfish nobles, but in other *TruthQuest History* guides we've studied the pitfalls of centralization. Sure, the communal, agrarian living of feudalism had some pluses: there was a simplicity and harmony with the seasons which was enjoyed. People felt part of one body, each doing their part–a teaching the church reinforced. But feudalism was also plagued by war, poverty, abuse, and bondage; people had almost become accustomed to it. When our focus shifts higher than questions of government, we see it was the sinful desires of mankind which had created the ruin and bloodshed. Safety and freedom would come only when God's beloved laws were obeyed.

The church had already had some good impact though. Think of this episode:

> He...captured the...Emperor and his young wife and son, and sent them off to separate convents. This shows the advance....A Merovingian monarch [of the earlier era] would at the least have killed the wife and son out of hand, and perhaps the emperor too.[72]

So, let's dig into this feudal system. In spite of how I introduced it, the topic is *not* boring! It's about lords and ladies and heavy cavalry and rough-hewn fortresses! And did I mention knights? Ms. Mills makes an interesting comment about them:

 Chivalry

> The ideals of the chivalry of the Middle Ages were essentially Christian: they were ideals of service, of loyalty, of fearlessness in the cause of right, of integrity in word and deed, of courtesy and generosity, of consideration for those in need or distress. The ideals of chivalry were not always lived up to, but in an age that was often rough and violent, they were a civilizing influence, and they set a standard that was deeply respected. Noblesse oblige expresses what was required of those who were bound by the obligations of chivalry.[73]

---

[72] Asimov 180-181.

[73] Mills 153.

I'm glad we can wrap up this section by talking about knights because they let us answer more happily our question–*Was Christianity having a positive effect?* Isn't a knight someone who is supposed to act not in his own interests but to instead do what is right in the eyes of God on behalf of others? Wasn't it almost unheard of in non-Christian cultures for men to use their strength to tenderly protect women rather than using it to lord over them?[74] And think of the spiritual ritual knights underwent the night before they were dubbed!

[Parents: it is my opinion that boys especially connect intuitively with the concept of knighthood because it touches on the very essence of their God-given nature: the desire to use their strength in harness to God on behalf of the needs of this world. You fathers will be powerfully moved by the book, *Raising a Modern-Day Knight*, by Robert Lewis, because it will help you and your wife work with your son's God-given nature rather than against it as you raise him in the Lord. Highly recommended... especially when your son is already probing the life of knights. Talk about a teachable moment!]

Well, let's get to digging in here! Few books specifically address the topic of feudalism, so you won't see many specific resources listed below. We will thus also list general overview books on the Middle Ages because they usually cover it. Enjoy! (*Begin ThinkWrite 6* now.)

ThinkWrite 6: "Feudalism"

Do some research on *feudalism*. Make sure you understand the concept and the terminology, such as *fief*, *vassal*, and *liege*.

Don't stop there; you want more than just knowledge. You must dig deeper and use discernment, because the establishment of feudalism shows us the *Big 2 Beliefs* of the 'power brokers.' Who did they *really* think was 'God?' In other words, who had the ultimate authority to determine the principles which other people lived by? How did that first belief affect the quality of life for everyone else? Had the rulers' deep beliefs changed much from the time when their barbarian ancestors were in power?

What does the Bible say about the treatment of employees in I Cor. 9:7-10 and I Tim. 5:18?

Your conclusions here will probably contribute to your *Investigation Supreme!* Don't forget it!

And, while you're learning about knights, make sure you understand *chivalry*. It sounds like a big word, but it's very important for boys, especially, to grasp. How does Scripture say men should treat women?

17a❧ Feudalism

*Story of the Middle Ages, by C. Miller & H.A. Guerber, Ch. XL-XLIII   Gr. 4-8
        Some of these chapters cover feudalism; others cover the crumbling of Charlemagne's empire.

---

[74] If you're exploring this topic with your sons, you may want them to seek out the Scriptural mandate for how women are to be treated. It is so different than the world's system of "might makes right."

Middle Ages, by Dorothy Mills, Ch. X, XII   Gr. 6-12

Dark Ages, by Isaac Asimov, pp. 175-218   Gr. 8-12
   Surprisingly, I really enjoy Asimov's book, as you've probably noticed. I think it's
   amazingly fair and interesting, but the section cited above could definitely be omitted
   if you're short on time. While it certainly mentions the development of feudalism, that
   topic is lightly covered and you can get that info elsewhere, if needed; Asimov focuses
   more on the civil wars which ensued for the next 150 years. Since almost everyone
   involved–generation after generation–was named Louis or Charles or Lothair or Pepin,
   it can get quite confusing. The point can easily be gained without this reading: there was
   chaos brought on by the selfish grasping for power and the people paid the price!
   Don't get me wrong, it is still helpful reading, but it can be omitted.

Child's History of the World, by V.M. Hillyer, Ch. 48   Gr. 1-4

Birthdays of Freedom: Vol. 2, by Genevieve Foster, pp. 17-18   Gr. 2-5

Knights and Castles and Feudal Life, by Walter Buehr   Gr. 3-12
   Buehr's book, though out-of-print, is worth seeking. He does a great job of explaining
   things in an interesting way.

Kings, Bishops, Knights, and Pawns, by Ralph Arnold   Gr. 4-12
   This book looks very interesting also.

Fiction/Historical Fiction

The old poem, *Pied Piper of Hamelin*, by Robert Browning, is apparently based on an event
which occurred during this time,[75] even though Browning set it in 1376, if anyone is interested.
I mention it only briefly because the tale is odd.

17b❧ General overview of the Middle Ages

Duke and the Peasant: Life in the Middle Ages, by Sister Wendy Beckett   All ages
   See medieval days, months, and seasons in this reproduction of an actual "Book of the
   Hours" painted during the Middle Ages.

The Middle Ages, by Gloria & Oriol Verges (Journey Through History)   Gr. K-2

---

[75] Asimov 216, though Asimov cites the author as Robert Southey.

First Book of Medieval Man, by Donald Sobol (First Books)   Gr. 2-7
     This is from the author of the beloved 'Encyclopedia Brown' books.

Hamster History of Britain, by Stanley Baron, illustrated by Janis Mitchell   Gr. 2-8
     The illustrations show events in English history, but the main characters are hamsters!

*How Would You Survive the Middle Ages? by Fiona Macdonald   Gr. 3-7

Castle, Abbey, and Town, by Irma Black   Gr. 3-10

*Middle Ages, by Susan Howarth (See Through History)   Gr. 4-9

*Middle Ages, by Giovanni Caselli (History of Everyday Things)   Gr. 4-10
     A colorful look at the details of medieval life.

Life in the Middle Ages, by Jay Williams (Giant Landmark)   Gr. 6-12

*Medieval Life, by Andrew Langley (DorlingKindersley)   Gr. 6-12

*Early Middle Ages, by James Corrick   Unknown

*Early Middle Ages, published by Raintree Steck-Vaughn   Unknown

Activities

*Coloring Book of the Middle Ages (Bellerophon)   Various

*Days of Knights and Damsels, by Laurie Carlson   Various
     This was formerly titled *Huzzah Means Hooray!*

*Knights & Castles: 50 Hands-On Activities..., by Avery Hart   Various

*Life in a Medieval Castle and Village Coloring Book (Dover)   Various

*Medieval Cookbook, by Maggie Black   Various

*Middle Ages: My World, by Peter Chrisp and Kate Hayden   Various

17c   Knights

You <u>must remember</u> that the knights at this early stage were much less elaborate and much less widespread than they would be in later medieval times, but most of the books about them show them at their later peak. If you don't keep this straight, you'll wonder why the knights had so little impact against the upcoming wave of invaders–the Vikings. It wasn't until the Viking menace had passed and other factors changed around 950, that the knights came into their fullness. By the way, there are so many books about knights at your library that I will just mention samples. Enjoy whatever is available.

Story of the World: Volume 2, by Susan Wise Bauer, Ch. 17a	Gr. 3-6
Middle Ages, by Dorothy Mills, Ch. XI	Gr. 6-12
Dark Ages, by Isaac Asimov, pp. 228-231	Gr. 8-12

        This refers to the development of knighthood *after* 950, when it came into its prime.

The True Book of Knights, by John Lewellen	Gr. K-2
Knights in Shining Armor, by Gail Gibbons	Gr. 1-3
Child's History of the World, by V.M. Hillyer, Ch. 49	Gr. 1-4
If You Lived in the Days of the Knights, by Ann McGovern	Gr. 2-5
Armor Book, by Michael Berenstain	Gr. 2-7

        You'll recognize the Berenstain name, but the topic is knightly body armor! It looks like a very interesting book with neat, detailed pictures.

Days of the Knights: A Tale of Castles and Battles, by C. Maynard (DK Reader 4)	Gr. 3-6
The Illustrated Book of Knights, by Jack Coggins	Gr. 3-7
Knights, by Carole Corbin (First Books)	Gr. 3-7
Knights & Armor, by Daisy Kerr (Worldwise)	Gr. 3-7
Knights in Armor, edited by John Clare (Living History)	Gr. 3-9
(Usborne Time Traveller:) Knights & Castles, by Judy Hindley	Gr. 4-8
Medieval Knights, by David Nicolle (See Through History)	Gr. 4-9
Knights, by Philip Steele (Kingfisher)	Gr. 4-10
Chivalry and the Mailed Knight, by Walter Buehr	Gr. 4-12

Heraldry: The Story of Armorial Bearing, by Walter Buehr	Gr. 4-12
*Knight, by Christopher Gravett (Eyewitness)	Gr. 4-12

Story of Knights and Armor, by Ernest Tucker	Gr. 4-12	
Men in Armor, by Richard Suskind	Gr. 6-12	If you'd like to learn more about *arms & armor*, see Dewey Decimal #739.7.
When Knights Were Bold, by Eva March Tappan	Gr. 6-12	
*World of the Medieval Knight, by Christopher Gravett	Gr. 6-12	

*Knights and Castles, by Richard Dargie	Unknown
*You Wouldn't Want to Be a Medieval Knight, by Fiona Macdonald	Unknown

Activities

*Cut and Make a Knight in Armor (Dover)	Various
*Cut and Make a Knight's Helmet (Dover)	Various
*Design Your Own Coat of Arms (Dover)	Various
*History of the Sword Coloring Book (Dover)	Various
*Knight's Handbook: How to Become a Knight in Shining Armor, by C. Gravett Each section includes a project or activity.	Various
*Medieval Jousts and Tournaments Coloring Book (Dover)	Various
*Medieval Knights Paper Soldiers (Dover)	Various
*Treasure Chest: Knights Kit contains activities, objects, stickers, etc.	Various

Fiction/Historical Fiction

*Knight and the Dragon, by Tomie dePaola	Gr. K-2	Just for fun!
Queen of the Tournament, by Neil Morris Kids enjoy this book, and it is probably still in many libraries.	Gr. K-2	**Cowardly Clyde*, by Bill Peet

Sir Kevin of Devon, by Adelaide Holl   Gr. 1-4

> This was a favorite of my husband's (and many other tykes) when he was a little boy!

A Tournament of Knights, by Joe Lasker   Gr. 1-4

> I'm very sorry to see this book is now out-of-print, but I bet most libraries still have it! It's a nice little gem.

*Minstrel in the Tower, by Gloria Skurzynski   Gr. 2-6

> This is a nice introductory story for early chapter readers.

*The Reluctant Dragon, by Kenneth Grahame   Gr. 2-6

> This is a classic story that has long been beloved. It's from the author of *Wind in the Willows*. It features a friendly dragon.

Tales of True Knights, by George Krapp   Gr. 5-12

> These tales are based on stories told by real medieval bards! It's very rare.

The Tournament of the Lions, by Jay Williams   Gr. 5-12

> The story of a young knight in training who learns the meaning of chivalry.

Knights and Champions, by Dorothy Heiderstadt   Gr. 6-12

> Chapter stories of famous knights, real and legendary, including Roland, Beowulf, King Arthur, El Cid, St. George, Sir Gawain, etc.

18 Viking Raids!

You knew it was coming! I told you in the last section Europe was on the eve of *yet another* invasion! "How is that possible!?" you ask. Well, we know that pagans—who let their own impulses rule as gods in their lives rather than acknowledging the supremacy of God and His laws—are quite happy to prey on the weak. That is barbaric. Do you see? Paganism automatically creates barbarism. Pound, pound, pound this truth into your head! When *you* are tempted to be your own god by acting on your own wrong impulses, remember that you would be acting like a pagan...which would lead you to do barbaric things, things which hurt others. When the world around you says it wants to be free of God's laws and makes that 'freedom' sound happy-go-lucky, a red flag better go up in your heart! For their quest is just a pretty description of paganism...which *will* lead to barbarism. And to what does barbarism lead? *Destruction! Suffering! Pain!*

Those three words describe all too well the new raids being unleashed on Europe by the pagan barbarians of the north—the Vikings. These Northmen (Norsemen) were horrifically cruel, for they held the Teutonic *Big 2 Beliefs* we studied earlier. They swept out of Scandinavia (Denmark, Norway, and Sweden) and brought indescribable waves of cruelty, devastation, and bloodshed which absolutely astounded Europe! Even the monasteries were not safe, for these pagans had no respect for Christianity. When the dreaded Viking ships were sighted, the monks bravely hurried to protect their precious illuminated manuscripts and silver chalices, but it was no use; the monasteries were chief targets due to their relative wealth. The Europeans quaked at the very word *Viking*, for their brutality shocked even the folks of the Dark Ages...and that's saying a lot! The peasants clung even more desperately to their feudal liege lords in hope of protection.

It wasn't just a handful of remote coastal outposts they hit, for their amazing boats–the longships–were faster than anything else on the water. They were also agile, and most importantly, they could run in extremely shallow waters. They dashed up the many rivers of Europe and struck in the very heartland! No one was safe! Not the folks in Scotland, England, Ireland, Spain, Frankland, Germany, southern Italy, or...[76] Well, you get the idea! The Vikings even established trading posts in remote parts of Russia, and it is said a Viking captain named Rurik ruled a great part of Russia himself; some Vikings even made it to Byzantium where they became bodyguards to the emperor![77]

Remember, the kings and dukes of Europe were busily pursuing their own goals–trying to get the other people's land–instead of obeying God's commands to govern rightly the lands they already had! This selfishness made them distracted, weak, disorganized...and foolish. When the first raids came they seemed to think they were a fluke and would never happen again; they went on their merry way, feathering their own nests. But don't we do the same? Aren't we out for what Francis Schaeffer calls "personal peace and affluence?" Aren't we more focused on feathering our own nests than quelling the world's growing dangers? Don't we assume trouble will come to other, faraway people: surely our shire can't be touched! Doesn't modern philosophy say there is no one to fear since there really is no evil (or else it would have to acknowledge the need for a Savior as well as the existence of a God who has the right to determine what is good and evil)? Well, let the 800s be a lesson to us: if we are selfish and distracted and weak, those who are cruel–and there *are* cruel people in this world–*will* take advantage. Remember what the Book of Ecclesiastes tells us: nothing is new under the sun.

Story of the World: Volume 2, by Susan Wise Bauer, Ch. 14a, 14c	Gr. 3-6
Story of the Middle Ages, by Christine Miller & H.A. Guerber, Ch. XLIV	Gr. 4-8
Middle Ages, by Dorothy Mills, Ch. VI, Pt. 1	Gr. 6-12
Dark Ages, by Isaac Asimov, pp. 189-193	Gr. 8-12

---

[76] Miller & Guerber 109.

[77] Miller & Guerber 110.

Vikings, by Kate Petty (Small World)   Gr. K-2

*Birthdays of Freedom, Vol 2, by Genevieve Foster, pp. 21-22   Gr. 2-5

Looking at History, by R.J. Unstead, pp. 53-54   Gr. 2-5
    This is listed for those following English history through this wonderful book.

Stories of the Norsemen, by Johanna Johnston   Gr. 2-7

*Growing Up in Viking Times, by Dominic Tweedle   Gr. 3-7

*Usborne Time Traveller Book of Viking Raiders, by Civardi/Graham-Campbell   Gr. 3-7

Viking Longboats, by Margaret Mulvihill   Gr. 3-7

The Everyday Life of a Viking Settler, by Giovanni Caselli   Gr. 3-8

*Going to War in Viking Times, by Christopher Gravett   Gr. 4-7

They Lived Like This: The Vikings, by Marie Neurath   Gr. 4-7

*Viking Times, by Antony Mason (If You Were There)   Gr. 4-7

*Viking Town, by Jacqueline Morley (Metropolis)   Gr. 4-7

*Viking World, by Julie Ferris (Sightseers)   Gr. 4-9
    Use this 'travel guide' to get around Viking territory.

Viking Warriors, by Tony Triggs   Gr. 4-10

*Technology in the Time of the Vikings, by Peter Hicks   Gr. 4-12

The Vikings, edited by John D. Clare (Living History)   Gr. 4-12
    This series is a favorite of mine, because photos of costumed re-enactors show many
    interesting aspects of daily life. It just went out-of-print, but is probably still in most
    public libraries.

The Northmen, by Thomas Chubb   Gr. 5-10

The Story of Britain, by R.J. Unstead, pp. 51-53   Gr. 5-12
  This is listed for those following English history through this wonderful book.

*Viking, by Susan Margeson (Eyewitness)   Gr. 5-12

*Viking Longship, by Lynda Trent   Unknown

*The Vikings, by Denise Allard (Picture of the Past)   Unknown

Activities

Food & Feasts with the Vikings, by Hazel Martell   Various

**Make This Viking Settlement Cut Out Model* (Usborne)   Various

**Story of the Vikings Coloring Book* (Dover)   Various

**Viking Ships to Cut Out & Put Together* (Bellerophon)   Various

*The Vikings, by Gillian Chapman (Crafts from the Past)   Various

**The Vikings Treasure Chest*   Various
  Kit contains activities, objects, maps, games, etc.

Fiction/Historical Fiction

Snorri and the Strangers, by Nathaniel Benchley (History I Can Read)   Gr. 1-3

**Yo, Vikings!* by Judith Schachner   Gr. 1-3
  I have not seen this, but have only read it described as a modern girl's exploration for info on Eric the Red...which leads to her getting a used Viking ship!

The Sailor Who Captured the Sea, by Deborah Lattimore   Gr. 1-4
  This is an exquisite book! Can our hero protect an illuminated manuscript from the Vikings?

*Viking Adventure, by Clyde Robert Bulla   Gr. 1-5
  Do not, do not, do not miss this wonderful story of a Viking boy's journey. Someone just brought it back into print!

The Falcon of Eric the Red, by Catherine Coblentz   Gr. 3-8

Hakon of Rogen's Saga, by Erik Christian Haugaard   Gr. 3-12
    Son of a slain chieftain must become leader in his father's place.

Pangur Ban, by Mary Stolz   Gr. 4-12
    This is the moving tale of one Irish boy's yearning to illuminate manuscripts and his
    heroic effort to save his works from Viking ravages. It has been *highly* recommended
    to me. It was in-print recently and is probably in many libraries still.

Sigurd & His Brave Companions, by Sigrid Undset   Gr. 4-12

Black Fox of Lorne, by Marguerite de Angeli   Gr. 5-12
    A truly wonderful story! I surely hope you can somehow find a copy of it.

Dublin Crossing, by Sandy Dengler (Heroes of the Misty Isle)   Gr. 5-12
    Christian series: Irish girl survives Viking raids.

Beorn the Proud, by Madeleine Polland   Gr. 6-12
    Viking teen encounters the Christianity of a captured Irish girl.

Blood Feud, by Rosemary Sutcliff   Gr. 7-12
    Boy is taken as Viking slave, travels to Byzantium/Constantinople.

Judith of France, by Margaret Leighton   Gr. 7-12
    Fictional tale of Charlemagne's granddaughter, whose adventure only begins when, due
    to Viking raids, she must hurry to her wedding with a Saxon king.

The Story of Rolf and the Viking Bow, by Allen French   Gr. 8-12
    Respected older story.

Viking's Dawn; Road to Miklagard; Viking's Sunset, by Henry Treece   Gr. 8-12
    Treece's books are always gripping and rugged. This one covers a young Viking and a
    captured Moorish slave.

Raiders from the Sea, by Lois Walfrid Johnson (Viking Quest)...and rest of series   Unknown
    This series of fictional tales, set in Viking times, is published by Moody Press!

19✥ England Reels Under Viking Attacks: Alfred the Great

It was in England that the Vikings first struck, decimating the Lindisfarne Monastery in 793.
After that, the Viking longships prowled the English and Scottish coasts on all sides, and the
Irish—who had not felt the lash of the Roman Empire—did not escape the Norse battle axes.

Shortly after the Lindisfarne attack, King Egbert (ruled 802-839) made his kingdom of Wessex (the West Saxons) dominant over the many smaller kingdoms of England which had been warring amongst themselves for so long. This meant it would fall to the Saxons to fend off the Vikings, if it could be done at all.

When there was nothing left to steal, the Danish Vikings helped themselves to farmland and settled down to live![78] Their region would soon be called the *Danelaw*, but their land-appetite seemed unquenchable.

Then, a great Saxon leader–grandson to King Egbert–became king in 871 at the young age of 22. He poured himself into stopping the Viking menace. His name was, rightfully, Alfred the Great. Much more than a brave warrior, Alfred was a sincere, devout believer, a humble man, a wise maker of laws, and an extremely diligent student who eventually translated the Gospels into the language of the Anglo-Saxons![79] And wait until you learn of his Christian influence on the Vikings! He is probably the greatest monarch England ever had!

Before we learn more about Alfred though, let me say one thing about the Anglo-Saxons. Rather, let me ask Ms. Mills to say it:

> *...they had certain characteristics and certain ways of ordering their tribal life that were to be of great importance in the history of England and of the English people* [which we can extend to Americans, Canadians, Australians, New Zealanders, etc.]. *They loved freedom and independence, and though they had some slaves, their civilization never rested on slavery as did that of Greece and Rome. They spoke a language that was later to develop into the English language. Each tribe governed itself by an assembly of the freemen, the* Folk Moot *or meeting of the people. When the tribes became united as a kingdom, these smaller folk moots developed into the* Witan *or assembly of wise men. These assemblies were not always very powerful and under strong kings they did little more than give him advice, which he did not always feel bound to take, but it was from these early assemblies that representative government developed.*[80]

Do keep in mind that while Alfred's efforts against the Danish Vikings resulted in a fifty-year truce, the Norsemen renewed their attacks after his death. Alfred's son, Edward, and his daughter, Ethelfleda, Queen of Mercia, renewed resistance to the Danes. We can then see Edward's son, Athelstan, win a major victory over them at Brunanburgh; Athelstan would later have the whole Bible translated into Anglo-Saxon. Athelstan's victory was not total, though, and the day would come (we'll peek ahead just a bit) when to keep the peace, the Saxon assembly (the Witan) offered the throne to a Danish chieftain, Canute (1016-1035). Turns out, he converted to Christianity and was a good king, but his sons were unable to keep the crown. The Witan chose a Saxon–Edward–as king (1042-1066), so once again a countryman was on the throne. Edward had been raised in Normandy, though, and had a decidedly un-Saxon style.

---

[78] Unstead 53.

[79] Miller and Guerber 118.

[80] Mills 93.

He was very interested in church ceremonies and church buildings, and poured himself into rebuilding Westminster Abbey.[81] He was thus nicknamed Edward the Confessor. There was a great deal of struggle during his reign. When he left no heir, the trouble boiled over...but you'll have to wait until later to find out what happened!

As an added bonus, I've tucked in a little side trip to Scotland in our topics below. No extra charge! Well, I had better stop talking so you can meet some of these people!

19a✤ Egbert the Saxon

Greenleaf's Famous Men of the Middle Ages, Ch. XII	Gr. 3-7

The Story of Britain, by R.J. Unstead, pp. 49-51	Gr. 5-12

19b✤ Alfred the Great

Story of the World: Volume 2, by Susan Wise Bauer, Ch. 15a-b	Gr. 3-6
Greenleaf's Famous Men of the Middle Ages, Ch. XIV	Gr. 3-7
Story of the Middle Ages, by Miller & Guerber, Ch. XLV-XLVII	Gr. 4-8
Middle Ages, by Dorothy Mills, Ch. VI, Pt. 4 & Ch. VII, Part 1b	Gr. 6-12

Child's History of the World, by V.M. Hillyer, Ch. 46	Gr. 1-4
Birthdays of Freedom: Vol. 2, by Genevieve Foster, pp. 19-20	Gr. 2-5
Looking at History, by R.J. Unstead, pp. 54-55	Gr. 2-5
Alfred the Great, by Mary Fitt	Gr. 2-6
I'm so excited! I just found a used copy of this precious old book. Looks perfect!	
A Book of Heroes, by Dorothy Heiderstadt, pp. 38-46	Gr. 3-6
Island Story, by H.E. Marshall, Ch. XV-XVII	Gr. 3-8
King Alfred the Great, by Eleanor Noyes Johnson	Gr. 4-9

---

[81] Unstead 72.

Seven Kings of England, by Geoffrey Trease, pp. 13-48   Gr. 4-10

Trial and Triumph: Stories from Church History, by Richard Hannula, Ch. 11   Gr. 5-12

Story of Britain, by R.J. Unstead, pp. 54-69   Gr. 5-12

Young Alfred the Great, by Naomi Mitchison   Gr. 7-12

The Right Line of Cerdic, by Alfred Duggan   Gr. 9-12

Ballad of the White Horse, by G.K. Chesteron   Gr. 10-12
    An epic poem, some call it the best in English, on the life and deeds of Alfred.

Fiction/Historical Fiction

A Maid at King Alfred's Court, by Lucy Foster Madison   Gr. 4-12

Alfred, King of the English, by Carola Oman   Gr. 5-12
    This book is very biographical.

Escape to King Alfred, by Geoffrey Trease   Gr. 6-12
    Trease's books are rare, but excellent. This one is also titled *Mist Over Athelney*.

Journey for a Princess, by Margaret Leighton   Gr. 6-12
    Alfred's daughter travels to Rome and receives a secret letter after a Viking prince
    pursues marriage.

Voyage to Coromandel, by Margaret Leighton   Gr. 6-12
    Viking hostages given to Alfred travel, fight pirates, etc.

The Dragon and the Raven, by G.A. Henty   Gr. 7-12

The High King's Daughter, by Theodora DuBois   Gr. 7-12
    I've not seen this but have read that it is about Alfred before he became king and relates
    to Viking invasions in Ireland.

The King's Jewel, by Erick Berry   Gr. 7-12

The Marsh King, by C. Walter Hodges   Gr. 7-12

The Namesake, by C. Walter Hodges   Gr. 7-12

Great Axe Bretwalda, by Philip Ketchum   Gr. 8-12
    I've not read this, but learned that it is set in the era of King Alfred; an Englishman and
    his friends who are enslaved by the Danes try to support the king.

19c☙ Alfred's descendants continue to resist the Vikings

*Story of the Middle Ages, by Miller & Guerber, Ch. XLVIII-XLIX, LI-LII   Gr. 4-8

Heroes and Saints, by R.J. Unstead, Ch. 8   Gr. 3-9

The Story of Britain, by R.J. Unstead, pp. 61-63   Gr. 5-12

19d☙ Ethelred the Unready and Edmund Ironside

*Island Story, by H.E. Marshall, Ch. XVIII-XIX   Gr. 3-8

Heroes and Saints, by R.J. Unstead, Ch. 9   Gr. 3-9

The Story of Britain, by R.J. Unstead, pp. 64-69   Gr. 5-12

Fiction/Historical Fiction

The Story of Elswyth, by Eileen Meyler   Gr. 8-12
    I've not seen this, but it is described as a youth novel about the time of Ethelred.

19e☙ Canute, the Danish king of England

**Greenleaf's *Famous Men of the Middle Ages*, Ch. XVI   Gr. 3-7

*Story of the Middle Ages, Ch. LXI   Gr. 4-8
    by Christine Miller & H.A. Guerber

Middle Ages, by Dorothy Mills, p. 102   Gr. 6-12

Looking at History, by R.J. Unstead, p. 56   Gr. 2-5
    There is only a very brief mention of Canute.

*Island Story, by H.E. Marshall, Ch. XX   Gr. 3-8

The Story of Britain, by R.J. Unstead, pp. 70-71   Gr. 5-12

> If you have extra time, a famous English legend tells of Havelok the Dane.
>
> *Havelok the Dane* Gr. 7-12 by Kevin Crossley-Holland
>
> *Havelok the Dane* Gr. 7-12 by Ian Serraillier

Fiction/Historical Fiction

The Ward of King Canute, by Ottilie Liljencrantz   Gr. 8-12

19f🍃 Edward the Confessor: England returns to a Saxon king

*Greenleaf's *Famous Men of the Middle Ages*, Ch. XVIII   Gr. 3-7

Story of the Middle Ages, by Miller & Guerber, Ch. LXII   Gr. 4-8

Middle Ages, by Dorothy Mills, p. 102   Gr. 6-12

Looking at History, by R.J. Unstead, p. 57   Gr. 2-5
    There is only the briefest mention of Edward.

Island Story, by H.E. Marshall, Ch. XXI   Gr. 3-8

The Story of Britain, by R.J. Unstead, pp. 72-75   Gr. 5-12

Fiction/Historical Fiction

Far Traveler, by Rebecca Tingle   Unknown
    I've not even seen this book and cannot comment on its content, but I learned that it is set during the reign of Edward the Confessor.

Audio/Video

Lady Godiva, starring Maureen O'Hara   Parental decision
    Alas, the cover art on my version of this film makes it look like the film is risqué, but this true story is handled modestly in the film. It tells of Lady Godiva's support for the Saxon folk, the punishment she received (riding unclothed through the town), and the way the community protected her. Alfred, Lord Tennyson, wrote a poem on the topic: *Godiva*. Parents, you will need to decide if this is an appropriate topic for your children.

19g🍃 Scottish focus: Macbeth and Queen Margaret

It was just before the reign of Edward the Confessor that the Scottish nobleman, Macbeth, about whom Shakespeare wrote, assassinated the Scottish king. The king's heir appealed to Edward for help. If you have the time and ability, you could read Shakespeare's *Macbeth* now, but there are also narrative retellings of the plot listed in the much-appreciated books below. (Parents: because this story includes an assassination, a guilty man haunted by his wrongful deeds, and the witches Shakespeare added as a literary device, you will need to decide the appropriateness of this topic for your children. Therefore, I've not listed any grade recommendations for the Shakespearean Macbeth stories. The retellings are often gentler, though.)

In quite a different direction, Queen Margaret's powerful influence on Scotland is amazing! I hope you can find information on this significant lady. I've been able to stand in her chapel in Edinburgh, and it was quite moving.

❧ Historical Macbeth

*Greenleaf's *Famous Men of the Middle Ages*, Ch. XVI   Gr. 3-7

Story of the Middle Ages, by Christine Miller & H.A. Guerber, Ch. LXII   Gr. 4-8

❧ Shakespearean Macbeth

Beautiful Stories from Shakespeare, by E. Nesbit
     This has been released under various titles.

Macbeth, adapted by Leon Garfield
     This book has darkish illustrations, but I've heard it's a good retelling.

Shakespeare's Stories, Vol. 1, by Leon Garfield

Stories from Shakespeare, by Marchette Chute

Tales from Shakespeare, by Charles and Mary Lamb

❧ Queen Margaret
Don't forget! Margaret is the subject of a major section of the Christian novel "Fields of Bannockburn."

Beggars, Beasts and Easter Fire, by Carol Greene, Ch. 7   Gr. 2-8

Fiction/Historical Fiction

Faraway Princess, by Jane Oliver   Gr. 4-12

Queen's Blessing, by Madeleine Polland   Gr. 8-12
     Queen Margaret helps orphans.

20 ❧ Frankland Reels Under Viking Attacks: Eudes, Rollo, and Hugh Capet

Did you notice that in 885 the Vikings were not only harrying England, Scotland, and Ireland, but had also sailed up the Seine River and laid siege to Paris itself?! King Charles the Fat (a "monument to inertia")[82] did nothing, so it was up to Count Eudes of Paris to defend the city. The kingship of Frank-land would eventually transfer to a great-nephew of Eudes (Hugh Capet) because the Franks were disgusted with Charles's failures and were proud of the brave resistance of Eudes, but we'll get to that later.

In the end, a weak Frankish king simply offered a big chunk of Frankland to the chief Viking, Rollo (Hrolf), if he would stop his attacks. Rollo accepted the deal in 911 and supposedly accepted Christianity![83] His Norsemen (mostly Danes, though Rollo was Norwegian) settled along the north coast, in what is now called the *Norman*dy area of France. Get it? Rollo became a fancy-dancy duke, and in just five generations, his descendant, William of Normandy, would.... Oh, I better shut up! You'll find out soon enough!

Midway between Rollo and William came Richard. He was part of helping the dying Carolingian dynasty to its final resting place since he supported the long push of Hugh Capet to the throne.

In Hugh's career can be seen *the* political issue of the late Dark Ages: the power struggle between the most powerful liege lords (nobles such as the Dukes of Burgundy, Normandy, and Aquitaine) and the struggling central kings who talked of building a unified nation which could better withstand attack, develop trade, and end civil wars. Ah, but I'm painting too rosy a picture. Many kings had no such ideals but simply wanted to boss everyone else! Of course, the same power-lust could be found in the nobles who didn't want to be ruled by kings, but who wanted to be kings outright in their own lands. Are you getting the picture?

This issue again raises key questions about what is appropriate government, for it seems the fracturing of Europe did indeed open it to horrendous invasions, horrendous civil wars, and horrendous economies. When Europe had been under the massive centralized empire of Rome, it had different problems: lack of human rights, lack of local control, the caesar's whims being imposed on the masses, the state becoming godlike, etc. Indeed, you may remember that as the Roman Empire was falling, the locals sometimes cheered the barbarian arrivals,[84] apparently thinking anything would be better than Rome's tyranny! This may even have helped them embrace the Germanic ideal of localness...and later feudalism, which has a local flavor.

---

[82] Asimov 209.

[83] Asimov 220.

[84] Keating 110.

Thinking deeper, though, we can see that *all* these problems relate not so much to the form of government as to the heart (*Big 2 Beliefs*) of those in government. The issue is this: does the king, noble, or chieftain see himself as a god—someone able to do what he wants, to please himself, to take what he wants at the expense of others, simply because he has the power to do so? (You've seen what horrors and suffering come from *that* line of thinking.) Or does he see his power as limited since he is acting only as a deputy of the God Who is the King of human kings? *This*, then, is precisely where the influence of the church was so desperately needed.

You've already been thrilled to see how virtually every barbarian tribe which set foot in Europe became Christian in the end (though one could sometimes question if their Christianity was real and biblical, especially when they were 'converting' others at swordpoint). Even so, this is an *enormous* thing! These barbarians were mightily changed over the many centuries it takes to alter the thinking of an entire, millennia-old tribe...and they soon settled down to being productive nations rather than marauding bands of bloodthirsty warriors! Alvin Schmidt has written an entire book (**Under the Influence*) about the amazing impact of Christianity on civilization. I've not had a chance to read it, but I hear it's wonderful!

Yes, Christianity had a profound impact on the barbarian tribes, but did it have as much impact as it could have? Did the church government (the papacy) show the secular governors the significance of purity and service? Ms. Guerber addresses this:

> *...things in Rome were in a sad state of affairs. The popes were by this time so powerful that ambitious men wanted to be pope, and there was bribery, fighting, and murder in order to gain the holy office.*[85]

Alas, where it could and should have been working to constrain the harshness and selfishness of dukes and kings, the church was too often competing with them in a life-and-death chess game with the poor peasant-pawns in the middle. This did have the tremendously good effect of limiting the power of kings, but what does it tell us about the *Big 2 Beliefs* of the church leaders who were corrupt and selfish? Ouch! And what of the fact that the church was trying to centralize its power and structure, and the kings were doing likewise? That's a hard question to ask, but we must, for *what the church is in one generation, the government will be in the next.*[86] Were things supposed to be different? I have no idea, but I do know God knows! Let's see how He would move things over the centuries working through people here and there. All I know is that the nations of Europe *and* the pope became much more powerful after the year 1000—the era called the 'High' Middle Ages. Since great power is often misused, you'll see the common people squeezed hard between.

One thing's for sure, you have plenty to think about: the impact and connection of paganism, barbarism, church authority, governmental authority, and the *Big 2 Beliefs* propelling them all. That's what your *ThinkWrite 1: Investigation Supreme* is all about! Get some of your current thoughts woven in there. Remember, we're seeking wisdom, not just knowledge!

---

[85] Miller & Guerber 135.

[86] Peter Marshall said this at a homeschooling conference I attended.

Oh, I almost forgot! We just nonchalantly mentioned the emergence of the 'High' Middle Ages. What began to end the 'Dark' Ages? Farming became more productive due to the invention of a better plow and the horse collar, and the strength of knights was better developed. But there was something much deeper at work, as you know. With the conversion of the Vikings to Christianity, most of the barbarians had now retired from their dreadful careers. We can thank Ansgar, the *very* courageous first missionary to the Vikings,[87] and we can happily and proudly answer our *what-was-the-impact-of-the-church* question! So instead of fleeing, dying, and repairing, Europeans could build! You probably cannot even begin to imagine what a Godsend this was–and I mean that literally! More solid nations sprang up everywhere, as well as more solid trade, more solid schools, and even more solid buildings as society moved from sticks to stones.[88] No one who knows history can say Christianity binds people. It frees people!

Phew! We've wandered far from our discussion of Hugh Capet, but then again, maybe not! This is what Hugh was facing. Interestingly, Hugh's descendants–the Capetian dynasty–would sit on that throne for the next 900 years, and we can now officially think of the land of the Franks as *France!* I'll ask Mr. Asimov to eulogize:

> *The great thing about the Franks, the enormous contribution they made to later culture, even at their most abysmally brutal and barbaric, was that they* survived! *They stopped the Moslems; they stopped the Norsemen. They were caved in and broken here and there, and they tore themselves apart in suicidal civil war, but they never collapsed completely.*

Let's dig in and see the new France which was emerging from the 'Dark' Ages...then we'll see the same happen in other European lands!

Greenleaf's Famous Men of the Middle Ages, Ch. XIII	Gr. 3-7
Story of the Middle Ages, by Miller & Guerber, Ch. LIII-LIV, LVIII	Gr. 4-8
Middle Ages, by Dorothy Mills, Ch. VI, Pt. 3 and Ch. VII, Pt. 2 (first half)	Gr. 6-12
Dark Ages, by Isaac Asimov, pp. 218-224 and Ch. 10	Gr. 8-12
Child's History of the World, by V.M. Hillyer, Ch. 50	Gr. 1-4

Fiction/Historical Fiction

Little Duke, by Charlotte Yonge   Gr. 5-12
   The classic story of the childhood of Richard the Fearless, grandson of Rollo and great-grandfather to William! When Richard was only nine years old... Oh, I had better not tell. Then there's the story of his escape attempt... Oops! I'll let you read it!

---

[87] S.M. Houghton, *Sketches from Church History* (Carlisle, PA: Banner of Truth Trust, 1980), 49-50.

[88] Asimov, Ch. 10.

21☙ Leif Erickson: A Big Discovery and a Bigger Change!

I know you've heard of him! Leif Ericson, that is. He is best known for setting foot–around the year 1000–on the shores of North America. He *was* indeed a brave explorer. Would *you* want to nose around the North Atlantic without charts or navigational tools in a small *open* boat?! Yes, that was courageous, but Leif was even more courageous than that, for he admitted the 'manmadeness' of Woden and Thor–the old Teutonic gods–and took Christianity not only to his own heart,

> **ThinkWrite 7:**
> *"Leif turns over a new leaf!"*
>
> What was the effect on Europe's history when the Vikings and other barbarians converted to Christianity?

but also to the Viking strongholds in Greenland.[89] I know you met the Vikings earlier in a general way, but it's now time to meet these specific men: Leif, his father, Eric the Red, his brother, and the many Viking explorers! (Do **ThinkWrite 7** while studying this.)

Story of the World: Volume 2, by Susan Wise Bauer, Ch. 14b	Gr. 3-6
Middle Ages, by Dorothy Mills, Ch. VI, Pt. 2	Gr. 6-12

Eric the Red & Leif the Lucky, by Barbara Schiller	Gr. K-3
Leif the Lucky, by Ingri & Edgar Parin d'Aulaire	Gr. K-3
This *don't-miss* book offers beloved illustrations and text which relate Leif's life and his conversion to Christianity.	
Leif's Saga, by Jonathan Hunt	Gr. K-3
Gorgeous illustrations! Recently in-print, it is probably in most public libraries.	
Child's History of the World, by V.M. Hillyer, Ch. 47	Gr. 1-4
Leif the Lucky: Discoverer of America, by Erick Berry (Garrard Discovery)	Gr. 1-5
Leif Ericson: Explorer, by Ruth Weir (Makers of America)	Gr. 2-6
Viking Explorers, by Rupert Matthews (Beginning History)	Gr. 2-6
A Book of Heroes, by Dorothy Heiderstadt, pp. 47-54	Gr. 3-6
Eric the Red, by Neil Grant	Gr. 3-6

---

[89] Katherine B. Shippen, *Leif Eriksson: First Voyage to America* (New York: Harper & Brothers, 1951) 88-89.

66

Viking Explorers, by Luigi Pruneti	Gr. 3-7
The Viking Explorers, by Walter Buehr	Gr. 3-8
The Story of Leif Ericson, by William O. Steele (Signature)	Gr. 3-9
The Vikings, by Elizabeth Janeway (Landmark) One of the few Landmarks in print, this focuses on Eric and Leif.	Gr. 4-10
Leif Erikson the Lucky, by Frederic Kummer Emphasizes adventure of Leif's voyage; extremely rare.	Gr. 5-12
Voyagers West, by Margaret Johansen Focuses on Eric the Red, father to Leif Ericson.	Gr. 6-12
Strange Footprints on the Land, by Constance Irwin Story of the Vikings in America.	Gr. 9-12
Eric the Red: The Vikings Sail the Atlantic, by Anne Millard	Unknown

Fiction/Historical Fiction

Door to the North, by Elizabeth Coatsworth (Land of the Free) A tale of the Vikings in North America.	Gr. 4-12

22 Off to Russia!

Do you remember learning earlier that the Vikings were in the city of Kiev (which is now capital of the Ukraine)? Well, the year 989 found Prince Vladimir ruling from Kiev. He no longer wanted to be a pagan, so sent official envoys to three religious capitals to see which had the grandest religion. It was the Byzantine envoy who returned with the most glowing tales, so Vladimir converted to the Eastern Orthodox Church and led the nation to do so as well! Ukraine and Russia have been Eastern Orthodox nations ever since! You may know that the famous St. Basil's Cathedral in Moscow was later built in the Byzantine style. (We'll not study much Russian history here; our focus is on the main section of Europe; but you can independently!)

Story of the World: Volume 2, by Susan Wise Bauer, Ch. 23a	Gr. 3-6

23 Off to Germany!

As we march around Europe at the turn of the millennium—when many folks feared the world was going to end—we must visit the eastern Frankish land which would become Germany. Do you remember? Few of Charlemagne's descendants had been able to hold together both the western and eastern Frankish halves because the culture and the language of the two had drifted apart. They would eventually become fully separate (and usually hostile) nations: France and Germany. After suffering under the same destructive civil wars and poor leadership as had the western section, a strong eastern leader came on the scene in 919: Henry the Fowler. Henry was a very active king—he trained his peasants to better resist the Magyars and he built walled cities (burgs) filled with supplies in case of siege. He conquered the Duke of Bohemia (in what is now the Czech Republic) and sent missionaries there. This was at the time of Duke Wenceslaus (of Christmas carol fame), who had already become a Christian through the training of his mother. This gives me the opportunity to remind everyone of the great impact of women on history by quoting the famous line: *the hand that rocks the cradle rules the world*

Anyway, Henry's son, Otto I, accomplished even more and would be given by the pope a new title: Holy Roman Emperor![90] In fact, this land would be called the Holy Roman Empire (not *Germany*) for some time. It was Otto who first well-employed armored knights,[91] and he gave the ever-raiding Magyars a great defeat. Eventually, the Magyars accepted Christianity and settled down in (what would be) Hungary. Otto also conquered many tribes to the north and east of him, including the Slavonic people in (what would be) Poland. In 966, Prince Mieszko I embraced Christianity on behalf of his people, and Poland has been devoutly catholic to this day![92]

It was Otto's grandson—Emperor Otto III—who boosted his former tutor, Gerbert, to the papacy. Gerbert, who, as secretary to a French archbishop helped Hugh Capet to the throne, was now Pope Sylvester II (999-1003). He brought into the church many of the great documents of Greece (mostly via the Arabs who had largely gotten them from Christian lands they had conquered). Sylvester/Gerbert also began usage of a better numbering system. You can see he had a positive impact on increasing the learnedness of the church.[93]

Since Otto III had no heirs, his cousin Heinrich became the next Holy Roman Emperor. Heinrich was very interested in continuing the spread of Christianity into eastern Europe. He continued work amongst the Slavonic tribes and he supported Stephen, Christian king of Hungary. The era ended with the passing of Heinrich, for he was the last Saxon emperor.[94]

*Greenleaf's *Famous Men of the Middle Ages*, Ch. XV	Gr. 3-7
Story of the Middle Ages, by Christine Miller & H.A. Guerber, Ch. LIX	Gr. 4-8
Dark Ages, by Isaac Asimov, pp. 221, 228-234	Gr. 8-12

---

[90] Asimov 231.

[91] Asimov 229.

[92] Carol Greene, *Beggars, Beasts & Easter Fire* (Batavia, IL: Lion Publishing, 1993) 57.

[93] Asimov 232-234.

[94] Miller & Guerber 141.

Good King Wenceslas, by Christopher Manson   Various
    This illustrated book contains the text of the famous Christmas carol which emphasizes
    Christian compassion.

Middle Ages: Cultural Atlas for Young People, by Mike Corbishley, pp. 36-37   Gr. 3-8

Good King Wenceslas, by Mildred Luckhardt   Gr. 4-10

Peasant Boy Who Became Pope, by Harriet Lattin   Gr. 7-12
    This is the life story of Gerbert.

24 ☙ Off to Spain!

We won't bother to make a trip to Italy for it was a fragmented mess with a great deal of conflict
between the various nobles, the Papal States, and more. Of course, the pope's power was great,
and he was based on the Italian peninsula, but the turmoil kept Italy itself in the shadows for
a long time.

So, we will make our final millennial tour stop in Spain. Don't get me wrong, though! Spain,
like Italy, was torn between competing kings and nobles, making it difficult for them to defeat
their Moorish overlords. These Moslem rulers were sometimes very tolerant of Christianity,
though not always, alas. Spaniards can be very proud of their martyr heroes, and their great
national hero, El Cid! In the middle of the eleventh century (1040-1099), this great knight came
to Spain's rescue and was instrumental in wresting key Spanish cities from the Moors.

    Story of the World: Volume 2, by Susan Wise Bauer, Ch. 18d   Gr. 3-6

    *Greenleaf's *Famous Men of the Middle Ages*, Ch. XVII   Gr. 3-7

    Story of the Middle Ages, by Miller & Guerber, Ch. LXIV-LXVI   Gr. 4-8

    A Book of Heroes, by Dorothy Heiderstadt, pp. 55-62   Gr. 3-6

    The Tale of the Warrior Lord, by Merriam Sherwood   Gr. 4-12

    El Cid, by Geraldine McCaughrean   Gr. 6-12

    Heroes and Warriors: El Cid, by John Matthews   Gr. 7-12
        Emphasizes the actual historical basis for the legends of El Cid.

The Legend of the Cid, by Robert Goldston   Gr. 7-12

El Cid, by Philip Koslow (Hispanics of Achievement)   Unknown

Audio/Video

El Cid, starring Charleton Heston
I call this a *don't-miss* film! It's one of my favorites!!

25❧ Phew: The Church at the Year 1000!

We have indeed made it to the year 1000! We've done our millennial tour around Europe! Did you see the 'Dark' Ages were beginning to be the 'High' Middle Ages? Yes, instead of centuries marked by barbarian invasions and folks living in mud huts, you'll now see more of what you imagine the Middle Ages to be: knights in

<table>
<tr><td>

ThinkWrite 8: "Darkness Lifts"

What influences and factors brought about the end of the Dark Ages?

</td></tr>
</table>

shining armor, damsels in distress, and mighty castles with flags unfurled. (Do *ThinkWrite 8* now before continuing with this section, if you please.)

History, though, is not just about dashing—or even *un*dashing—people. It's not the story of beautiful buildings and famous events. History is His-story; it's Who *God* is, what He's doing, the truth that is His very essence, as well as what people believe (their *Big 2 Beliefs*) and do in response! Interesting! So don't get swept away with all the glamour of the Middle Ages; don't be overwhelmed by the grit, either. Keep probing for the hand of God; He is always at work in history to bring about His own plan!

As we seek to understand the beliefs of medieval people, we see something amazing! Almost all Europeans believed the same thing because they were members of the same church. This makes the Middle Ages one of the most unified times in history and it shows the great impact the church had already had. Ms. Mills explains:

There was only one church in the Middle Ages, all Christians belonged to it and in all parts of it the teaching and the worship were the same. The Church influenced almost every part of the life of a medieval man. If he went to school, it educated him, for nearly all schools were connected in some way or other with the Church. If he lived in the country, once a year...he marched in procession with all the people of the parish round the fields praying for a blessing on the crops. If he lived in a town and were a craftsman, the gild to which he belonged maintained a chapel in the...church to which the members of the gild went in procession on their annual festival. If he were of noble birth, he kept vigil in the church the night before he was made a knight, and the religious side of the ceremony was the most important. Whether he lived in castle or manor or town, he attended Mass on Sundays and Holy Days....All through the year the chief holidays were the holidays of the church, such as Christmas, Easter and Whitsuntide, Midsummer's Day...and Michaelmas Day.

70

The ideal of the medieval Church was that of a great spiritual society that should include all Christendom, and for many centuries it seemed as if the ideal were to be realized. As the pagan peoples of Europe became converted to Christianity they took their place in the organization of the church; an organization that represented the old civilization [the Roman Empire] *in its details of discipline and order.*[95]

You've already seen the impact of the local priests all across Europe; they worked hard to teach and minister to the community, care for the poor and sick, and so much more. You know the role monasteries played in preserving the Scriptures and the important writings of civilization. You've seen the incredible change in Europe as the barbarian tribes converted and settled down to become productive members of society! Truly amazing!

Interestingly, we've been seeing that several of the kings and nobles—as in England (Alfred), France (Pepin the Short, Charlemagne, Louis the Pious, and Robert), the Holy Roman Empire (Otto I and other Ottonians, including Heinrich), Hungary (Stephen), and Bohemia (Wenceslas)—were actually quite devout! They were trying to build Christian nations,[96] though their understanding and implementation was often highly flawed.

What is especially interesting about these devout kings is that they were extending the church at a time when the popes were the weakest, as you've seen.[97] So let's do a church check! That way we can *really* take Europe's temperature! It will not be hard, for there was just one Christian church in the Middle Ages—the one which had grown up from the early church and was thus called *catholic* (the Latin word for *universal*), as you've seen.[98] This means we're checking our *own* ancestral church—whether we are what is now called Catholic or Protestant. (The division of the church into Roman Catholic and Protestant branches occurred after the time period we're studying now; only then is *Catholic* capitalized since it then refers to a specific church rather than the general church of the Middle Ages. We'll study all this later.)

We've picked a uniquely good time to do a church check, because many Europeans thought the year 1000 was the end of time. They didn't bother to plant crops, and many gave their worldly goods to the church, thinking it wouldn't hurt to be *extra good* right before meeting their Maker. Of course, the year 1000 came and went, and the world was still here. Maybe there had been an earlier calendar error, they assumed; Judgement Day must be coming in the next couple years certainly. Again, no crops were planted and even more was given to the church. It was finally decided Judgement must be 1000 years after Christ's death, not His birth, so the

---

[95] Mills 111-112.

[96] Jackson 85.

[97] Jackson 85.

[98] One small denomination takes exception to this statement, saying they can trace their history back to the apostles separately from the mainstream *catholic* church of the Roman Empire and Middle Ages, but the statement is at least true for the vast majority of us.

world waited–treading water–for another thirty years.[99] (Of course, Jesus Christ had cautioned against such behavior, but that doesn't mean we obey!) Eventually, it was realized time was rolling on, so Europe again settled down to the business of planting and building. Good thing! There had been major famines during the years of idleness, and things were pretty run-down.[100]

Do the math, though! Folks had been giving land to the church and it now owned 25% of all Europe![101] It had the money to begin magnificent cathedrals (which we'll talk about later). It was a feudal lord itself! The pope had already been governing the Papal States and had his own army, but now local churches, monasteries, and bishops were estate and title holders too![102] They were an intricate part of the feudal economy and the political power structure, especially since the church was almost the only source of educated officials. The kings needed the power, structure, and endorsement of the church, but the church now had mixed motives in deciding what role to play because it had its own real estate and income at stake. Sticky business! While Christianity had made great impact on Europe, it does seem the church was now focusing more on its own earthly kingdom than on God's kingdom! There were even times when wealthy men "invested" in a parish and then hired unscrupulous, uneducated, immoral priests to run it for them, keeping most of the profits (baptism fees, burial charges, feudal incomes, and the new required tithe to the church).[103] What a mess! How the devoted priests must have cringed! Mr. Jackson describes it:

> *As long as the church thrives in the orbit of the secular power as the supplier of administrators...and accepts a share of the spoils...it will tend to make spiritual values take the back seat.*
>
> *It is possible to exaggerate the number of gimlet-eyed opportunists among the dignitaries of the church. But even a few would be too many. And these had unique occasion for gain. Their cooperation with the local prince frequently meant he would turn a blind eye to their public depredations.*[104]

Yes, the church was spending much of its time and effort sparring with kings to build its own earthly kingdom–an ever stronger *monarchy* with the pope ruling as unchallenged king. Spiritually, this was far from the local, intimate churches of the New Testament era. Politically,

✒ Monarchy

the kings began to feel mistrustful and defensive toward the church because it was trying to get lands and income *from* the king *for* itself! Think of a king who finds one-quarter of the people and lands in his realm belonging to a different king–a pope with his own army, his own agenda, and without

---

[99] Mills 180, and Miller & Guerber 136.

[100] Miller & Guerber 136.

[101] Jackson 83.

[102] Mills 115.

[103] Jackson 83.

[104] Jackson 82-83.

accountability–while the kings had to watch for backlash from their nobles, the populace, and the pope! As an example, you'll see Pope Gregory VII's subjugation of Emperor Henry IV. This papal restraint on the power of kings could have been fantastic, except it was used more often for papal gain than the protection of the people! *That's* the problem! Over the course of the High Middle Ages, it was the popes who, by far, had the most power and wealth, but these assets were rarely used to benefit the starving, downtrodden people. On the contrary! They were extracted from them!

Remember, the secular kings were watching the popes, determining what must be acceptable behavior in God's eyes. That's why it has been said that what the church is, the nation will become. Remember...the church cannot avoid its leadership position: it is always modeling to the world, whether for good or evil. Put simply, the church cannot *not* lead!

But there's a side to this which is more profound than the political and economic impacts we've been discussing, though these made life harder for folks every single day. There was an even more powerful spiritual impact, though. The church began presenting itself as the only way to reach God, because God was being shown as increasingly remote, guilt-obsessed, and abstract. I don't want to admit it, but it seems a strong likelihood that the motive for these 'distortions'[105] was protection of position and income...because those had been the strongest impulses in most of the top church leadership for some time, and this is just the purpose that was accomplished. Certainly it was not to benefit the common folk, for they were losing the intimacy with God that had been a hallmark of the New Testament era and the earlier Middle Ages when people felt close to the Lord and His creation.

How can such suspicions be drawn? Well, the lay people were no longer allowed to take the cup, some spiritual principles were now called "holy mysteries," Latin was still used for mass even though most common people no longer understood it, and church art became increasingly otherworldly, as Byzantine art had done.[106] It was only 'professional churchmen' or 'otherworldly saints' who could approach God on behalf of the people, so the communion table moved behind a screen. Simply put, the church was driving a wedge between God and people which would leave an aching void in the hearts of men. Where would they seek to fill that void, especially after the church stripped medieval Christianity of its intimacy and folks wrongly concluded true Christianity had no answers? You'll see in the next *TruthQuest History* guide! For now, though, you can know the issues we're talking about–because they are spiritual–are huge! They are history-changing!

Is it any wonder the secular kings soon felt they too were professionals who–like the medieval church–were above God's laws for the treatment of others? Yes, when both church and king ignored God's laws on service, purity, humility, honesty, and compassion, life could get very unpleasant. Can you see that some *Big 2 Beliefs* must have changed? Remember, a pagan and

---

[105] Francis Schaeffer uses this word to convey the concept, p.56 and throughout Ch. 2.

[106] Schaeffer 31 and Jackson 84, 95.

a humanist is anyone who acts as if there is no God.[107] I guess we must admit that selfish, greedy, prideful people both inside and outside the church can make that mistake.

Before we end this section, I'd like to hit a more positive note. I'd like to reiterate again all the things God had accomplished through the church so we're not too discouraged: Christianity had totally penetrated European society, there was a tremendous Christian consensus (as Mr. Schaeffer puts it), God's presence was felt in all of life (nature, seasons, harvest, etc.), He was given His rightful place as Creator, the power of kings had been limited, great artworks had been commissioned to teach the people, usury had been limited, price gouging and hoarding had been banned, and *trial by ordeal* had been abolished![108] Surely you also know there were still many church workers committed to purity and service. You'll see many step forward to attempt reforms. God was surely not going to let His church fall apart! Seeing again the good of the church, you can realize afresh how much was at stake.

I leave you, then, with the challenge of keeping two conflicting pictures in your mind: first, that of the common people of the Middle Ages–many of whom were barbarians just decades before–enjoying strong unity and a rich sense of God warmly ruling over every detail of their world. Think of how this is shown in the lovely, cherished *Book of Hours* devotionals created by families during this time. It's sad to know this intimacy was being eroded. At the same time, political and financial undercurrents were corrupting the church–which had become a sort of monarchy. You know the dangers of

> ## *ThinkWrite Reminder:*
>
> You're working on your *Investigation Supreme* throughout this guide, remember? You are probing for the *Big 2 Beliefs* which fueled the church and secular kings. You're trying to see the good they did (yeah!) as well as the times they slipped into a selfish drive for unlimited human power, as the Romans and barbarians had, and which always results in hurtful (barbaric) actions.

monarchy because we've already said *power corrupts and absolute power corrupts absolutely.* I don't honestly know how much political power the church *should* have had or what form that power should have taken, but I know the world needs the church to act courageously and rightly!

*Greenleaf's *Famous Men of the Middle Ages*, Ch. XX   Gr. 3-7

Story of the Middle Ages, by C. Miller & H.A. Guerber, Ch. LVII, LX, LXX   Gr. 4-8

Middle Ages, by Dorothy Mills, Ch. VIII and IX, Pts. 1-3   Gr. 6-12

---

[107] Jackson 82.

[108] Jackson 99.

☞ Your library may have a *Book of Hours*. These were created by individuals, so vary widely.

> How beautiful on the mountains are the feet of those who bring good news, who proclaim peace, who bring good tidings, who proclaim salvation...(Is. 52:7a).

26☙ Norman Conquest!

When we last saw England, King Edward the Confessor had died without an heir. Harold Godwinson, an Anglo-Saxon, was chosen to take the throne by the Witenagemot. He did *not* have an easy time of it, though. He had to face Vikings under Harald Hardrada at the Battle of Stamford Bridge, and that was only the beginning of his problems! Edward's feisty relative, William, Duke of Normandy, wasn't going to let Harold have the kingship without a fight. He claimed that Edward had promised it to him, and that Harold had too! The pope believed William's story and threw his support behind the Norman cause. I hope you remember that William had descended from Rollo the Viking, but the Normans were now considered more French than Viking. You can bet the English didn't cotton to the idea of a French-Norman ruling them. Did that bother William? Not much, apparently. He attacked.

William's undertaking is one of the most famous events in English history! Have you heard of it? It began with the Battle of Hastings in 1066, one of the few dates I'll ask you to remember (if you're ever on Jeopardy, you'll thank me!)...and culminated in the Norman Conquest! William claimed England and pushed it toward his Norman ways, Norman nobles, and Norman (Romanesque) architecture (as in his White Tower in the Tower of London, which may be England's most famous building), *but* there was still Anglo-Saxon and Viking-Dane resistance, as well as resistance (rightly so!) from church leaders such as Anselm. Even after

William's death, when his nasty descendants fought amongst themselves horrifically, there was continued resistance from the barons (even the Norman barons), the Vikings, and locals such as Hereward the Wake. It was a war-torn time, and folks claimed "God and His saints slept."[109] Well, you want to hear the stories for yourself! (You might run across mention of the Crusades while learning of William's sons; we'll cover them in the next section.)

26a♣ Harold Godwinson and William the Conqueror (conquest, reign, descendants)

Story of the World: Volume 2, by Susan Wise Bauer, Ch. 15c, 16	Gr. 3-6
*Greenleaf's *Famous Men of the Middle Ages*, Ch. XIX	Gr. 3-7
Island Story, by H.E. Marshall, Ch. XXII-XXIX	Gr. 3-8
Story of the Middle Ages, Ch. LXVII-LXIX, LXXII-LXXIII, LXXV-LXXVI by Christine Miller & H.A. Guerber	Gr. 4-8
Middle Ages, by Dorothy Mills, Ch. VII, Part 1c	Gr. 6-12

Child's History of the World, by V.M. Hillyer, Ch. 50	Gr. 1-4
Birthdays of Freedom, Vol. 2, by Genevieve Foster, pp. 22-23	Gr. 2-5
Looking at History, by R.J. Unstead, pp. 57-59, 69-90	Gr. 2-5
William the Conqueror, by L. DuGarde Peach (Ladybird)	Gr. 2-6
The Norman Conquest, by C.W. Hodges	Gr. 3-8
William the Conqueror, by Thomas Costain (Landmark)	Gr. 3-8
The Bayeux Tapestry, by Norman Denny	Gr. 3-12
Hastings, by Philip Sauvain (Great Battles and Sieges) The usual two-page spread method of imparting info. Not narrative.	Gr. 4-7
Life in the Time of Harald Hardrada and the Vikings, by Peter Speed Harald Hardrada did more than just attack England, as you can see! He was also king of Norway.	Gr. 4-12
Norman Britain, by Tony Triggs (History in Evidence)	Gr. 4-12

---

[109] R.J. Unstead, *Looking at History*. (London: A. & C. Black, Ltd., 1968) 90.

The Normans, by Peter Chrisp (Look into the Past)   Gr. 4-12

The Normans, by Hazel Martell (Worlds of the Past)   Gr. 5-12

The Story of Britain, by R.J. Unstead, pp. 76-87   Gr. 5-12

Battle of Hastings, by William Lace (Battles of the Middle Ages)   Gr. 6-12

Growing Up with the Norman Conquest, by Alfred Duggan   Gr. 6-12
> Duggan's books are usually quite interesting; this one shows the nature of childhood during this era.

William the Conqueror, by Elizabeth Luckock   Gr. 6-12

Great Invasion, by Clifford Alderman (Messner/Milestones)   Gr. 7-12

William the Conqueror, by Hilaire Belloc   Gr. 8-12

Fiction/Historical Fiction

The Striped Ships, by Eloise MacGraw   Gr. 5-12
> Girl survives battle and helps with Bayeux Tapestry.

Man with a Sword, by Henry Treece   Gr. 6-12
> A gripping novel of the tremendous turmoil within England after William's attack when key figures–Harold Godwinson, Hereward the Wake, and Harald Hardrada– sought to oust him.

Heart's Conquest, by Gladys Malvern   Gr. 7-12
> This book would only be enjoyed by girls. It tells of uprisings just after the conquest.

**King's Shadow*, by Elizabeth Adler   Gr. 7-12
> This story of Harold Godwinson has been highly recommended to me.

*Wulf the Saxon, by G.A. Henty   Gr. 7-12
> This is also available in an audio format!

Knight's Fee, by Rosemary Sutcliff   Gr. 8-12
> This gripping novel is set in the era when England is trying to fight off William's sons.

Shield Ring, by Rosemary Sutcliff   Gr. 8-12
> This gripping novel is set in the era when England is trying to fight off William's sons.

Golden Warrior, by Hope Muntz   Gr. 11-12
> This is a very in-depth, and supposedly accurate, novel on the life of Harold Godwinson and the events of 1066. Very few students would have time to read it, though.

26b🍀 Tower of London and Norman-Romanesque architecture

Norman architecture was a form of Romanesque *architecture, meaning it derived from the Roman style. It has distinctive qualities you will enjoy being able to identify! Any book on the history of architecture will cover this style, and will probably include mention of William's White Tower also!*

Child's History of Art, by Hillyer & Huey (*Architecture* section, Ch. 12)   Gr. 2-8
<u>OR</u>, *Young People's Story of Architecture: 3,000 BC - Gothic Period*, pp. 106-113

**The Tower of London*, by Leonard Everett Fisher   Gr. 2-8
    The first section of this excellent book covers William the Conqueror's part in the
    building of the White Tower portion.

**Romanesque Art and Architecture*, by Ana Martin   Gr. 4-12

26c🍀 Anselm

**Trial and Triumph: Stories from Church History*, by R. Hannula, pp. 77-82   Gr. 5-12

**Invitation to the Classics*, by Louise Cowan & Os Guinness, p. 90   Gr. 8-12

26d🍀 Hereward the Wake

This is not an essential subject; feel free to omit it if you need more time.

*An Island Story, by H.E. Marshall, Ch. XXV   Gr. 3-8
    This chapter was also cited above.

**Hereward the Wake*, by Charles Kingsley   Gr. 11-12
    I've not seen this, but Kingsley is a highly-reputed author; it might be a *very* lengthy read.

27🍀 Castles

Okay! I can hear you chomping at the bit. Learning only about William's tower isn't going to satisfy your craving to know more about castles, is it?! What is it about castles, anyway? We all seem to find them terribly fascinating, whether they be the simpler *donjons* and keeps of the 'Dark' Ages or the massive stoneworks of the 'High' Middle Ages!

Well, have at it! You'll find plenty of books about castles at your library, so I've listed only a few samples below. There are also fun coloring books, models to build, and much more. You could even construct your own castle out of Legos, blocks, snow, or sand! These buildings were such feats of engineering and architecture that they surely are part of the reason the High Middle Ages were *high!*

The Story of a Castle, by John S. Goodall   PreK-2
      This is a beautifully-illustrated wordless book which is probably in most libraries.

*Three-Dimensional Medieval Castle, by Willabel Tong   PreK-2
      I've not seen this but it sounds fun. There is a dragon piece you may want to remove.

*Medieval Feast, by Aliki   Gr. 1-4
      This wonderful picture book shows a castle household at work preparing a feast. I'd
      definitely call it a *don't-miss* book!

*What Were Castles For? by Phil Cox (Usborne Starting Point)   Gr. 1-4

*Castles, by Gillian Osband   Gr. 1-5
      I'm not exactly sure of the age-grouping on this, but it looks like a picture book.

The Truth about Castles, by Gillian Clements   Gr. 1-5

Child's History of Art, by Hillyer & Huey (*Architecture* section, Ch. 13)   Gr. 2-8
<u>OR</u>, *Young People's Story of Architecture: 3,000 BC - Gothic*, pp. 114-123

*(Usborne) Time Traveller Book of Knights and Castles, by Judy Hindley   Gr. 2-8

*Castle Diary: The Journal of Tobias Burgess, Page, by Richard Platt   Gr. 2-10
      Kids are crazy about this brand-new book! Though set with fictional characters, it
      vividly shows the life of a castle page. I know of very young children who have enjoyed
      it being read aloud to them, including my four-year-old son.

Norman Castles, by Graham Rickard (Beginning History)   Gr. 3-7

The Castle Book, by Alfred Duggan   Gr. 3-8

*Castle, by Mark Bergin   Gr. 3-9

The Art and Industry of Sand Castles, by Jan Adkins   Gr. 3-10
      What an amazing book! I think you could learn more about castles from this book than
      any other, because while it supposedly is showing us how to make incredible sand
      castles, it is actually teaching the development and details of castle design. Great
      illustrations, great concept, great book!

Castle, by Struan Reid   Gr. 3-10

*A Medieval Castle, by Fiona Macdonald (Inside Story)   Gr. 3-10

Castle at War, by Andrew Langley   Gr. 4-10
    See the real activities of a castle under siege.

Castles, by Philip Steele (Kingfisher)   Gr. 4-10

Castle, by Christopher Gravett (Eyewitness)   Gr. 4-12

Castle, by David Macaulay   Gr. 4-12
    Don't let *anyone* miss this one, especially your boys!

Cross-Sections: Castle, by Richard Platt and Stephen Biesty   Gr. 4-12
    Amazingly intricate cut-away views fascinate students.

The Castle, by Kathryn Hinds (Life in the Middle Ages)   Gr. 5-12

Medieval Castle, by Don Nardo   Gr. 6-12
    A more in-depth look at the development and utilization of castles.

Life in a Medieval Castle, by Tony McAleavy   Unknown

Audio/Video

Castle, by David Macaulay   Various
    Mr. Macaulay hosts this intriguing video version of his book, giving extra commentary.

Activities

Castles: Facts, Things to Make, Activities, by Rachel Wright   Various

Castles of the World Coloring Book (Dover)   Various

Cut & Assemble a Medieval Castle (Dover)   Various

Easy-to-Make Playtime Castle (Dover)   Various

Make This Model Castle (Usborne)   Various

Model Medieval Castle   Various

28🕮 Crusades!

You know what? There is something I would *really* like to know. Well, there are a *lot* of things I would like to know, but there's a biggie right here. What did God think of the Crusades?

The Crusades. Well, maybe you're not familiar with them. It's rather simple, I guess. Europeans went to the Holy Land to wrest it away from its Muslim occupiers. How and why it happened are a little harder to understand.

We've said Europe was intensely Christian. Whether French or English or Spanish or German or Italian or Polish, Europeans seemed to think they were 'born' into Christianity. We're not discussing here how one becomes a Christian; our focus is on history and I am merely saying–in a simple way–what was widely believed. This born-into-Christianity view did breed strong unity and the penetration of Christianity into (and therefore the improvement of) many facets of life. Great! But it did something else too, something Mr. Jackson says better than I can:

> *If there is no distinction in being a believer, because everybody is, then emphasis will tend to fall on rank (as a church official, for example) or upon particular and often stereotyped signs of exceptional holiness....*[110]

Do you understand what he's saying? People felt a need to do something more than simply be 'born' into Christianity. (Different families will view this process in a different light; we're just looking at motivations behind historical events.) For example, it was considered very significant to make a difficult trip–a *pilgrimage*–to an important religious site, such as the shrine to a saint's relics, the city of Rome, or even Jerusalem! How does this tie into the Crusades, you ask? Well, Jerusalem fell to the (Islamic) Seljuk Turks in 1065 and they were less tolerant of Christian pilgrims in Jerusalem than the earlier Islamic occupiers had been.[111] They harassed, or even killed, the pilgrims and were disrespectful to important Christian sites.

🕮 Pilgrimage

Constantinople feared Seljuk invasion and said it would rather be ruled by Latins than by Muslims, so an appeal was sent to Pope Urban II in Rome, who had also heard about the problems in Jerusalem. He cried out to the people of Europe, calling on them to roust the Turks.[112] Another voice was commissioned by the pope to preach holy war, that of a French monk, Peter the Hermit, who had been to Jerusalem on pilgrimage and seen the Muslim hostility in person. By 1096, the first wave was ready to head out, but they met disaster, and Peter the Hermit was one of the few survivors! The emperor in Constantinople was hardly excited about this first group which contained too much rabble, some of whom stole and

---

[110] Jackson 95.

[111] Miller & Guerber 169.

[112] Mills 181.

81

murdered along the way.[113] A second wave, a more military band, under Godfrey of Bouillon, recaptured Jerusalem in 1099 and set up 'crusader states' where they ruled over the local lands and people.

This brings in one of several questions about the Crusades. *Should they have been waged?* I'll not answer that one flat out, for they can't even be lumped together; various Crusades and various crusaders had different goals. Too, folks thought differently then (though God's principles are timeless). Europeans knew Islam had captured vast sections of the known world and insisted at swordpoint that the residents–including Christians–become Muslim; they also knew Muslims had tried to invade more of Europe. But if that was the real concern, why wasn't something done sooner? And what type of resistance was godly? All I know is that God alone sees it fully. But even *if* each of the various Crusades were right (and that's a huge *if*), it surely does not say they were handled rightly, for the mercilessness of the crusaders both against Muslim civilians, Jews (whom they called "Christ killers"), and even fellow Christians was horrific!

So, what were the motivations? Were they only to free Jerusalem? Well, as you've already seen in history, all is not what it seems. Mrs. Mill explains:

Why were men so moved as to go on Crusades? Motives were probably very mixed. Before the first Crusade, the desire to free the holy places from the infidel was a very honest and a very real one, and countless crusaders set out with no other thought in their minds. The popes probably furthered the Crusades as part of their policy of a world-wide Christian empire, and it is possible that the leaders of the Church saw in the Crusades the opportunity to use the fighting spirit of the eleventh century to the thirteenth centuries to some better account than in private warfare. They had done something to this end by the Truce of God, the Crusades gave them the opportunity to turn the fighters away from Europe. For ambitious knights and barons the Crusades offered the lure of kingdoms and lands in the east where they heard that wealth was to be had beyond anything that they knew in Europe. Italian towns, such as Venice and Genoa, seized on the Crusades as a means by which they might extend their commerce and acquire eastern products more easily and cheaply. Then there were the adventurers and the restless, those who found life dull, those who found it evil, those who at any time will seize upon anything that is new and exciting and that seems to offer them a carefree life, to such men the east spoke of wealth and luxury and endless possibilities of success.[114]

Also, keep in mind that a large percentage of the crusading knights were younger brothers who would not inherit land, so they brought their families with them on Crusade, apparently hoping to settle in newly won lands, which they often did.[115] I'm recalling now a portion of the speech given by Pope Urban issuing the call for the First Crusade, as given by one of the many listeners who recorded it:

---

[113] Miller & Guerber 170.

[114] Mills 183-184.

[115] Jackson 96.

...this land which you inhabit, shut in on all sides by the seas and surrounded by the mountain peaks, is too narrow for your large population; nor does it abound in wealth; and it furnishes scarcely food enough for its cultivators. Hence it is that you murder and devour one another, that you wage war....[116]

What of the Fourth Crusade which saw Venetians (folks from Venice) crushing and destroying fellow-Christians in Constantinople, with whom they were competing for eastern trade?! Constantinople had withstood many a pagan assault, and had protected Christian Europe to the west of it in the process, but the Fourth Crusade devastated it. Mr. Jackson wryly notes: "What the pagan had so far not been able to do, the Christian accomplished."[117]

Then there was the Children's Crusade! Yes, children! They were promised special spiritual blessings if they would march to the Holy Land and preach to the Saracens. I recall Pope Urban's words again:

Undertake this journey eagerly for the remission of your sins, with the assurance of the reward of imperishable glory in the kingdom of heaven.[118]

Were the promises biblical? Or was the church—which was struggling in its success to keep God's word strictly at the helm, and which was also drifting toward its own humanistic definitions of church power—making its own salvation promises? Anyway, you'll be deeply saddened when you see what happened to the children; most of the Germans died on the trip and most of the French were sold *by fellow Europeans* into slavery in Egypt! What on earth was going on?!

In closing, let me say the Crusades are still deeply resented by Muslims and Jews, who feel their history every moment of the day. This is hard for us westerners to realize. We hardly remember what happened last year! While we need to stand up for the true faith and be honest about hostilities against us, it would also be good for us to own up to any mistakes done in the name of our religion. Well, let's dig into a general overview of the Crusades and a look at both the First Crusade and the Children's Crusade in particular. We'll cover the others later, but always be watching for side-effects of the Crusades, such as vassals (sometimes an entire town or city) being able to buy their freedom from liege lords selling holdings to raise money for a Crusade.[119] Isn't history amazing?! (Do *ThinkWrite 9* after studying this topic.)

> ## *ThinkWrite 9: "Crusade!"*
>
> What were some of the results of the Crusades? How did they affect the crusaders, the Muslims, the Jews, and all of Europe, both then and now?

---

[116] Mills 182.

[117] Jackson 97.

[118] Mills 182.

[119] Miller & Guerber

28a ❧ General overview

Story of the World: Volume 2, by Susan Wise Bauer, Ch. 18a-c   Gr. 3-6

Greenleaf's Famous Men of the Middle Ages, Ch. XXI   Gr. 3-7

Story of the Middle Ages, by Christine Miller & H.A. Guerber, Ch. LXXI   Gr. 4-8
> You can also jump ahead to Ch. XCVII to see the effects of the Crusades, but we will cite this chapter later in our study also.

Middle Ages, by Dorothy Mills, Ch. XIII   Gr. 6-12

Child's History of the World, by V.M. Hillyer, Ch. 51   Gr. 1-4

Birthdays of Freedom: Vol. 2, by Genevieve Foster, pp. 24-25   Gr. 2-5

Looking at History, by R.J. Unstead, pp. 92-93   Gr. 2-5

Crusaders, by Joanne Jessop   Gr. 2-6

Crusades, by Chris Rice (DK Discoveries)   Gr. 3-8

Crusades, by Anthony West (Landmark)   Gr. 3-8

Fire Upon the Earth, by Norman Langford, pp. 80-83   Gr. 4-8

The Crusades, by Walter Buehr   Gr. 4-12

Cross and Crescent, by Richard Suskind   Gr. 6-12

The Crusades: Failed Holy Wars, by Cherese Cartlidge   Gr. 8-12

No Other Foundation: The Church Through..., by Jeremy Jackson, Ch. 8   Gr. 11-12
> This book is too difficult for most students, but is valuable, so I mention it nonetheless. This chapter was also cited previously, but includes information on the Crusades.

Activities

My dear friend, Gina Snyder, gathered several families together for a crusader evening. She draped sheets from the ceiling to make a crusader tent, we all sat inside on strewn pillows while the kids–dressed as various crusade figures–told their stories in first person. We all enjoyed medieval food and then watched DeMille's film, "The Crusades." Fun, fun, fun!

*Paper Soldiers of the Middle Ages: The Crusades (Bellerophon)   Various

Fiction/Historical Fiction

Boy of the Lost Crusade, by Agnes Danforth Hewes   Gr. 4-10

The Land Beyond, by Ruth Knight   Gr. 5-10

Marching to Jerusalem, by Ruth Langland Holberg   Gr. 7-12

Perilous Pilgrimage, by Henry Treece   Gr. 8-12

*Celtic Crusade trilogy: *Iron Lance, Black Rood, Mystic Rose*, by Stephen Lawhead Gr. 8-12
    Many of you are already familiar with the high drama of this Christian author. At times, he does include topics which are for mature readers.

28b⁊ Persecution of Jews in Europe

On this sad subject, I'll quote Mr. Jackson:

> *When the crusaders were moving south through France and Germany to the various assembly points for embarkation, there were frightful pogroms. After all, was not the Jew an enemy of the Cross nearer home? Was not his guilt greater than that of the Moslem? To be fair, men like Bernard of Clairvaux [whom we'll meet later], as well as several popes and various sovereigns, struck out hard against these atrocities. But it was the start of a wave of violence which would pulsate down through the years to our own century.*[120]

Yes, this is an entire topic in itself, but I'll just list a couple books below. Feel free to explore more deeply if you have time and resources.

---

[120] Jackson 97.

29🐾 The Plot Thickens!

Are you ready to tackle the convolutions of European royalty during the 1100s? Even though
you may need a flow chart, don't be overwhelmed; our focus is always on the Higher King!
Human kingdoms wax and wane, but His authority and principles for nations are changeless.
So don't just look at the various kings and scoundrels, some of whom were *both!* Instead watch
for their *Big 2 Beliefs* and how they responded to God's truth for law, government, human
worth, etc. Ready?

In France, Philip I was king; then came his son, Louis VI; then came *his* son, Louis VII.

In England, Henry I was king because he was the only one of William the Conqueror's three
sons to survive the conflict between them. William Rufus had died suspiciously and Robert had
been blinded and imprisoned in a castle. Sounds like a movie, doesn't it?!

In Germany, Heinrich V was Holy Roman Emperor, and Maude was his empress; she just
happened to be daughter to the Henry I of England we just met. She was known in England,
naturally, by her English name, Matilda. Keep track of this Matilda-Maude; she was a busy
lady! When Heinrich died, she returned to England, while a battle raged in the Holy Roman
Empire (Germany and Italy) for the emperorship. There were two parties, the Welfs and the
Waiblings, one more supportive of kingly rule, the other more supportive of papal rule. In the
end, a man named Conrad won all, including respect for his chivalry at the Hill of Weibertrue
(Woman's Truth).

Let's go back to Matilda. Her mother was Saxon royalty, her father was Norman royalty; she
was a grandchild of William the Conqueror. Mighty impressive bloodlines if you're into that
sort of thing, and people in the 1100s *were* into that sort of thing. Her father, King Henry I,
arranged for her to be Queen upon his death—the first female ruler of England. She did not
remain a widow, but married Geoffrey Plantagenet, Duke of Anjou of France. Problem is, she
didn't remain Queen either, because her cousin Stephen, also a grandchild of William the
Conqueror, immediately fought her for the throne. Years of battles and nail-biting escapes

ensued, and the English people and countryside were ravaged. She and Geoffrey managed to have a son, Henry II. After Matilda finally gave up her queenly claims, Henry II continued the fight, but was finally forced to let Stephen have the throne until he died.

Then Henry II became king, and what a king! What a wife! What children! Let's begin with the wife: Eleanor of Aquitaine. Now, Eleanor was no daisy. The lands she owned, the duchy of Aquitaine, were fabulous and large, though. That must have made her seem a whole lot more charming *before* the wedding! In fact, Henry II and Eleanor together controlled more land in France than did the King of France (who was uncomfortably sandwiched between them), which shows you how messy the feudal system could become. But get this! Before Eleanor married King Henry, she *had been* married to the new king of France, Louis VII! Yes, clever Louis VI had hoped to bring Aquitaine into his realm, so had arranged the union. Louis VII, however, got fed up with Eleanor's un-daisy-like ways and divorced her. (Is this sounding like a soap opera?) That's when she married Henry, who probably regretted his decision quite quickly. Indeed, Eleanor soon backed their sons in waging war on him! What a family!!

As I said, Henry II and Eleanor had four sons and a daughter (another Matilda), and they were doozies! Richard, Henry, Geoffrey, and John. Somehow Geoffrey and Henry missed the fame bus, but you know Richard–Richard the Lionheart! And you know John–Bad Prince John of Robin Hood and Magna Charta infamy! Yup. I thought you'd see the light at the end of this tunnel!

Now everyone started dashing around trying to take each other's land...and the sons waged war on their father with their mother's help, as I mentioned...and Henry was involved in the murder of England's top churchman, Thomas à Becket...and the Second and Third Crusades started up and several of these characters were *extremely* involved...and while Richard the Lionheart was in the Holy Land winning his famous, but horrific, victory at Acre, John was tormenting England so that Robin Hood (or whomever is the basis of the legend, if its true at all) had to come to the rescue...and the English barons got King John to sign one of the most important documents of all time, the *Magna Charta*...and a powerful chap named Frederick Barbarossa came to power in Germany by uniting some of the smaller principalities, though he was resisted by one duke named Heinrich who was married to Henry and Eleanor's daughter, Matilda, whom I just mentioned...and Frederick was in on the Crusade too...and there were two *mighty* churchmen in France–Bernard of Clairvaux and Abbe Suger...and Abbe Suger built a fabulous new cathedral at St. Denis which initiated the truly Gothic cathedral that is the quintessential medieval style which still takes our breath away...and, well, I'm losing my breath just telling you about it all! Let's slow down and see these key moves in instant replay! So much was happening so fast!

Remember what I said at the beginning of this litany, though, that history is not about the shenanigans of feisty kings and queens as much as it is that straight line of God and His truth which shoots through all these messes. In contrast, I think of something said by my beloved sister, Karen: "Look how badly humans flop when they act upon the ideas they have. We always fall for the trick that if we thought it up it must be good." One thing's certain, our messes make God and His ways look even more beautiful! "More is He to be desired, yea, than much fine gold!" as the Psalmist said.

87

30๛ A *Crazy* Couple: Henry II and Eleanor of Aquitaine

Since I just talked about this duo in the last section, I'll just say here that King Henry II ruled from 1154-1189. Though he descended from William the Conqueror on his mother's side, Henry II's reign began England's Plantagenet dynasty, named for his French father.

30a๛ Henry and Eleanor

*Greenleaf's *Famous Men of the Middle Ages*, Ch. XXIII, Part I Gr. 3-7

Story of the Middle Ages, by Miller & Guerber, Ch. LXXIX Gr. 4-8

Looking at History, by R.J. Unstead, pp. 102-105 Gr. 2-5
    These pages simply explain the legal system in England and changes made by Henry II.

Middle Ages: Cultural Atlas for Young People, by Mike Corbishley, pp. 42-43 Gr. 3-8

The Story of Britain, by R.J. Unstead, pp. 88-103 Gr. 5-12
    Includes information on Henry I, Stephen, and Matilda.

Queen Eleanor: Independent Spirit of the Medieval World, by Polly Brooks Gr. 8-12
    I've not read this, and thus cannot comment on its content.

Eleanor of Aquitaine, by Zoe Kaplan Unknown

Devil's Brood, by Alfred Duggan Unknown
    This covers the lives of Henry II's family.

Fiction/Historical Fiction

Eleanor: Crown Jewel of Aquitaine, France, 1136, by K. Gregory (Royal Diaries) Gr. 3-8
    These fictional diaries often display very *modern* attitudes, if you know what I mean.

A Proud Taste for Scarlet and Miniver, by E.L. Konigsburg Gr. 4-12
    Eleanor looks back on her life from purgatory. While families have varying views about the scriptural legitimacy of purgatory, keep in mind that here it is not a theological issue; it is a literary device. The book is much enjoyed both by Protestants and Catholics for its lively look at Eleanor and her family.

30b❧ Henry II and Archbishop Thomas à Becket

Henry–king of the largest realm in Europe at the time–had many power struggles with the church and specifically with Thomas à Becket. You see, back when Becket was merely Henry's capable, fun-loving, and high-living friend, Henry had made him Lord Chancellor of England, the second highest position in the realm! They got along famously! When the leading church position (Archbishop of Canterbury) became available, Henry thought he could control both the state and the church if he made his buddy Archbishop, which he could get away with since Becket was a priest. Problem! Becket took his new job as archbishop very seriously, gave up his wild ways, and switched his highest loyalty to the interests of the church. Now, that made Henry mighty mad, and it cost Becket his life in the end (1170). This is a prime example of the church working to temper the domineering rulership of a king...and of kings not wanting the church officials in their realm more beholden to the pope than to the king.

An Island Story, by H.E. Marshall, Ch. XXX-XXXI   Gr. 3-8

Story of the Middle Ages, by Miller & Guerber, Ch. LXXX-LXXXI   Gr. 4-8

Fiction/Historical Fiction

If All the Swords in England, by Barbara Willard   Gr. 4-12
   Happily, this fascinating book is being reprinted by Bethlehem Books! It is the story of English boys who get involved with Becket and King Henry II, and is from one of England's top youth authors.

Hidden Treasure of Glaston, by Eleanore Jewett   Gr. 6-12
   Another wonderful book which is being reprinted by Bethlehem Books!

Murder in the Cathedral, by T.S. Eliot   Gr. 11-12
   Classic English drama based on death of Becket.

30c❧ Henry II conquered portions of Ireland (1169-1172)

As you know, Ireland had been spared much of the ravages of earlier European history due to its isolated geography. It had also been a strong beacon of Christianity after the work of St. Patrick. Yet, the pagan Druid religion had not been completely abandoned by some either. The island was torn by these opposing forces as pagan and Christian chieftains battled each other, and the church struggled to maintain a purity of doctrine in such a mystical land. To add to their woes, one Irish chieftain asked some Norman knights for help; when the Irish leader died, the Normans stayed and ruled despotically. These Norman atrocities gave Henry II the excuse he wanted to subdue portions of

Ireland under his *own* control. His brutal invasion was followed by the placement of notoriously tyrannical governors. For centuries since, many Irish have resented the British presence which exists to this very day! Any resource on Irish history will cover these events.

An Island Story, by H.E. Marshall, Ch. XXXII   Gr. 3-8

Price of Liberty, by Wayne Whipple, pp. 6-11   Gr. 5-12
      If you like *Price of Liberty*, you can follow it through history!

Fiction/Historical Fiction

Cargo for a King, by J.S. Andrews   Gr. 7-12
      Man faces Irish pirates during time of political unrest.

Sword of Clontarf, by Charles Brady   Gr. 8-12
      This covers one of the earlier battles between pagan and Christian forces. I may recall hearing this story was rather mediocre.

31 Richard the Lionheart

Richard, whom we introduced earlier, is known not only for being king of England, but also for his leading role in the Third Crusade (1189-1193), which began when the Saracens retook Jerusalem in 1187. We talked about Richard and the Crusades previously, so I'll say no more here, though you'll certainly want to hear what happened to Richard on his way home from the Crusades and the brave service supposedly rendered by his faithful minstrel, Blondel. And we must mention Saladin, the leader of the Moslems who was famous both for his military prowess and his amazing chivalry. Those people not able to go on the Third Crusade were told to pay one-tenth of their wealth to support it; the tax was called Saladin's Tithe.[121] You may also want to know about the great crusader fortress, Krak des Chevaliers, in what is now Syria. Well, you'll find plenty of good reading on these topics!

31a King Richard

Story of the World: Volume 2, by Susan Wise Bauer, Ch. 19a   Gr. 3-6

Greenleaf's Famous Men of the Middle Ages, Ch. XXIII, Part II, III   Gr. 3-7

---

[121] Miller & Guerber 199.

An Island Story, by H.E. Marshall, Ch. XXXIII-XXXIV   Gr. 3-8

Story of the Middle Ages, by Miller & Guerber, Ch. LXXXV-LXXXIX   Gr. 4-8

Story of Liberty, by Charles Coffin, pp. 18-19   Gr. 5-12
    Mr. Coffin presents a much different view of Richard than usually given in youth
    literature; he exposes gritty realities in this very important book.

Middle Ages, by Dorothy Mills, Ch. XX, Pt. 2a   Gr. 6-12
    Includes information on Richard, though mostly covers his French counterpart, Philip
    Augustus.

Child's History of the World, by V.M. Hillyer, Ch. 52   Gr. 1-4

Crusader King: Richard the Lionhearted, by Richard Suskind   Gr. 4-8

Seven Kings of England, by Geoffrey Trease, Ch. 3   Gr. 5-12

Story of Britain, by R.J. Unstead, pp. 104-107   Gr. 5-12

Richard the Lionhearted, by W.N. Pittenger (Immortals of History)   Gr. 8-12

Lionheart: Richard Coeur-de-Lion, by George Baker   Gr. 9-12

Knight in Battle, by Ewart Oakeshott (section on Battle of Arsuf)   Unknown
    This book has a major section on a key battle between Richard and Saladin.

Fiction/Historical Fiction

Minstrel in the Tower, by Gloria Skurzynski   Gr. 1-6
    Kids must search for their baron-uncle after the Crusade.

We Were There with Richard the Lionheart at the Crusades, by Robert Webb   Gr. 3-8
    Fictional children participate in real historical events.

Knight Crusader, by Ronald Welch   Gr. 7-12
    The first in a series of novels following one family through English history. This begins
    with the family in the Kingdom of Jerusalem in 1187. The hero, Philip, meets Richard
    the Lionheart at Acre, etc.

Winning His Spurs, by G.A. Henty   Gr. 7-12
    Older versions are entitled *Boy Knight* and *Fighting the Saracens*.

Ivanhoe, by Sir Walter Scott   Gr. 9-12

   A classic piece of English literature, which is rather difficult to enter into, but is *well* worth it overall. So many people have enjoyed it...for centuries! There are also many abridged versions for younger children, so all your students can enter this tale!

Talisman, by Sir Walter Scott   Gr. 9-12

Audio/Video

The Crusades, a very old film by Cecil B. DeMille

Ivanhoe, the version starring James Mason is excellent

Ivanhoe, there is also an older version starring Robert Taylor and Elizabeth Taylor

31b▰ Saladin

Saladin: Noble Prince of Islam, by Diane Stanley   Gr. 2-8
   Like all Stanley books, this is beautifully illustrated.

Saladin and the Kingdom of Jerusalem, by Lee Hancock   Unknown

31c▰ Krak des Chevaliers

Cut & Assemble a Crusader Castle: Krak des Chevaliers, by A.G. Smith   Various

Architecture, by Neil Stevenson, pp. 30-31 *(DK Annotated Guides)*   Gr. 7-12

32▰ Prince John, the Magna Charta, and Robin Hood!

John is probably known to you, not by his given name, but by one of his nicknames, such as *Bad Prince John*. At least, that's what *I* call him! I'm sure he was called worse in his day! Does that name ring any bells? There's a good chance you younger children will answer this question more easily than your older siblings! Yes! He was the evil ruler in the Robin Hood stories!

He had another nickname too—John Lackland—for he inherited no lands. I'm telling you! There is no guy grouchier than one who wants very much to be a king but doesn't have anyone to rule! So, while Richard was away on Crusade, John began helping himself to England and frightfully abusing the English people! (John later became king after the death of both Richard and the rightful heir, Geoffrey's son, under very suspicious circumstances.) There was resistance to John's abuses, though, both from the barons (who usually had the ignoble motives of wanting a bigger piece of the pie for themselves) and *maybe* from someone who was the basis of the Robin Hood stories (if the legends have any historical basis at all). You know Robin Hood, right? Well, if you don't, you will! Whether or not there was a Robin Hood, we can see the yearning of beleaguered people for a rescuer, which reminds us that we need to make our life count, for God's truths are always a blessing to this world. That's why we're studying all this, so *we* are ready to pitch in! We're going to lift Him high, speak the truth, vote, and dare to care. We won't ignore needs, but will seek God for our role in working toward solutions. Where will you be? Public office? The business world? The justice system? The media? Raising a godly family? These are *all* mission fields. Wherever you serve, be known for your compassionate Christlikeness...with a little dash of Robin Hood's courage!

But before we jump in, let's talk more about the *Magna Charta* (Magna Carta), which means *Great Charter*. What was so great about it? Or are you asking a different question: what on earth was it?! To answer, think of what you already know: there had been power struggles aplenty between the kings and nobles of Europe. Well, England's barons were pressing for a written charter confirming the longstanding (but abused) protections provided by earlier English law, especially that under Edward the Confessor.[122] (Do you remember, too, that King Alfred had sought godly law principles for England earlier? See the legacy?) So even though the English barons may not have been acting on behalf of the common people, but rather for their own benefit, something happened with the Magna Charta over the centuries. The principle behind it–limiting the power of rulers by law–would, over subsequent centuries, be increasingly claimed by common Englishmen, in spite of the fact that the pope tried to nullify the Magna Charta. In the end, therefore, the Magna Charta came to be one of history's most important documents, because the power of kings (since they have sinful human natures) *must* be limited! Otherwise, there cannot be freedom and respect for all. Along with the arrival of Christianity, then, the Magna Charta would contribute to the painstakingly slow growth of freedom in England...and its later colonies (that's us!) Yes, freedom came slowly, but it came to other European nations even more slowly! Doesn't it strike you funny that one of England's worst kings was forced to sign one of history's best documents?!

Because of its significance, you again need to do something I rarely ask: remember a date. You must know the Magna Charta was signed in 1215 in the field at Runnymede.

32a⚜ Prince John and the Magna Charta

Story of the World: Volume 2, by Susan Wise Bauer, Ch. 19b	Gr. 3-6
Greenleaf's Famous Men of the Middle Ages, Ch. XXIII, Part IV	Gr. 3-7
An Island Story, by H.E. Marshall, Ch. XXXV-XXXVI	Gr. 3-8

---

[122] Mills 285.

Story of the Middle Ages, by Miller & Guerber, Ch. XCIII   Gr. 4-8

Story of Liberty, by Charles Coffin, Ch. 1   Gr. 5-12

Middle Ages, by Dorothy Mills, Ch. XX, Part 1 (first section)   Gr. 6-12

Child's History of the World, by V.M. Hillyer, Ch. 54   Gr. 1-4

Birthdays of Freedom: Vol. 2, by Genevieve Foster, pp. 26-27   Gr. 2-5

Looking at History, by R.J. Unstead, p. 93   Gr. 2-5

King John and the Magna Charta, by L. DuGarde Peach (Ladybird)   Gr. 3-7

Magna Carta, by C. W. Hodges   Gr. 4-9

The Magna Charta, by James Daugherty (Landmark)   Gr. 5-12

Price of Liberty, by Wayne Whipple, pp. 20-31   Gr. 5-12

Story of Britain, by R.J. Unstead, pp. 108-112   Gr. 5-12

That Men Shall Be Free: The Story of the Magna Carta (Messner/Milestones)   Gr. 8-12
    by Clifford Alderman

Fiction/Historical Fiction

The Lost Baron, by Allen French   Gr. 6-12
    Boy lives in castle with missing baron; set in Cornwall in the year 1200.

Leopards and Lilies, by Alfred Duggan   Gr. 8-12
    I have not read this book, but only know it is from a knowledgeable author who has
    written both appropriate and inappropriate books for youth.

32b☙ Robin Hood

Your library is sure to have many books about Robin Hood; this is only a sample listing.

Story of the World: Volume 2, by Susan Wise Bauer, Ch. 19c   Gr. 3-6

Robin Hood and Little John, by Barbara Cohen   Gr. K-3

Robin Hood Stories, by Edward Dolch   Gr. 1-3

Adventures of Robin Hood, by Harry Ross (Bullseye Step Into Classics)   Gr. 1-4

Robin Hood, by Margaret Early	Gr. 2-5
Robin Hood's Arrow, by Eugenia Stone	Gr. 3-8
*Robin Hood of Sherwood Forest, by Ann McGovern	Gr. 3-10
Bows Against the Barons, by Geoffrey Trease Robin Hood battles Norman barons.	Gr. 7-12
*Robin Hood, by Paul Creswick This version is illustrated by N.C. Wyeth, student of Howard Pyle.	Gr. 7-12
*Robin Hood, by J.W. McSpadden	Gr. 7-12
*Adventures of Robin Hood, by Roger Lancelyn Green	Gr. 8-12
*Merry Adventures of Robin Hood, by Howard Pyle This is a classical version.	Gr. 8-12

Audio/Video

*Adventures of Robin Hood, starring Errol Flynn
    The classic Hollywood-style epic of yesteryear.

*Robin Hood
    Disney's fun animated version, produced when Disney was safer, though in one scene,
    Robin poses as fortune-teller to get the king's carriage to stop.

*The Story of Robin Hood, starring Richard Todd
    This is a very nice, older version.

33 France in the Twelfth Century...and the Birth of Gothic Cathedrals!

We already introduced you to the kings Philip, Louis VI, Louis VII, and Philip (II) Augustus, as well as the Second Crusade. The readings below will give you more info on events, such as Philip Augustus regaining Normandy from Bad Prince John, the completion of Notre Dame Cathedral in Paris, and the beginning of the Louvre. In our discussion here, though, let's meet the two important churchmen mentioned earlier, Bernard of Clairvaux and Abbe Suger.

Bernard was from a wealthy Burgundian family, but he renounced all to become part of a wave of reform which spawned new monasteries; the earlier ones had become successful and then flabby. (You see throughout history that God is always stirring reform.) Bernard preached so powerfully that many men joined upon hearing him, until it was said, "Mothers hid their sons from him, wives their husbands, and companions their friends!"[123] That's some preaching!

Bernard also deserves credit for courageously chastising kings, popes, and anyone else mishandling high positions! Remember, Bernard lived at a time when there were, in essence, two competing monarchies in each land: the king wanted to make the church an extension of his power, while the church wanted to make the king an extension of its power (as its protecting and enforcing sword). Sometimes the two monarchies worked in tandem and Europe seemed like a sort of *theocracy*,[124] but more often the two monarchies vied for political and financial supremacy. Ah, that's the way of humans, our sin natures desire more and more power since we innately want to make ourselves as God (*Big Belief #1*). I suppose God understands this more readily than we do because He didn't want the Israelites to have a king when they wanted to be like their neighbors.[125] Whatever the nations and church were meant to be, we know we're each part of one body, and the Lord is the head. It is really that headship, not the style, that is my concern.

Theocracy

Here's the storm cloud—at first only the size of a man's hand[126]—that we've seen building on the horizon in a sky that *had* been sunny with the great good of the church. It began when the church leaders started acting like human kings, seeing armies as their only protection, and being motivated by earthly ambitions. They ignored God's laws—actually making themselves higher than God's laws—by fighting for the papacy, waging *un*holy wars, propping up cruel kings which benefitted the church, harshly taxing the poor, and selfishly amassing mind-numbing wealth. But things got even more serious. The church was giving its human leaders the authority to declare *new* means to salvation and forgiveness of sin! For example, Pope Urban promised eternal life to crusaders,[127] and folks were told any sin could be forgiven if one visited Christ's tomb.[128] This overrode God's authority with human authority. This was *humanism*.

Elitism

What does humanism always bring? *Elitism.* Since the humans at the top are making their own laws and deciding the worth of non-elites, the law benefits the

---

[123] Jackson 107.

[124] Jackson 87.

[125] I Samuel 8:5

[126] I Kings 18:44

[127] Mills 182, quoting Pope Urban II's announcement initiating the First Crusade: "Undertake this journey eagerly for the remission of your sins, with the assurance of the reward of imperishable glory in the kingdom of heaven."

[128] Miller & Guerber 198.

humans at the top. God's laws, on the other hand, bless everyone because He is no respecter of persons. The elite, however, were far above and the common man was far below, mired in guilt. The completed sacrifice of Jesus Christ was no longer portrayed as the only way to salvation; now, one needed the elite, professional humans of the church to intercede, or one needed to accomplish some superhuman achievement such as a Crusade, pilgrimage, or self-punishment to be rid of guilt. But you see that these things all revolved around humanity's reach for God, not Jesus Christ's 'reach' for mankind.

Even with Bernard—whose devotion, compassion, and piety were amazing—it seems:

> ...for all that he spoke powerfully about the love of God, it seems that he strove more for kindling in himself a love for God, than for a positive dynamic recognition of the love of God.[129]

You may not see the point in my mention of this now. It may sound like theology, but *here* it is history. Why? Because when people felt increasingly distant from God, when the sacrifice of Jesus wasn't seen as the only way, when folks felt small, guilty, and hopeless before God while still being Christians...well, they would gradually search for meaning *outside* of Christianity! This search would contribute to the end of the Christian Middle Ages and would begin a humanist age! So how is it that what the church is, the nations will become? Because, by *baptizing* humanism, by implying it was true, the church led the nations to seek humanism too. This was a slow process, but I'm tipping you off early so you can watch for it.

But Christ is the Head of the Church; He knows our humanness and loves us still. You'll see Him patiently call, prod, and chastise His Church. Ack! I was supposed to be talking about Bernard...though we really were! While some of the church's errant thought may have seeped into him (we're all in the same boat with our own churches), the reason we're introducing him here is because he had such a passion to address the flaws of his beloved church. Great!

On a different note, Bernard was the key preacher (1146) of the Second Crusade and he helped develop the emphasis on the Virgin Mary; we'll leave that latter matter alone, for it is theological, not historical. Families will want to teach their own values there.

Now, on to the other French churchman of note: Abbe Suger. He was quite a character! He helped strengthen the French monarchy and even ruled the nation (1147-1149) when the king was on the Second Crusade! Suger wrote many books, but we could say his *magnum opus* was building the church of St. Denis in Paris. From that labor of love was birthed a new, inspiring, soaring architecture. It featured light and height, as well as incredible rib vaults, pointed arches, flying buttresses, and rose windows. Bask in pictures of these awesome buildings...or ask your parents for a 'field trip' to Europe to tour some! This magnificent style of architecture was called *Gothic* by later humanistic commentators, who felt anything medieval—when people were very religious—was backward and barbaric. But there is nothing backward or barbaric about the breathtaking cathedrals of the Middle Ages! In fact, these feats of engineering, design, artistry, and piety were one more reason the High Middle Ages were high!

---

[129] Jackson 107.

Do you have any Gothic churches in your town? If so, ask if you can sit quietly in them for a few minutes. How does the building make you feel? You'll discover that architecture, like other art, is almost a living thing, for it represents the thoughts, ideals, and *Big 2 Beliefs* of a human designer. These ideas reach out to you. That's the purpose and power of art–to communicate thoughts and feelings in a creative way. It reminds me that we're made in the image of our Creator, who artfully made this universe to represent *His* thoughts and values!

So, what direction does your soul go when you see Gothic architecture? When I was able to visit Europe, my attention was first captured by the cathedrals' tremendous beauty, intricacy, and size. I instantly thought of God's majestic enormity. After a while, though, another impression dawned on me: I felt small, even ant-like. Maybe my impressions are unfair since I live in an age when the cathedral is not our chief way of 'seeing' God represented, but the cathedrals seemed to imply God is dishearteningly unreachable. In fact, when in Paris's Sacre Coeur cathedral, I wanted to embrace the other visitors and say:

> *The nature of God you're seeing represented in this cathedral is true. He is majestic; He is awesome; He is beautiful; He is infinitely higher than us. But that's not all! He also loves us personally–loves you personally. He bridged the gap and came to you and me. There is no veil, no screen, no separation between you and Him if you surrender to His loving, forgiving Son and have faith in the sacrifice He made for us. We don't have to face God on our own; we can go right to Him confidently, humbly, and thankfully, through the blood of Jesus Christ–the total and complete sacrifice–to which we can add nothing. Intimacy with Jehovah is possible because of what He did. What a good God! Hurrah!*

Maybe it was that very spirit of celebration–rather than the elitism we just discussed–which the cathedral builders were trying to capture in stone. If so, awesome! He *is* worthy of our glory, and I applaud the folks of the Middle Ages who sacrificed to build those incredible works of art adorned with excellent sculpture! Most still felt great respect for the Lord and they used these great buildings, and even their interior layout,[130] to communicate God's majesty.

33a❧ Doings in France

Story of the Middle Ages, Ch. LXXIV, LXXVIII, XCI-XCII by Christine Miller & H.A. Guerber	Gr. 4-8
Middle Ages, by Dorothy Mills, Ch. VII, Pt. 2b & Ch. XX, Part 2a	Gr. 6-12

Fiction/Historical Fiction

Red Keep, by Allen French This is a tale of high adventure in Burgundy in the year 1165.	Gr. 6-12

---

[130] Jackson 111.

33b🔖 Bernard of Clairvaux and Abbe Suger

Glass, Stones, and Crown, by Anne Rockwell   Gr. 5-12

*Trial and Triumph, by Richard Hannula, Ch. 13   Gr. 5-12

*Invitation to the Classics, by Louise Cowan & Os Guinness, p. 90-91   Gr. 8-12

33c🔖 Magnificent medieval cathedrals

Middle Ages, by Dorothy Mills, Ch. IX, Pt 4   Gr. 6-12
----
*Child's History of the World, by V.M. Hillyer, Ch. 53   Gr. 1-4

Cathedrals: Stone upon Stone, by Brigitte Gandiol-Coppin (Young Discovery)   Gr. 1-5

Child's History of Art, by Hillyer & Huey   Gr. 2-8
(*Sculpture* section, Ch. 12; *Architecture* section, Ch. 14-17)
OR, *Young People's Story of Sculpture*, pp. 58-61 **and** *Young People's Story of Architecture: Gothic-Modern*, pp. 10-33

Everyday Life of a Cathedral Builder, by Giovanni Caselli   Gr. 3-8

*Medieval Cathedral, by Fiona Macdonald (Inside Story)   Gr. 3-10

*Cathedral, by David Macaulay   Gr. 3-12
    What an awesome book! In fact, it's so popular there's even a book about how
    Macaulay's *Cathedral* was made! It's called **Building the Book 'Cathedral'*, and is also by
    David Macaulay.

Made in the Middle Ages, by Christine Price, Part II   Gr. 5-12

The Cathedral Builders, by Marie-Pierre Perdrizet   Unknown

Audio/Video

*Cathedral, by David Macaulay   Various
    Mr. Macaulay hosts this intriguing video version of his book, giving extra commentary.

Fiction/Historical Fiction

Book of Hugh Flower, by Lorna Beers   Gr. 5-12
    The story of a stone mason working on an English cathedral.

33d☙ Stained glass windows
Yet another reason the High Middle Ages were high, in my opinion! Wow!

Middle Ages: Cultural Atlas for Young People, by Mike Corbishley, pp. 44-45   Gr. 3-8

Singing Windows, by Mary Young   Gr. 3-12

Activities

Ancient Arts: Stained Glass, by Sarah Brown   Various
> This is an activity kit for independent older children, or for younger children under supervision. You might want to have a field trip to a stained glass studio, or take a tour of any churches in your town which contain these gems!

Cathedral Stained Glass Coloring Book   Various

33e☙ Notre Dame Cathedral of Paris

Architecture, by Neil Stevenson, pp. 32-33 *(DK Annotated Guides)*   Gr. 7-12

34☙ Germany in the Twelfth Century and Frederick Barbarossa

We already mentioned the two vying factions in the Holy Roman Empire: the Welfs and the Waiblings. Well, upon his death, wise Conrad called not for his young son to be king but for his nephew, Frederick, who had a Welf mother and a Waibling father. Yes, Conrad actually put the interests of the nation before his own family pride, which was quite rare in those days! Frederick–called *Barbarossa* for his red beard–ruled from 1152-1190. He was very busy dealing with 'robber barons' in both Germany and Italy (especially in Milan and Lombardy). Frederick had intense conflict with the popes as well. Alas, Frederick was very cruel in how he maintained order, as were most of the kings of the age, but he was amazingly chivalrous to the daughter of Henry II of England (the younger Matilda) who had married a resistant German noble. Frederick was also part of the Third Crusade with Richard Lionheart, and it can be said he founded Munich, an important city in Germany to this day![131]

---

[131] Miller & Guerber 191-194, for the material in this entire paragraph.

Fiction/Historical Fiction

35 Medieval Towns

One thing Frederick Barbarossa did achieve in German lands was the redevelopment of towns. I can imagine what you're saying: "Towns?! Haven't there *always* been towns?"

Actually, you already know the answer! Just think about what you've learned! You saw that the flaws in late Roman government and economics, the horrific barbarian and Viking attacks, the lack of education and freedom, as well as civil wars between competing barons and kings all worked to devastate Europe's towns and instead foster the feudal system. This found people living and working on feudal estates, each of which had to produce all that was necessary for life. Thus, supplies were often meager and specialties could hardly develop since everyone was needed for subsistence farming.

Now think a minute. In Romans 13:3-4, God gives us a simple truth: governments must reward the righteous and punish evildoers so people are secure. Do you see? Only in a stable and upright nation can farmers bring produce to an honest market and merchants bring unique goods from other regions and climates. But during this time of mostly poor government and barbarian raids, it wasn't safe enough for travel and trade.

With the life-changing spread of Christianity among the barbarians, though, serious kings such as Frederick Barbarossa and Philip Augustus of France could finally begin to rebuild towns. Though this development would be very slow, people in towns could buy food produced on outlying farms (when there was finally an excess due to improvements in agriculture) rather

| Division of labor | than raising their own food. These townsfolk could instead make a living with their skills or could develop trade. Higher productivity was generated by this *division of labor.* |

Keep your eyes open! You'll see that the towns' artisans and merchants gradually became a political force, for they had more independence, creativity, confidence, and often more education. They weren't just 'surviving,' as so many peasants were. Think about it: any nation comprised of only a few aristocrats and masses of downtrodden serfs will not see a high level of freedom and inventiveness. Beleaguered peasants, living from one meal to the next, are hardly able to hold political and spiritual leaders accountable to God's higher laws or tinker with creative ideas. Mind you, there is nothing wrong with farming; we all depend on it! The problem was how farming was carried out under the feudal system.

This political power was very real in the growing cities, especially in the Holy Roman Empire where the weakness of self-indulgent kings after Frederick Barbossa made it possible for the cities to organize themselves. For example, eighty cities along the North Sea, with Lubeck and Hamburg at the head, bound themselves by treaty to do business together and protect each other. This was known as the Hanseatic League. Even within each city, the artisans and merchants gained power as they bound themselves together in *guilds* which governed the quality of their work, trained apprentices, and gave members a stronger voice.

| Guilds |

ThinkWrite 10: "Division!

Yes, I hear you yelping at me, "This is history class, not math class! Why are we talking about division?"

Well, do you understand the concept of *division of labor?* Do you know why it's important?

If you're old enough, think about the connection between economic and political freedom. Do they relate at all with spiritual freedom? Though we've talked about these ideas somewhat in earlier *TruthQuest History* guides, we'll further develop them in later guides, so don't worry if it is not clear now.

Information for this *ThinkWrite* is found in: *Whatever Happened to Penny Candy?* by Richard Maybury, for Gr. 5-12, or in other resources about simple economics.

Several Italian cities, such as Venice and Genoa, would also become very powerful, especially in trading for the eastern goods which had so impressed the crusaders. These two Mediterranean cities would fight many times over the centuries for control of that rich trade.

These changes would be very slow, but they had at least begun! Markets and fairs were springing up. More folks were able to deal directly, rather than passing everything through the feudal manor. You can bet the feudal lords were not very excited about releasing their hold. But you may also recall that many of these nobles–trying to raise money for Crusades–allowed certain towns and fiefs to buy their freedom. All these factors worked together to bring this gradual change. Fascinating! (Do *ThinkWrite 10* while learning about the development of towns.)

35a❧ General overview

Story of the Middle Ages, by Miller & Guerber, Ch. XCVII-XCIX   Gr. 4-8

Middle Ages, by Dorothy Mills, Ch. XIV-XV   Gr. 6-12

Birthdays of Freedom: Vol. 2, by Genevieve Foster, pp. 28-29   Gr. 2-5

Looking at History, by R.J. Unstead, pp. 113-128   Gr. 2-5

Marguerite Makes a Book, by Bruce Robertson   Gr. 3-7
> As an example of a non-church artisan, such as lived in medieval towns, you can enjoy this magnificently illustrated story. It features a girl who helps her father make illuminated manuscripts. The book itself looks gilded!

Medieval Town, by Daisy Kerr (Worldwise)   Gr. 3-7

Fourteenth-Century Towns, by John Clare (Living History)   Gr. 3-10
> Though about later towns, you can enjoy this excellent book now.

Life in the Middle Ages, by Jay Williams, Ch. 3 (Landmark Giant)   Gr. 5-12

Activities

Make This Model Town (Usborne)   Various

Fiction/Historical Fiction

Walter Dragun's Town, by Sheila Sancha   Gr. 4-10
> This unusual book shows budding merchants at work in an English town.

35b❧ Guilds and the Hanseatic League

Lebek: A City of Northern Europe Through the Ages, by Xavier Hernandez   Gr. 4-12
> This book focuses on what life would have been like in a Hanseatic League city; it features interesting drawings.

Fiction/Historical Fiction

Turn in the Road, by Cateau DeLeeuw   Gr. 6-12
> A young Dutch apprentice must protect children on the way to a fair.

The Secret Fiord, by Geoffrey Trease   Gr. 7-12
    Trease's books are always a great hit!

35c⟡ Venice and Genoa
Any books about Italian history will contain info on these two key cities if you want to dig deeper.

Story of the Renaissance and Reformation, by C. Miller & H.A. Guerber, Ch. II   Gr. 4-8

This is Venice, by Miroslav Sasek   Gr. K-3
    A lovely 'visit Venice' book in a rare, but beloved, series. If you have it, enjoy!

Venice: Birth of a City, by Piero Ventura   Gr. 3-9
    I bet many public libraries still have this.

Incredible Explosions, by Richard Platt & Stephen Biesty, pp. 24-25   Gr. 4-12
    These two pages show an intriguing, expanded view of Venice.

Rival Cities, by M. Gregg Robinson   Gr. 9-12

Venetians: Merchant Princes, by Thomas Chubb   Gr. 9-12

Fiction/Historical Fiction

The Lion of St. Mark, by G.A. Henty   Gr. 7-12

Swords on the Sea, by Agnes Danforth Hewes   Gr. 7-12
    A novel of the battles between Venice and Genoa from a good author.

36⟡ Good 'Ol Stories

Do you need a break? Here are some fictional stories which are not associated with a particular historical person or event, but give a good glimpse of life in the Middle Ages. You can enjoy a couple now, or any time! Just refer back to this list when desired!

36a⟡ General topics

Harald and the Giant Knight **and** *Harald and the Great Stag*, by Donald Carrick   Gr. 1-3
    Long-beloved stories of boy knight. There are a few in the series, I think.

Prince Valiant stories, by Harold Foster   Gr. 1-6
    There are *many* Prince Valiant stories!

Merry Ever After, by Joe Lasker   Gr. 2-6
    A fun and beautiful picture book about two medieval weddings! It was recently in-print,
    so is probably still in your public library.

Saint George and the Dragon, by Margaret Hodges   Gr. 2-6
    Many families enjoy this classic tale taken from Spencer's version of the legendary
    dragon-slaying hero and patron saint of England. Illustrated by Trina Schart Hyman.

Knight of the Lion, by Constance Hieatt   Gr. 3-8

Luttrell Village, by Sheila Sancha   Gr. 3-10
    See daily life in a fictional village.

Marvelous Misadventures of Sebastian, by Lloyd Alexander   Gr. 4-10

Gaudenzia, by Marguerite Henry   Gr. 4-12
    This story, from a beloved horse author, honors a medieval horse event.

Twelve Bright Trumpets, by Margaret Leighton   Gr. 4-12
    A collection of short stoires.

Red Falcons of Tremoine, by Hendry Peart   Gr. 5-12

Three Red Flares, by David Divine   Gr. 5-12
    Modern children find a medieval map that launches them on adventures.

One is One, by Barbara Picard   Gr. 6-12
    Everyone thinks the Earl's son is a coward, but is he?

Jackaroo, by Cynthia Voight   Gr. 7-12
    I have not read this, and cannot comment on its content, but only know it's the story
    of a 13th-century innkeeper's daughter who wonders if she's met someone very famous.

Kristin Lavransdatter, by Sigrid Undset   Gr. 8-12
    A very long novel about a medieval Norwegian girl by a famous Norwegian author.

Saint Julian, by Walter Wangerin, Jr.   Gr. 10-12
    This is not so much flatly historical, from what I understand, as much as it uses the
    themes of the Middle Ages—the privilege of the nobles, the power of the church, the
    conflict of the Crusades—to tell a gripping story of personal Christianity.

Audio/Video

Court Jester, starring Danny Kaye
  Warning! While some families greatly enjoy this funny spoof, others reject it since one of the plot devices is the casting of spells.

Inspector General, starring Danny Kaye
  What a funny film!

36b❧ Kings and queens, princesses and peas, and wonderful kingdoms
Some of these stories are quite fanciful, but you've had plenty to read about the reality of the Middle Ages. Remember, these books are all fiction/historical fiction.

The King's Wish, by Benjamin Elkin	Gr. K-2
The Sugar Mouse Cake, by Gene Zion	Gr. K-2
The very funny story of a king's pastry chef.	
Forever Laughter, by Don Freeman	Gr. K-3
A court jester tries to cheer a gloomy king. Jesters actually came later, but it fits now.	
Gillespie and the Guards, by Benjamin Elkin	Gr. K-3
This is the very funny story of a boy and the king's guards.	
The Princess and the Pea, by Hans Christian Andersen	Gr. K-3
The Simple Prince, by Jane Yolen	Gr. K-3
A prince finds the 'simple life' is not so easy!	
The True Princess, by Angela Hunt	Gr. K-4
In this *wonderful* story, a princess learns the meaning of service.	
Duchess Bakes a Cake and *Baron's Booty*, both by Virginia Kahl	Gr. 1-3
The warm, funny story of a family with 13 princesses! It's a Five-in-a-Row book.	
The 500 Hats of Bartholomew Cubbins, by Dr. Seuss	Gr. 1-5
What a funny story!	
Coll and His White Pig, by Lloyd Alexander	Gr. 1-5
Tale of Alain, by Edward Ormondroyd	Gr. 2-8
A younger prince learns to be strong.	

The Whipping Boy, by Sid Fleischman   Gr. 2-8
   The powerful, moving story of a boy forced to take the punishment due a spoiled
   prince. Boys especially appreciate this story.

A Cavalcade of Queens, by Eleanor Farjeon   Gr. 3-9
   Short stories about queens

*Adam of the Road, by Elizabeth Janet Gray   Gr. 4-12
   This is definitely a don't-miss story! A boy searches for his father in 1294 England.

*The Wonder Clock, by Howard Pyle   Gr. 4-12
   I've heard *rave* reviews about this collection of short stories by a highly-respected author
   and illustrator.

The Red Cape, by Rachel Varble   Gr. 5-12
   A princess must escape in order to save her country.

36c✿ Falconry

Fiction/Historical Fiction

The King's Falcon, by Paula Fox   Gr. 3-10

Ice Falcon, by Rita Ritchie   Gr. 6-12
   A boy falconer travels to Iceland.

The Earl's Falconer, by Ursula Williams   Gr. 9-12
   I've not seen this but it is supposedly a novel which reveals the lives of young squires
   being trained in falconry.

36d✿ Minstrels, bards, and troubadours
Remember, these stories are all fiction/historical fiction.

The Truthful Harp, by Lloyd Alexander   Gr. 2-6
   In this story, a minstrel learns to tell the truth.

The Troubadour, by René Guillot   Gr. 4-12
   A knight poses as troubadour to oust usurpers.

The Minstrel Knight, by Philip Rush   Gr. 5-12

37 ❧ New Voices in the Church: Dominic, Francis of Assisi, and Others

Do you remember? We said God is always working to revitalize and purify His church, and His work never seems to be done...because one century's reforms seem to get stale in the next. For example, the newly dedicated monastic orders of the 1100s had become luxurious and passive by the 1200s, a process we've seen occurring throughout the years.[132] It was time for another wave of reform!

Enter Dominic and Francis! Dominic, a Spanish churchman, was grieved about heresy such as he saw gripping the Cathars. He founded the Dominican monasteries, which were devoted to rooting out heresy. Alas, they would later be involved in the Spanish Inquisition. Prior to that, though, their emphasis on learning bred important intellectuals such as Albertus Magnus and Thomas Aquinas (whom we'll meet later).

As for Francis, after dramatically abandoning the wealth of his Italian family and giving his life to the Lord, he became a friar and urged simplicity, purity, and the love of God in His creation. He was soon joined in his cause by a former friend, Clare, also of Assisi, who began a similar movement for women. Mr. Jackson points out two excellent qualities in Francis:

> *What is so attractive about Francis is that he did not lose the openness of his preconversion personality.... Distinctive again of Francis was his great reluctance to institutionalize what he stood for....He knew the downfall of the other orders.*[133]

Not every attempt at reform was welcomed by the church; even Francis was resisted at first. In fact, few reformers were welcomed. As a case in point, look at the life and work of Peter Waldo (Valdes) of Lyon France, whose followers were known as Waldensians. They suffered great persecution for their call to purity. The reform-minded voices best heard by the church were those of noble birth. Ironically, even reformers who were persecuted would, after becoming accepted and institutionalized, persecute other reformers! Let us all remember, then, to carefully seek spiritual freshness and a heart that is responsive to correction.

There were others of note, too, such as Hedwig of Poland. We can even point out believers who accomplished works in diverse fields, such as Theodoric, a monk who experimented in science. (Later, when you learn about Gregor Mendel, who is considered the father of genetics, you won't be surprised to discover he was a monk!) Also, don't forget that the monks and nuns were still illustrating manuscripts, caring for the sick and poor, and providing most of Europe's education!

---

[132] Jackson 108.

[133] Jackson 109.

37a✤ St. Francis and Clare of Assisi

As with many heroes of history, legends have been added to the real life story of St. Francis. Because Francis and Clare are treated together in some books, we'll list them together here.

*Greenleaf's *Famous Men of the Middle Ages*, Ch. XXV, Part I	Gr. 3-7
Story of the Middle Ages, by Christine Miller & H.A. Guerber, Ch. LXXXIV	Gr. 4-8
Middle Ages, by Dorothy Mills, Ch. XVII. Pt. 1	Gr. 6-12

Saint Francis, by Brian Wildsmith	Gr. K-3
Brother Francis and the Friendly Beasts, by Margaret Hodges	Gr. 1-4
Saint Francis Celebrates Christmas, by Mary Walsh	Gr. 1-5

This book tells of Francis setting up a nativity scene, and how that became a custom.

Francis: Poor Man of Assisi, by Tomie dePaola	Gr. 1-6
A Book of Heroes, by Dorothy Heiderstadt, pp. 63-73	Gr. 3-6
Beggars, Beasts and Easter Fire, by Carol Greene, Ch. 10-11	Gr. 2-8
Wolf of Gubbio, by Michael Bedard	Gr. 3-6

This is the story of St. Francis calming a fierce wolf.

God's Troubadour: St Francis of Assisi, by Sophie Jewett	Gr. 3-8
St. Francis, by Pelagie Doane	Gr. 3-8
Brother Sun, Sister Moon: The Life and Story of St. Francis, by Margaret Mayo	Gr. 4-8

This book relates facts about Francis's life, as well as legends. It also includes information on Clare of Assisi.

Fire Upon the Earth, by Norman Langford, Ch. 9	Gr. 4-8
Francis and Clare, Saints of Assisi, by Helen Homan (Vision)	Gr. 4-12

This is in a distinctively Catholic series.

Trial and Triumph: Stories from Church History, by Richard Hannula, Ch. 15	Gr. 5-12
Message of St. Francis, edited by Sister Nan	Gr. 6-12

The words of St. Francis, along with stories and legends about him.

St. Francis of Assisi, by G.K. Chesterton   Gr. 10-12
     This highly-respected author relates the life of St. Francis.

Saint Francis of Assisi, by Mary Alves (Encounter the Saints)   Unknown

St. Francis of Assisi: The Happiest Man Who Ever Lived, by Robert Kennedy   Unknown

Fiction/Historical Fiction

The Work of St. Francis, by MacKinlay Kantor   Gr. 4-8
     Boy gets involved with St. Francis.

Big John's Secret, by Eleanore Jewett   Gr. 6-12
     Boy with a family mystery meets Francis of Assisi at a Crusade.

The Road to Damietta, by Scott O'Dell   Gr. 7-12
     Story (especially for girls) of a young woman who loves St. Francis from afar.

The Bright Thread, by Jack Steffan   Gr. 8-12
     I've not seen this, but have learned it is a novel about Clare of Assisi.

Audio/Video

Brother Sun, Sister Moon
     Some families enjoy this film, others do not...because it includes the scene in which–true
     to life–Francis renounces his wealthy life and tears off his clothing, since his father had
     made his fortune selling clothing textiles. I saw the film years ago, but don't remember
     it being handled offensively. Since I recall so little, that doesn't help much!

37b ❧ St. Dominic

*Greenleaf's *Famous Men of the Middle Ages*, Ch. XXV, Part II   Gr. 3-7

Story of the Middle Ages, by Christine Miller & H.A. Guerber, Ch. XC   Gr. 4-8

37c ❧ Monks & Nuns
We covered this general topic previously. I'll just list a couple resources that are more pertinent to this era.

Looking at History, by R.J. Unstead, pp. 94-99   Gr. 2-5

Child's History of Art, by Hillyer & Huey   Gr. 2-8
(*Architecture* sect., Ch. 11; *Painting* sect., Ch. 6b)
OR, *Young People's Story of Fine Art: 15,000BC-1,800AD*, pp. 28-31, **and** *Young People's Story of Architecture: 3,000BC-Gothic*, pp. 100-105

Fiction/Historical Fiction

*A Rare Benedictine, by Ellis Peters (Brother Cadfael Mysteries)   Gr. 9-12
   The Shearers of Greenleaf speak highly of most of the books in this series about a mystery-solving monk of 12th-century England.

**Trilogy: *Hawk and the Dove; Wounds of God; Long Fall*, by Penelope Wilcock   Gr. 9-12
   A Christian trilogy regarding the dear souls at an English monastery in the 1300s.

37d✿ Peter Waldo (Valdes) and the Waldensians

*Trial and Triumph: Stories from Church History, by R. Hannula, pp. 89-93   Gr. 5-12

37e✿ Theodoric

Theodoric's Rainbow, by Stephen Kramer   Gr. 1-6
   This book is *so* fascinating, and was recently in-print, so is probably at your library.

37f✿ Other Christian figures

A Book of Heroes, by Dorothy Heiderstadt, pp. 74-83   Gr. 3-6

Beggars, Beasts and Easter Fire, by Carol Greene, Ch. 9, 12-15   Gr. 2-8
   There are several light chapters covering medieval Christians of note, such as Catherine of Siena, Elizabeth of Hungary, Sergius of Radonezh, Hedwig of Poland, and Bridget of Sweden. I don't know details of their lives or theological stances, and they're not touched on in this book.

*Trial and Triumph: Stories from Church History, by R. Hannula, pp. 101-106   Gr. 5-12
   This chapter is about Elizabeth of Hungary.

St. Catherine of Siena, by Mary Fabyan Windeatt   Gr. 5-12

The Flame: Catherine of Siena, by Jeanette Eaton   Gr. 9-12

Fiction/Historical Fiction

So Young a Queen, by Lois Mills   Gr. 8-12
        The story of Jadwiega of Hungary, who married a prince of Lithuania, led him and his
        nation to convert to Christianity, and was also a queen of Poland!

38✍ Terror Strikes Europe: Genghis Khan and the Mongol Invaders!

**Throughout the Middle Ages, the threat of Muslim/Saracen invasion had always hung over
Europe, but now there was a new menace on the horizon, literally! Word spread like wildfire
that the rumbling earth and cloud of dust off in the distance signaled waves of Mongol warriors
under their fierce master, Genghis Khan, and later his sons and grandsons. They conquered
land from Korea to Poland, including lands in India, Iraq, and Iran! The cruelty and
devastation wreaked by Genghis were unthinkable; there was absolutely no respect for the value
of human life! At the peak time of European invasion (1213-1227), folks easily feared their entire
civilization was going to be annihilated!**

Story of the World: Volume 2, by Susan Wise Bauer, Ch. 21a   Gr. 3-6

Story of the Renaissance and Reformation, by C. Miller & H.A. Guerber, Ch. VIIa Gr. 4-8

A Child's History of the World, by V.M. Hillyer, Ch. 55a   Gr. 1-4

Genghis Khan and the Mongol Horde, by Harold Lamb (Landmark)   Gr. 3-8

Genghis Khan, by Judy Humphrey (World Leaders Past and Present)   Gr. 8-12

Genghis Khan, by Brenda Lange (Ancient World Leaders)   Gr. 9-12

Genghis Khan, by Harold Lamb   Gr. 11-12
        Few students would need to take the time necessary to read this large book.

Fiction/Historical Fiction

A Gift for Genghis Khan, by Frances Alberts   Gr. 2-7
        Story of boy who meets Genghis Khan.

Arrow Messenger, Messenger from K'itai, both by D.R. Burleigh   Gr. 4-8
        Stories of messenger boy for Genghis Khan.

Secret Beyond the Mountains; Golden Hawks of Genghis Khan; and *Year of the Horse*   Gr. 7-12
Three separate novels about the Mongols, all by Rita Ritchie.

Sons of the Steppe, by Hans Baumann   Gr. 8-12
A novel about Genghis Khan's grandsons.

39🕮 The Thirteenth Century

Eventually, the massacres of Genghis Khan came to an end, and life in Europe during the 1200s rolled on. Let's look at a happier miscellany of topics.

39a🕮 Food, clothing, and homes

Looking at History, by R.J. Unstead, pp. 129-142   Gr. 2-5

Clothing, Houses, and *Food,* all by Piero Ventura   Gr. 3-10
Each of these three books contain information helpful to students seeking further information on these topics.

Growing Up in 13th Century England, by Alfred Duggan   Gr. 5-12
See what was it like to be a kid in the 1200s.

Illustrated Encyclopedia of Costume and Fashion from 1066 to the Present   Various
by Jack Cassin-Scott (Contains some low-cut necklines.)

Activities

Knights & Ladies (Costumes for Coloring)   Various

Medieval Costumes Paper Dolls (Dover)   Various

Medieval Fashion (Dover)   Various
A coloring book.

39b🕮 A great mathematician: Leonard Fibonacci (Leonard of Pisa)

You'll be fascinated to meet this amazing mathematician who introduced Arabic numerals to Europe in 1202 and discovered Fibonacci numbers, among other accomplishments.

Mathematicians are People, Too: Vol. 2, by Luetta & Wilber Reimer, pp. 16-23   Gr. 3-8

Leonard of Pisa and the New Math of the Middle Ages, by Joseph & Frances Gies Gr. 7-12

39c☙ General medieval handcrafts and art

Duke and the Peasant: Life in the Middle Ages, by Sister Wendy Beckett   All ages
    See medieval days, months, and seasons in this reproduction of an actual "Book of the Hours" painted during the Middle Ages. (This was also cited earlier.)

Medieval Cats, by Susan Herbert   All ages
    What an unusual book! The illustrator presents actual medieval paintings and illuminated manuscripts, with the 'slight' alteration that the main characters are cats! It captures the essence of the art, while the cats grasp the attention of even those students usually uninterested in art.

Made in the Middle Ages, by Christine Price   Gr 5-12

39d☙ Knights
We talked about knights previously, but these books are set in later medieval times, so they fit better here!

Knights, by Catherine Daly-Weir (All Aboard Reading 2)   Gr. 1-2

The Making of a Knight, by Patrick O'Brien   Gr. 1-4

Knight in Battle, by Ewart Oakeshott   Unknown

Fiction/Historical Fiction

In the Time of Knights, by Shelley Tanaka   Gr. 4-10
    This tells the true story of William Marshal, reputed to be the best knight ever, and who played a role in the reigns of several English kings. Greenleaf highly recommends this!

39e☙ Frederick II

Fiction/Historical Fiction

King's Road, by Cecelia Holland   Gr. 4-10
    This is a highly esteemed story about the grandson of Frederick Barbarossa. Frederick II led the Fifth Crusade.

Bright Hunter of the Skies, by Herbert Best
A novel about Frederick II and his falconry.

Gr. 7-12

40 Louis, King and Saint!

It's time now to meet Louis IX, grandson of Philip Augustus. His father, Louis VIII, died early, so Louis IX was raised by his mother, who reigned in his stead until he came of age. Her name was Blanche of Castile, and she was an excellent mother! That's why, by the standards of the day, Louis was an excellent king, and was later made a saint! In fact, you may know this Louis by his nickname, Louis the Pious. His rule began in 1236, and as long as his mother lived, he sought her advice.

Fulfilling a vow made while ill, Louis set out on the Seventh Crusade, during which he captured Damietta in Egypt, hoping to work his way toward the Holy Land. That was his last success, though, and many hardships came. Even his return voyage was difficult, but he showed a respect for the value of human life—at least for the lives of his countrymen—which was unusual for his day.

> *On his way home his ship ran against a rock, and it seemed as if all on board would perish. The king was urged to leave the vessel with his family, but nobly replied that the lives of the five hundred people with him were as precious in the sight of the Lord as his own, and that if he left, a panic would surely seize the remainder of the passengers, while if he remained, everything would be done to save them all. Thanks to his steadfastness, the ship was saved from its perilous position, and all on board were rescued.*[134]

Another attribute of Louis made him rare: he sought peace with his neighbors rather than conquest. He even returned to England land on which he believed the French had no rightful claim. Louis helped establish Sorbonne University (which is still in operation), hospitals, and the first asylum for the blind. It was on the Eighth Crusade in Tunis that Louis succumbed to the plague in 1270; he was sainted just twelve years later. His son, Philip III (Philip the Bold) succeeded him.[135] Charles of Anjou, brother of Louis, was asked by the pope to drive the Germans out of Sicily, which the son of Frederick Barbossa had gained when he married into one of the Norman families who had settled and ruled for centuries.

---

[134] Miller & Guerber 217.

[135] Miller & Guerber, Ch. XCVI.

*Greenleaf's *Famous Men of the Middle Ages*, Ch. XXIV	Gr. 3-7
Story of the Middle Ages, by Miller & Guerber, Ch. XCIV-XCVI	Gr. 4-8
Middle Ages, by Dorothy Mills, Ch. XX, Part 2b	Gr. 6-12

St. Louis and the Last Crusade, by Margaret Hubbard (Vision) This is in a distinctively Catholic series.	Gr. 4-12

Fiction/Historical Fiction

Where Valor Lies, by Adele & Cateau DeLeeuw A French boy goes on a Crusade with Louis IX.	Gr. 5-12

41🙶 England Gets a Real Parliament!

After years of struggle with King Henry III (son of Bad Prince John), the nobles were fed up and the Magna Charta gave them authority to seek changes. The strongest noble, Simon de Montfort the Younger, led the struggle against the king and his son, Edward. They clashed at the Battle of Evesham in 1265. The result was the founding of a new parliament, which included some common citizens. These were able to assemble in what would be called the House of Commons, giving representation and voice to a wider group of Englishmen for the first time in centuries! This is considered the beginning of the modern English parliament which tried—sometimes more successfully than others—to limit the power of the king by the authority of the common folk. What a breakthrough, even though feeble at first! I wish I could tell you that Simon de Montfort was a nice guy, but I can't. He persecuted Jews and severely dealt with others.

An Island Story, by H.E. Marshall, Ch. XXXVII-XXXIX	Gr. 3-8
Story of the Middle Ages, by Christine Miller & H.A. Guerber, Ch. C-CI	Gr. 4-8
Middle Ages, by Dorothy Mills, Ch. XX, Pt. 1 (second section)	Gr. 6-12

Looking at History, by R.J. Unstead, p. 106	Gr. 2-5
The Story of Britain, by R.J. Unstead, pp. 113-115	Gr. 5-12

Fiction/Historical Fiction

High Courage, by Rosemary Weir   Gr. 5-12
        A boy is involved in the struggle between Montfort and Henry III.

Baron's Hostage, by Geoffrey Trease   Gr. 7-12
        This great author spins a tale of Montfort at the Battle of Evesham.

42❧ Medieval Learning: Thomas Aquinas and Roger Bacon

As you already know, the church was the main source of education in Europe during the Middle Ages. Whole monastic orders, such as the Dominicans, were focused on learning. So, before we get to the 'explosive' story of Roger Bacon (hint, hint), we will first meet one of the most famous Dominicans: Thomas Aquinas (1225?-1274). His impact on history has been enormous!

Thomas Aquinas was an extremely intelligent, hardworking, and prolific scholar of the Scholastic movement who impressed everyone even as a boy! He taught in major universities and authored massive works on church doctrine.

Before we think about his work, though, we must remember that folks are profoundly affected by the *Big 2 Beliefs* of their world...because the beliefs seem so 'obvious' and 'normal' that they are rarely questioned (though question them we must if we want our minds renewed).[136] Anyway, we know the medieval beliefs were gravitating toward the preeminence of human authority (*Big Belief #1*), just as the beliefs of the Greeks and Romans had done. Yes, in the time of Thomas Aquinas, Europe was all about the authority of popes and cardinals, bishops and kings, queens and dukes, barons and counts. The church had *baptized* humanism, as we've seen.[137] Our goal is not to gloatingly point fingers when we say this, because we face the same struggles and this church we're discussing is the ancestral church of us all. So, without hostility, judgment, or offensiveness, we can applaud the great effort of Thomas Aquinas, and also admit a crack in the works.

Working from the *Big 2 Beliefs* of his age, and seeing that the power of human reasoning had been neglected as the medieval church became more mystical and abstract, Aquinas set out to bring the two powers together–Christianity and the human mind. He believed Christian thought could sustain intense intellectual analysis, and he wrote many books in that vein.

---

[136] Romans 12:2: "And be not conformed to this world: but be ye transformed by the renewing of your mind, that ye may prove what is that good, and acceptable, and perfect, will of God." (KJV)

[137] Jackson 122.

But one of the greatest impacts of his work came from the flipside (unintentionally, I imagine) of his point about Christianity and the human mind. I'll say it very specifically, because it's worth understanding well: Aquinas knew God had created human reasoning, and he didn't think the mind had been corrupted at the Fall,[138] so he believed that what a well-used mind discovered could be trusted as true.[139] Furthermore, he held Aristotle–the ancient Greek philosopher and scientist–to be a prime example of what human reasoning had discovered. So, it was Aquinas's firm belief that what Christianity said about higher matters and what non-Christian[140] Aristotle had said about earthly particulars would jive perfectly.[141] He made it his life's work to prove that. The result was his book: *Summa Theologica*.

Now, we know God did indeed make our minds capable of learning truth, and we know all truth comes from Him since He doesn't just say the truth, but *is* the truth.[142] But it seems Aquinas was saying something more than that, and you *must* understand this difference if you're going to understand all the rest of western history. So, take a deep breath as we tackle it!

You see, Aquinas gradually began "placing revelation (God's words) and human reason (Aristotle) on an equal footing."[143] This is *very* different from saying the latter is a tool of the former. In a church already chasing humanism, his "system became the accepted orthodox theology of the...church"[144] and "to question it was a heresy."[145] Think: when in later centuries the church would punish Galileo and Copernicus, it was for differing *scientifically* with Aristotle about such things as the earth rotating around the sun. Do you understand? The words of Aristotle–a human–were given the status of infallibility, as only the Bible has in fact. The church was making science into an elite monarchy which brooked no accountability; no one could question the King of Science.

Do you wonder if Aristotle's words really had that much authority? Here is the impassioned comment of Averroës, a Spanish scholar active just before the time of Aquinas:

> *Aristotle was the wisest of the Greeks and constituted and completed logic, physics, and metaphysics....I saw that*
> *he put the finishing touches on these sciences, because none of those who have succeeded him up to our time, to wit,*

---

[138] Schaeffer 52.

[139] Mills 269.

[140] This descriptive term and concept is from: Cowan and Guinness 98.

[141] Schaeffer 73-74.

[142] John 14:6 says, "Jesus saith unto him, 'I am the way, the truth and the life....'" (KJV)

[143] Schaeffer 43 (parenthetical phrases in the quote are mine).

[144] Jackson 111.

[145] Mills 268.

during nearly fifteen hundred years, have been able to add anything to his writings or find in them any error of any importance. Now that all this should be found in one man is a strange and miraculous thing, and this privileged being deserves to be called <u>divine</u> rather than human.[146] (emphasis mine)

Once that door was opened, 'distortions' in the church became more and more widespread, as Francis Schaeffer puts it, because Scripture was no longer bedrock, it was no longer supreme, it was no longer superior to human notions and impulses, some of which have brought suffering to millions of people who would emphatically testify to the *fallibility* of human thinking. But this shift to believing human reason could determine truth independently of God would have a *galactic* impact! Top church leaders, kings, and intellectuals had already moved in the direction of humanism; then they exploited Aquinas's loophole.

In so doing, they were ending the Christian Middle Ages and launching a new age–the Renaissance (Latin, *rebirth*)–when folks looked backed longingly on the humanist values of ancient Greece and Rome.[147] Of course, in craving the rebirth of all things Greek and Roman, they were conveniently ignoring ancient bondage. They were even ignoring the progress of the Christian centuries, and were blaming medieval problems on Christianity, when in fact the problems sprang from remaining strongholds of humanism–the very thing they were chasing! And guess what?! Even today, people come to the same wrong conclusion! This drastic error has impacted history during all

> *ThinkWrite Reminder!*
>
> I hope you're weaving your learning on this topic into your *ThinkWrite–Investigation Supreme!* We won't give many new *ThinkWrites*, so you can focus on the biggie!

the intervening centuries, as you'll see throughout *TruthQuest History*. I'd sure like you to set the record straight for your generation! That's why we're doing this!

Let me quickly add something. It *is* good to be a thinking, intellectual Christian, as Aquinas was. I'm asking *you* to be one right now by contemplating all this! It's just important that we not put our thinking on an equal plane with God's, "For {as} the heavens are higher than the earth, So are My ways higher than your ways And My thoughts than your thoughts."[148] To give our own thoughts great authority–which is humanism indeed–is something we must not do. His Word is the only flawless standard, because He spoke it and watched over it and brought it to be. That same Bible says we must not add or take anything away from its message.

In great contrast, then, we come to Mr. Roger Bacon, a Franciscan friar at England's Oxford University during the latter 1200s. *Kaboom!* Mr. Bacon carried on some experiments with gunpowder which probably shook up the neighborhood. Happily (or not), his work with lenses was less dramatic, but his ideas were so new and his science so misunderstood, it was assumed he dabbled in dark magic! In fact, he spent ten years of his life in prison!

---

[146] Mills 268.

[147] Schaeffer 52.

[148] Isaiah 55:9 (NASB)

119

Interestingly, Bacon is now considered the "first modern scientific thinker."[149] Why? Because he didn't go in for the medieval preoccupation with human authority figures. He felt the truths of science were open to any and all who cared to observe, whether or not your name was Aristotle. Though I don't know where Mr. Bacon stood personally in his spiritual walk, his scientific view came from the 'Christian consensus,' as Mr. Schaeffer calls it. What consensus? I'll answer carefully, for this view would contribute to the dramatic Scientific Revolution coming soon. It was, quite simply, this: God—who is totally consistent—has created the world; thus, scientific truth is consistent and can be consistently observed by anyone throughout repeated experiments.[150]

Now, take that thought deeper. It also means there could be no monarchs or divinities in science, even if they were named Aristotle. There could be no one whose findings were above testing (accountability) through the experiments of others. Do you see the modern *scientific method* right here? Do you? Do you understand that the *Big 2 Beliefs* of Bacon and those of the church made their science completely different? I'm telling you! These *Big 2 Beliefs* are at the bottom of everything...because they are spiritual! Want more proof? Think of the *Big 2 Beliefs* of the Romans. Their human authority mindset led them to declare the earlier Greeks as authorities on pure science; thus, the Romans only memorized Greek discoveries, making virtually none of their own in 1,250 years of civilization! (Sound like modern science education?)

Here is how one author describes Bacon's thoughts:

> *He taught that human error was due to an undue regard to authority, to a false idea of what knowledge was, to prejudice and to habit which encouraged mental laziness. He declared that the only way to find out truth was not merely to argue, but to observe and experiment, because it is by observation and experiment that conclusions can be tested.*[151]

With that point of view, you will see why Bacon envisioned so many scientific breakthroughs and inventions correctly, when everyone else thought he was nuts! You'll also be interested to see how gunpowder changed European history and even helped end feudalism. Keep your eyes open!

42a🍂 Thomas Aquinas
This topic is beyond the understanding of most young children. Don't feel pressed to find resources.

Middle Ages, by Dorothy Mills, Ch. XIX, Pt. 1   Gr. 6-12

---

[149] Mills 271.

[150] Schaeffer 131.

[151] Mills 270.

Twelve Great Philosophers, by Howard Ozman, pp. 16-18   Gr. 3-8
> The reading level of this book can be handled by young children, but I hesitate to list this book because it has a humanist orientation and is thus not honest about humanistic problems. Consider it 'relevant, but not recommended.'

St. Thomas Aquinas: The Story of the Dumb Ox, by Mary Fabyan Windeatt   Gr. 5-12

Saint Thomas Aquinas and the Preaching Beggars, by Brendan Larnen (Vision)   Gr. 7-12
> This is in a specifically Catholic biography series.

Invitation to the Classics, by Louise Cowan & Os Guinness, pp. 93-96   Gr. 9-12

St. Thomas Aquinas, by G.K. Chesterton   Gr. 10-12

42b Roger Bacon

Few youth books have been written on Bacon, so you may want to check an encyclopedia.

Middle Ages, by Dorothy Mills, Ch. XIX, Pt. 2   Gr. 6-12

Child's History of the World, by V.M. Hillyer, Ch. 56   Gr. 1-4

Looking at History, by R.J. Unstead, p. 109   Gr. 2-5

Story of Britain, by R.J. Unstead, pp. 116-117   Gr. 5-12

Gunpowder, by Richard Worth & Sandra Weber   Unknown

Fiction/Historical Fiction

The Magician's Apprentice, by Sidney Rosen   Gr. 4-12
> Exciting story of fictional boy who is forced to spy on Bacon because he is considered a magician due to his wondrous experiments.

The Black Rose, by Thomas Costain   Gr. 11-12
> A novel of Bacon, Edward I (whom you'll meet soon), Bayan, Crusades, etc. This is a lengthy novel of unknown content, but Costain has many fans. Few students need take the time to read it.

42c ☙ Medieval thought and education

Middle Ages, by Dorothy Mills, Ch. XVIII-XIX   Gr. 6-12

No Other Foundation: The Church Through..., by Jeremy Jackson, Ch. 9-10   Gr. 11-12
    This book is too difficult for most students, but is so valuable I mention it anyway!

43 ☙ Marco Polo

The ideas of men like Bacon and Aquinas were changing the world and expanding Europe's horizons. One man who *literally* expanded Europe's horizon was Marco Polo of Venice!

Actually, it was Marco Polo's father and uncle who first made the great voyage to little-known China (Cathay). They made the incredibly arduous journey and were received by Emperor Kublai Khan, a Mongol descendant of Genghis Khan who was ruling China and other parts of the Far East. The Khan was intensely curious about European life. Mrs. Mills tells us something amazing:

> *When the Grand Khan heard all that they had to tell him, he begged them to return to Europe and ask the Pope to send him a hundred missionaries who would convert his people to the Christian faith. The Venetians returned, but they found that the Pope had died and his successor was not yet elected. After a time they decided to return to China, though without the hundred missionaries. Two friars went with them, but they grew fearful in Armenia and turned back.*[152]

Oh, if only the missionaries had gone! How different would things be for the billion people in China today, as well as the people of Mongolia and the other lands Kublai conquered?!

It was on this second journey that Nicolo's son, Marco, went along (1271). It is Marco's part of the journey which is best known because, while later imprisoned during a war between Venice and Genoa, he wrote about his journey. His tales would spark the imaginations of many Europeans, including Christopher Columbus two hundred years later! Yes, the story of Polo's trek added fuel to the cultural stirrings being felt foremost in Italy, stirrings which would soon develop into a new epoch in history. Let's relive Polo's amazing journey!

43a ☙ Polo's journey
Your library will have many choices; here we've listed only a few samples.

Story of the World: Volume 2, by Susan Wise Bauer, Ch. 21b-22a   Gr. 3-6

*Greenleaf's *Famous Men of the Middle Ages*, Ch. XXVII   Gr. 3-7

---

[152] Mills 238.

122

Story of the Renaissance and Reformation, by C. Miller & H.A. Guerber, Ch. III   Gr. 4-8

Middle Ages, by Dorothy Mills, Ch. XVI, Pt. 3   Gr. 6-12

**Child's History of the World*, by V.M. Hillyer, Ch. 55b   Gr. 1-4

**Marco Polo*, by Charles Graves (Garrard World Explorer)   Gr. 1-5
    This is now being reprinted by Chelsea House.

Marco Polo, by Gian Paolo Ceserani   Gr. 3-6

**Marco Polo: A Journey through China*, by Fiona Macdonald   Gr. 3-7

Adventures and Discoveries of Marco Polo, by Richard Walsh (Landmark)   Gr. 3-8
    This is one of the few Landmarks that kids tell me is not interesting.

The Story of Marco Polo, by Olive Price (Signature)   G. 3-8

The World of Marco Polo, by Walter Buehr   Gr. 3-8
    Buehr's books are always fascinating.

**Marco Polo: His Notebook*, by Susan Roth   Gr. 3-12
    Interesting adaptation of Polo's own journal and a favorite resource for many.

Marco Polo, by Manuel Komroff (Messner)   Gr. 7-12

**The Travels of Marco Polo the Venetian*, by Marco Polo   Gr. 9-12
    Polo's own journal.

**Marco Polo*, by Kathleen McFarren (FactFinders)   Unknown

**Marco Polo*, by Struan Reid   Unknown

**Marco Polo*, by Robert Strathloch   Unknown

Activities

**Marco Polo for Kids*, by Janis Herbert   Various
    Warning: this book includes some projects which dabble in eastern religion. You must be selective if you use this!

Fiction/Historical Fiction

**He Went with Marco Polo*, by Louise Kent   Gr. 5-12
    Fictional boy travels with Marco Polo. I've heard this series is being reprinted.

43b✤ Kublai Khan

Kublai Khan: Lord of Xanadu, by Walker Chapman   Gr. 8-12

Kublai Khan, by Kim Dramer   Unknown

44✤ Giotto

While the Middle Ages had few painters of individual note, there were a couple stand-outs. Most notable was Giotto. He was known for his paintings of St. Francis, but this Italian could do much more than just paint. He was trained by another Italian artist–Cimabue. While Cimabue has his own fame, you need to make special note of Giotto (1267-1337) because he followed and furthered his teacher–and the good side of Aquinas's teachings[153]–in moving medieval art away from the flat, otherworldly, Byzantine style which had dominated for so long due to the church's presentation of a remote God. But Cimabue, and especially Giotto, began to bring a vital quality back into art.

*Greenleaf's *Famous Men of the Renaissance & Reformation*, Ch. 2   Gr. 3-7
    Because Giotto transitioned between the medieval and Renaissance period, he is actually
    covered in Shearer's Renaissance book.

A Boy Named Giotto, by Paolo Guarnieri   Gr. 1-4
    Wonderful illustrations actually look gilded!

Giotto, by Mike Venezia (Getting to Know the World's Great....)   Gr. 1-4

Child's History of Art, by Hillyer & Huey (*Painting* section, Ch. 7)   Gr. 2-8
OR, *Young People's Story of Fine Art: 15,000 BC - 1800 AD*, pp. 32-35

Giotto Tended the Sheep, by Sybil Deucher and Opal Wheeler   Gr. 2-8
    Precious and rare antique book.

Giotto and Medieval Art, by Lucia Corrain (Masters of Art)   Gr. 4-12
    Covers Giotto and other medieval arts and art forms.

---

[153] Schaeffer 57.

Glorious Impossible, by Madeleine L'Engle   Gr. 5-12
       L'Engle tells the story of Christ with reproductions of Giotto's frescoes.

Fiction/Historical Fiction

Knight of Florence, by Margery Evernden   Gr. 7-12
       A story about an apprentice to Giotto who gets involved in the struggles of Florence.

45🐾 The House of Hapsburg

If you're at all familiar with European history, you've probably heard of the famous Hapsburg dynasty. It was powerful for centuries. Rudolf, its founder, was made king in Germany (1273) after Frederick Barbarossa's line lapsed into dissipation and civil war. Interestingly, this chaos had the effect of allowing even greater freedom to the independent cities, even the Italian cities such as Venice and Genoa, which had been ruled by the German emperors of the Holy Roman Empire. Through a later turn of events, the Hapsburgs gained control of Austria, and Vienna was eventually their capital.

       Story of the Middle Ages, by Christine Miller & H.A. Guerber, Ch. CVIII-CIX Gr. 4-8

46🐾 Epic Battle: William Wallace & Robert Bruce Face the Edwards of England

While you were gallivanting with Marco Polo and lolling in Giotto's studio, a lot was happening in England and Scotland! For example, Edward I (nicknamed 'Longshanks,' son of Henry III, and grandson of Bad Prince John) conquered Wales[154] (in spite of the brave resistance of Llewellyn and David), fought Philip IV in France, persecuted and then expelled the Jews from England, and set his roving eye, as well as his powerful English armies, on Scotland. He suffered a shocking defeat to the Scots at the Battle of Stirling Bridge in 1297, one of the more dramatic battles in history! Still determined, though, his dying words to his son, Edward II, were to take Scotland at all costs. That is just what the new king set out to do.

But the Scots who resisted them—William Wallace and Robert Bruce—are more famous than both the Edwards put together! Their struggle to protect Scotland, and their famous battles at Stirling and Bannockburn against impossible odds, make for a powerful story. If Wallace's name doesn't seem familiar, you may know him as the subject of the film *Braveheart*. I'm not

---

[154] David Macaulay's book *Castle* is actually set during Edward's conquest of Wales.

recommending the film–it's too violent and inappropriate, in my opinion–but I mention it to help you place Wallace. You'll not weasel out of me the ending of this stirring story. Find out yourself!

*Greenleaf's *Famous Men of the Middle Ages*, Ch. XXVI	Gr. 3-7
An Island Story, by H.E. Marshall, Ch. XL-XLIV	Gr. 3-8
Story of the Middle Ages, by Miller & Guerber, Ch. CII-CVII	Gr. 4-8
A Book of Heroes, by Dorothy Heiderstadt, pp. 84-90	Gr. 3-6
Story of Britain, by R.J. Unstead, pp. 118-127	Gr. 5-12
Robert Bruce: King of Scots, by Nina Brown Baker	Gr. 6-12
Outlaw King: Story of Robert the Bruce, by P.J. Stephens	Gr. 7-12
Young Robert Bruce, by Jane Oliver	Gr. 7-12

Fiction/Historical Fiction

Red Towers of Granada, by Geoffrey Trease	Gr. 5-12

    The story of an English boy and a persecuted Jewish doctor on an errand to Spain for Queen Eleanor, wife of Edward I.

In Freedom's Cause, by G.A. Henty	Gr. 7-12
Scottish Chiefs, by Jane Porter	Gr. 8-12

    Esteemed classic about Wallace's & Bruce's struggle for Scottish freedom. This book is moving and unforgettable, but it is written in a flowery, chivalrous style!

Young Man with a Sword, by Jane Oliver	Gr. 9-12

    A novel about Robert the Bruce.

47✤ William Tell

William Wallace wasn't the only William challenging despotic rulers. Around the year 1300, in the cantons of Switzerland, William Tell was courageously insisting on good government in the face of great risk. The initiator of the tyranny was the son of Rudolf the Hapsburg, who did not rule nearly as well as his father. The only thing most people know about William Tell is the incident of the apple and arrow, but you're going to hear the rest of the story! By the way, you should listen to the famous music composed by Rossini in Tell's honor–the *William Tell Overture.* I bet you'll recognize it right away!

Greenleaf's Famous Men of the Middle Ages, Ch. XXIX	Gr. 3-7
Story of the Middle Ages, by Christine Miller & H.A. Guerber, Ch. CX	Gr. 4-8

William Tell, by Margaret Early	Gr. 1-6
The Legend of William Tell, by Terry Small	Gr. 1-8
William Tell, by Leonard Everett Fisher Fisher's books always feature strong illustrations.	Gr. 2-7
A Book of Heroes, by Dorothy Heiderstadt, pp. 91-100	Gr. 3-6
William Tell, by Katharine Scherman (Legacy Books)	Gr. 3-8
The Apple and the Arrow, by Mary & Conrad Buff This is a don't-miss book! Kids love it!.	Gr. 3-9

48🙠 John Wycliffe

May I introduce you to someone of great significance in church history? Well, it's not like I know him personally, but I sure know *of* him! Mr. John Wycliffe!

Wycliffe, an English priest and professor at Oxford University, lived (1320?-1384) during one of the low periods of the church. First there was the so-called Babylonian Captivity (1305-1377), when the French king put up his own pope in the French city of Avignon. Then there was the Great Schism (1378-1415), when two or three men claimed to be pope.[155] How could Europe obey the pope when there were two or three of them?

This is a bigger question than you think. Remember, the Middle Ages had become focused on human authority, and that authority extended much further than you can imagine, because you haven't lived under it. In fact, one of the reasons *why* you haven't lived under it is coming up right here, so pay attention!

---

[155] Miller & Guerber 166.

Let's nail down what we know. The Middle Ages was now about the authority of the elite. This elite, partly in response to the implications of Aquinas, gradually claimed the right to declare truth as it saw truth (even separately from the Bible). Everyone else had to agree...or pay the consequences. Do you recall the examples we've seen? The church had proclaimed new means of salvation and forgiveness; it had made the science and philosophy of Aristotle supreme. No one could disagree. Likewise, people who questioned kings found themselves "pushing up daisies." People had to believe what they were told to believe, and do what they were told to do. Only professional churchmen and ruling aristocrats could understand and implement truth.

But what happened when there were two or three popes? Who were folks to believe and obey? How could they all be speaking the truth if they were disagreeing with and excommunicating each other?[156] How could the pope be 'above it all' if he was put in place by a French king, ruled from a French city, and often made decisions to the political benefit of France? What was an English, German, or Bohemian churchgoer to think?

This is just the sort of muddle created when human authority–which changes with the times and goals of humans–is placed over biblical authority. Only God's Word is sure, timeless, fair, and infallible. And that's just what John Wycliffe believed.[157] But he went a step further. He began to say (others developed the thought more fully in subsequent years) that God had written His Word so that each individual could not just read it, but could also grasp the truth!

Do you remember? This was Roger Bacon's point in science–that it wasn't even right to have authorities 'declare' scientific truth and then require everyone to believe it. The conclusions of just one person, no matter how brilliant, can be wrong (as many of Aristotle's were). Science shows its truths to any who seek them. Thus many people can learn, and together there is an accountability and a confirmation of truth.

You probably will not be able to really fathom the differences here, at your young age. The teachings of Roger Bacon and John Wycliffe made folks see both God and themselves in a new way. He had made truth to be directly knowable for He *is* truth and wants to be directly known. He reveals Himself to the hearts of everyone, not just professional churchmen or kings. With this belief, Wycliffe and his team began a translation of the Bible in the language of the neighbors, as you'll see in a minute.

Before we move on with Wycliffe's story, though, we must explain that the church was horrified by his teachings! While there were earthly reasons for its fierce opposition, there were religious ones as well. The church felt it had long been the guardian of God's Word. It had allowed people to read the Bible, but had been the one to interpret its meaning, thinking Scripture would be confused and abused in the hands of ignorant peasants and untrained professionals. At great cost, the church *had* indeed saved, copied, and beautified biblical manuscripts down through the years. The church *had* taught the Word, but it would increasingly be seen that it

---

[156] Jackson 116.

[157] Mills 332.

128

was God at work in all. Both Church and Word were His; the church had not gained its own authority over Scripture in the process. Likewise, God was in charge of revelation; the church was His tool. But we had better stop here–these are deep and sensitive issues.

In the end, Bacon would turn science upside down and Wycliffe would (for many) turn religion upside down. Since what is believed about authority, truth, and the common man in the spiritual realm is what will soon be believed in the political realm, you can guess that great changes would come to nations too...as you'll see in later *TruthQuest History* guides.

Why Wycliffe? Others *had* spoken out earlier along these lines, but they were mostly silenced. Wycliffe, though, had the protection of young King Richard II's regents, especially John of Gaunt. When one of the popes issued five bulls against Wycliffe calling for his arrest, no one acted on them. No one went to arrest him! This would have been unthinkable just a short time earlier, but the kings of Europe knew they could no longer give spiritual obedience to political popes. Mr. Jackson says:

> *Between 1200 and 1300 the balance had tipped: the spiritual debasement of church leadership had coincided with the first flush of confident royal power.*[158]

Wycliffe was able, then, to continue work on his translation in East Midlands Middle English (there were many dialects at the time). It is fascinating to learn that the works of both Wycliffe and Chaucer–whom you'll meet later–made their dialect the dominant English of their day and ancestor to our modern English![159] Indeed, Wycliffe's translation was one of the earliest non-poetical books in English, and thus forged English prose, though every copy was hand made![160]

In fact, Wycliffe wanted even more change. He called for the church to become more like the original churches of the New Testament by releasing its vast wealth and feudal lands so it could spend its time tending to people's souls, not its own feudal estates.[161] He even questioned the legality of King John having earlier given England to the pope as a fief.[162]

Yes, Wycliffe had some protection, but was still in plenty of trouble...even *after* his death. His followers, derisively nicknamed Lollards, would face even more persecution. They went around the countryside preaching Wycliffe's message, reading the Bible, and ministering to the needy. Certainly, there were some who went a little overboard. Eventually, many of the Lollards were burned at the stake. Even Wycliffe's Bibles were hunted down and torched.

---

[158] Jackson 116.

[159] Charles Coffin, *The Story of Liberty* (Gainesville, FL: Maranatha Publications, 1987) 43-44.

[160] Mills 334.

[161] Mills 332.

[162] Mills 332.

In closing, let's take a peek at the church itself. The Babylonian Captivity and the Great Schism had renewed wider calls (the *concilar movement*) for a council of bishops to share leadership with the pope. Indeed, a council had to be called (Council of Constance, 1415) to decide who should be the real pope. Again, I quote Jackson:

> *Conciliarism did, in any case, receive a boost from the Great Schism. For how could you end the Schism, how could you decide between rival popes, without invoking a body superior to the papacy?*[163]

> **ThinkWrite 11:**
> **"What's up with Wycliffe?"**
>
> After studying the life of Wycliffe, please put into your own words the impact of his spiritual teachings, and if you can, discuss how they would make political changes as well. Don't worry, though. We'll cover this subject deeply in the next *TruthQuest History* guide.

Of course, the subsequent pope condemned the council and little came of it right away,[164] but the battle would rage to bring accountability to top church officials (and later royal officials). *Something* had to be done, because the church was now the butt of public jokes,[165] especially on issues of purity and money. Great change was afoot, and Wycliffe and his followers–though imperfect themselves–were part of it. (Do *ThinkWrite 11* after learning about Wycliffe.)

Story of the Renaissance and Reformation, by C. Miller & H.A. Guerber, Ch. IV-VI Gr. 4-8
    Jan Hus will be discussed in our next guide, *Renaissance/Reformation*.

The Story of Liberty, by Charles Coffin, Ch. 2 Gr. 5-12
    Don't miss this important chapter! (I wish it would mention more of the good aspects of the church though. Coffin really focuses on the things that needed to be changed, because it was the response to those needs that so profoundly shaped history.)

Middle Ages, by Dorothy Mills, Ch. XXII, Pt. 2 Gr. 6-12

Beggar's Bible, by Louise Vernon Gr. 4-8

Fire Upon the Earth, by Norman Langford, Ch. 10 Gr. 4-10

John Wycliffe, by Ellen Caughey (Heroes of the Faith) Gr. 5-12

Morning Star of the Reformation, by Andy Thomson Gr. 5-12

---

[163] Jackson 117.

[164] Jackson 118, referring to the *Execrablis* bull of 1460.

[165] Jackson 118.

Trial and Triumph: Stories from Church History, by Richard Hannula, Ch. 17   Gr. 5-12

No Other Foundation: The Church Through..., by Jeremy Jackson, Ch. 10   Gr. 11-12
          This book is too advanced for most students, but I mention it because of its value.

Audio/Video

John Wycliffe: The Morning Star

49🙠 The Hundred Years' War Begins!

Here's a recipe! In a bowl, place Wycliffe's questioning of church government and his encouragement to Bible authority, the church's moral and spiritual flaws, the society-shaking Great Schism, the impact of the Magna Charta in England, the growing strength of kings and trade, the broadening travel of the Crusades and Marco Polo, the growth of more independent cities, Roger Bacon's challenge to blindly accepting 'facts' (even those of Aristotle), and, lastly, Aquinas's impetus to greater intellectualism, humanism, and reverence for Greek thought. What'chya cooking up? Major change! *The end of an age!*

Ah, but ingredients alone do not make a cake. There must be heat to fuel the chemical reaction! Would a plague and the Hundred Years' War work? You betcha!

Yes, it's sad, but true. Both a wave of bubonic plague and a protracted war occurred during the 1300s. I think you'll see that humans contributed directly to these horrors, yet our amazing, involved, loving, *active* Father brought good even out of these tragedies. I hope you never forget that He is in charge and is always working toward His own ends!

Let's first tackle the opening of the Hundred Years' War (1337-1338) and two of its key players: King Edward III of England (son of the hated Edward II who lost his throne to his wife, Isabella, sister of the French king, and Roger Mortimer, an English baron who had escaped Edward II's earlier cruelty)...and Edward's son, also named Edward, but better known as the Black Prince. Edward III's thirst for military adventure was foiled in his first attempt to wrest Scotland from Robert Bruce's son, so he looked to France for opportunity. Thus began the Hundred Years' War, which was really an endless string of smaller wars, beginning with the incredible sea battle at Sluys in 1340 and on through the battles and sieges at Crécy (1346, with the loss of 30,000 Frenchmen), Calais (1347, which saw the heroics of Queen Philippa), etc.

Though I don't think much of his reasons (not that anyone asked me...), Edward spouted patriotic-sounding motivations for war: 1) a claim by bloodlines to the French throne which had no clear heir, 2) a desire to regain former English holdings in France, and 3) anger with France over their aid to the Scots during England's fight for Bruce's throne, though England was supporting Flanders in its revolt against French tyranny. Can you keep this soap opera straight? The French and Scots were united in hatred of England; the English and Flemings were united in hatred of France and in a thriving wool trade.[166] (The most famous medieval tapestries were made in Flanders.)

What were the *real* motivations for most of this nonsense? Power-hunger and money-hunger. Of course, we think of France and England in their current, settled forms, but it was not so at the time. Portions of what is now France had been under English control (in the convolutions of feudalism) since the time of William the Conqueror. Though it may seem ironic, Edward III of England was also a Duke and Count of France, and thus one if its peers.[167] There were other connections between the two nations, besides constant intermarrying. Earlier Brits (true Celts) had escaped tumult in their native land during the post-Roman invasions by settling in what is now the French province called Brittany! So, the English king may have felt England's borders were yet to be determined. Of course, this doesn't make his deeds heroic, mind you! I'm just explaining the difference in outlook.

Anyway, to thicken the plot, the wool merchants sided with Edward against the French king who was their despised and harsh overlord. The pope–who was then backing France, whose new capital was sometimes in Avignon (a French city), and who was sometimes under the influence of the French king–commanded the wool merchants to support the French king and pay him lots of money![168] Speaking of money, Edward 'up and decided' to refuse the taxes due the pope because he feared they would be used to arm the French against him,[169] a refusal which would have been unthinkable a short time earlier! The kings of Europe knew the pope usually had his own political and financial motives, and they were growing bolder in resisting him. Of course, the motives of the kings were hardly biblical either. There were no 'white hats' and 'black hats' here. Spiritual renewal–which alone causes men to treat others well–was needed desperately!

Phew! We've discussed only the first portion of the war (up through the plague cessation), when the Edwards were at the helm. We will get to the later portions, certainly, but we'll be discussing other events in between. If you're reading any books which cover the whole war, you might want to pause when we do. Let's dig in!

---

[166] Desmond Seward, *The Hundred Years War* (New York: Atheneum, 1978) 31, and, Miller & Guerber 255-256.

[167] Seward 21.

[168] Mills 303.

[169] Mills 331.

49a ❧ General overview

We'll look at not only the first stage of the war, but the soap opera leading up to it!

Greenleaf's Famous Men of the Middle Ages, Ch. XXVIII	Gr. 3-7
An Island Story, by H.E. Marshall, Ch. XLV-XLVII	Gr. 3-8
Story of the Middle Ages, by Miller & Guerber, Ch. CXI-CXIX	Gr. 4-8
Middle Ages, by Dorothy Mills, Ch. XXI, Pt. 1	Gr. 6-12
Child's History of the World, by V.M. Hillyer, Ch. 57	Gr. 1-4
Looking at History, by R.J. Unstead, p. 107	Gr. 2-5
Stories of Famous Sea Fights, by Frank Knight, pp. 31-35 Covers the Battle of Sluys (Sluis).	Gr. 4-12
Story of Britain, by R.J. Unstead, pp. 128-134	Gr. 5-12
Hundred Years' War, by William Lace	Gr. 7-12
Boy's Froissart, by Sidney Lanier This is an abridged version of *Chronicles of Froissart*, an eyewitness report!	Gr. 8-12
Hero Tales from the Age of Chivalry, by Jean Froissart This is an abridged version of *Chronicles of Froissart*, an eyewitness report!	Gr. 8-12
Chronicles of Froissart, by Jean Froissart The original version.	Gr. 10-12

Activities

Paper Soldiers of the Middle Ages: The Hundred Years' War (Bellerophon)	Various

Fiction/Historical Fiction

The White Company, by Sir Arthur Conan Doyle Don't miss this fabulous tale of Black Prince Edward and a teen in the war, from the famous author of the *Sherlock Holmes* stories!	Gr. 5-12

Bowman of Crécy, by Ronald Welch   Gr. 7-12
      This is the second Welch novel following the d'Aubigny family. I've heard good reports!

*St. George for England, by G.A. Henty   Gr. 7-12
      The story of a teen battling at the Battles of Crécy & Poitiers.

All Men Tall, by Thomas Wheeler   Gr. 7-12
      A novel about the struggle of Baron Roger Mortimer and Queen Isabella against Edward II, and the impact of newly-discovered gunpowder.

Ride into Danger, by Henry Treece   Gr. 9-12
      A boy at the Battle of Crécy uses gunpowder for the first time.

49b🕭 Flanders and conflict over wool trade

Made in the Middle Ages, by Christine Price, pp. 46-53   Gr. 5-12
      This book provides a look at medieval tapestries.

Fiction/Historical Fiction

Shuttle and Sword, by Hawthorne Daniel   Gr. 5-12
      This novel includes the great figures at the center of the Flemish struggle.

50🕭 Bubonic Plague!

Do you remember the other catastrophe we mentioned? The Plague. The Bubonic Plague. The Black Death. Ugh. It is hard to comprehend a disease sweeping across Europe, killing one-third to one-half[170] of its residents between 1348-1350, but that's just what happened. There were other waves of plague over the centuries, but this was a biggie. Germany was hardest hit:

    ...whole villages were left without a single inhabitant, and even the cats, dogs, and pigs died.[171]

But something good came out of even this, besides bringing a temporary halt to the Hundred Years' War:[172] Since so many people had perished, there was a shortage of serfs to work the fields. This meant that in some areas of western Europe, the surviving serfs could demand

---

[170] Jackson 120.

[171] Miller & Guerber 262.

[172] Miller & Guerber 261.

rightful pay...and get it! For the first time in centuries, poor peasants walked down the road toward a life of their own making. In other words, the Plague further weakened feudalism.[173] (Sadly, feudalism wasn't outlawed in eastern Europe and Russia for another four hundred years!) While there may have been a sense of community in feudalism, it must have felt good to be paid for weeding the same cabbage rows worked by Great-great-great-grandpa, instead of being owned like the land and veggies themselves.

The Great Plague also reduced the power of the church, for folks could see that all their pilgrimages and observances had mattered little.[174] Another rivulet of questioning bubbled into society. This questioning would become a fast-flowing river of change in the next age of history, and you're seeing one of its springs right now.

The tantalizing scent of freedom was now blowing from several sources: the economic opportunity created by the erosion of feudalism and the growth of cities, the move to curb the unrestrained power of the church and kingly governments, and the growing idea that individuals should seek out God's truths, not just authority figures. Soon the yearning for freedom bubbled into peasant revolts in England (1381), France (1358), and Germany, as you'll see after we meet the new king of France!

Story of the World: Volume 2, by Susan Wise Bauer, Ch. 25	Gr. 3-6
Middle Ages, by Dorothy Mills, Ch. XXII, Pt. 1	Gr. 6-12
Looking at History, by R.J. Unstead, p. 110	Gr. 2-5
Black Death, by James Day (Great Disasters)	Gr. 5-8

51✿ Charles the Wise

Though a treaty (which turned out to be only temporary) was signed with the English in 1360, France's problems were far from over. You've probably guessed that the many years of war created great suffering, devastation, and chaos in France. Well, you're right. (When did you get so smart?!) Dukes, especially Charles of Navarre, had plundered and grasped. The peasants were desperate! Some hid in holes in the ground when horrendously destructive soldiers—idled by the plague-induced truce—swept through![175] Their victims were the same poor peasants who had been devastated by the 'total war' of the English king[176] and the war taxes of

---

[173] Mills 324-329.

[174] Mills 331.

[175] Miller & Guerber 270.

[176] Seward 38.

the French king. Well, it wasn't long before the pot boiled over. The 'John Does' of France–the 'Jacques Bonhommes'–started a peasant revolt cleverly known as the Jacquerie.[177] This revolt came in 1358, just after the disastrous French loss in the Battle of Poitiers, when Black Prince Edward captured France's new king, John II, and his son. The French uprising, like the English revolt, was poorly run. Even women and children were slaughtered mercilessly by furious fellow Frenchmen.[178]

It was left to the son of King John (the king who had been captured at Poitiers) to pick up the pieces. Charles V, though he didn't look like much, successfully did just that.[179] He got the country on an even keel and boosted learning. Translations of the Bible were made at his order, as well as certain Greek and Rome classics. He even began a library at the Louvre. Ah, a man after my own heart.... He was involved with another famous building in history too, for he oversaw the beginning of the Bastille fortress which became a famous (or *infamous*) prison in Paris. Beyond that, he turned the tide (one of *many* tides) in the Hundred Year's War, which was about to flare up again. How so?

> *Instead of oppressing his people by constantly asking for more funds, this ruler actually remitted a large part of the taxes they had hitherto paid, so as to enable them to strengthen the walls of their cities, and equip themselves properly. Thus, you see, he was quietly preparing to renew the old conflict with England, but this time with far better chances of success.*
>
> *His opponent, Edward III, less prudent than he, was meanwhile devoting most of his energies to pleasure, so when Charles finally used the complaints of the southern lords [those in regions owned by the English king under the waning feudal system] as a basis for renewing the war, England was ill prepared to meet it. Charles began by sending a messenger to the Prince...summoning him to appear in Paris, to answer the charges made by the discontented lords.... The English prince grimly retorted that he would certainly come, but with a helmet on his head and escorted by a force of sixty thousand men!*[180]

You'll be fascinated to know that under little Charles V's rule, England lost virtually all it had gained in France during the war and even earlier. It now held just five cities, and I can't say it was losing graciously. What Edward the Black Prince did in Limoges is heartbreaking.[181] How did England lose so much so fast? And what did reading have to do with it?[182] You'll find out!

---

[177] Miller & Guerber 269.

[178] Seward 96 and Miller & Guerber 269.

[179] Seward 103-104 and Miller & Guerber, Ch. CXXI.

[180] Miller & Guerber 274.

[181] Mills 315-316.

[182] Miller & Guerber 275.

52☙ Peasant Revolts!

It wasn't just France which had a peasant revolt. There was an uprising in England also. In fact, the pressure on peasants throughout Europe would lead to much turmoil in the coming centuries.

Like the French uprising, the handling of the English revolt was hardly glorious. It was led by Wat Tyler (1381), whose daughter had been attacked by a tax collector.[183] This began a series of events which led to common folk marching behind Tyler to London, demanding relief from unbearable taxes. Alas, many committed acts of violence along the way and in the city itself. They even captured and beheaded the Archbishop of Canterbury—leader of the English church!

May I comment? It takes great spiritual purity and wisdom, as well as a knowledge of the truth about laws and government, to appropriately carry out a political upheaval; this was not common in the 1300s. But think! Had the top churchmen and kings modeled purity, selflessness, humility, and restraint? Since most of the population was unable to read the Bible or even understand the Latin church services, was it not harder for them to know the principles of honorable political actions?

In any event, Richard II, the very young son of Edward the Black Prince (Edward died before he could become king), was king of England during the Peasant Revolt. It was he who faced Mr. Tyler, making promises which were not kept for a variety of reasons. Mrs. Mills comments:

> ...though in 1381 the revolt failed, the cause of the peasants was not lost. Slowly they gained more independence, statutes were passed bettering their condition, especially in the matter of wages, until by the end of the fifteenth century, nearly all labour had become free. The peasants still worked for landlords, they were still dependent on the landlord, they were still poor, but they were no longer serfs. A long period was to go by before they were regarded as citizens with equal rights with the townsmen and before they were allowed to vote. But with the passing of the serf from English life, one of the distinctively medieval characteristics had disappeared.[184]

---

[183] Miller & Guerber 280.

[184] Mills 329.

An Island Story, by H.E. Marshall, Ch. XLIX   Gr. 3-8

Story of the Middle Ages, by Miller & Guerber, CXXIV-CXXVI   Gr. 4-8

Middle Ages, by Dorothy Mills, Ch. XXII, Pt. 2   Gr. 6-12
      This chapter was also cited in the section of John Wycliffe, for it has info on both.

Looking at History, by R.J. Unstead, pp. 111-112   Gr. 2-5

Story of Britain, by R.J. Unstead, pp. 135-139   Gr. 5-12

Flame of Freedom: Story of the Peasant's Revolt   Gr. 7-12
      by Clifford Alderman (Messner/Milestones)

Fiction/Historical Fiction

Fire, Bed and Bone, by Henrietta Branford   Gr. 4-8
      An English hunting dog 'tells' of his people's involvement in the Peasant Revolt; this
      is a new book and I've not yet heard feedback about its contents.

Crispin: The Cross of Lead, by Avi   Gr. 5-12
      This is a new book, and I've not yet heard any feedback; I'm unaware of its contents,
      but know it's about a young man uncertain about his origin during the Peasant Revolt.

Son of the Land, by Ivy Bolton   Gr. 5-12
      A serf boy fights in the English Peasant's War.

March on London, by G.A. Henty   Gr. 7-12
      Wat Tyler leads the English Peasant's Revolt.

53❧ A Young King and a Young Cousin–Richard II and Henry Bolingbroke

You saw that King Richard II of England was just fifteen years old when he went out to meet Wat Tyler during the Peasant's Revolt. Can any of you fifteen-year-olds imagine doing the same?! Can any of you eight-year-olds imagine becoming a queen?! Well, that's just how old Isabella (a French princess) was when she became Richard's second wife; he knew she would grow up some day. In the meantime, Richard actually played dolls with her![185]

---

[185] Miller & Guerber 287.

Though Richard's reign was short, it seems he wanted to make a difference. With most of the power in the hands of his uncles, such as John of Gaunt, and with his own weakness, he didn't actually accomplish much other than temporarily halting England's part in the Hundred Years' War. England was changing, though, as some of you may have read in the last section. The first battles of the Hundred Years' War had united the Normans and Saxons of England; they had fought *together*, rather than against each other. In fact, the speaking of English became increasingly common in high circles, in place of Norman French.[186]

So, why was Richard's reign short? Ask Henry Bolingbroke! Well, I'll give you a clue. Henry B. would soon be known as King Henry IV, for he officially broke the Plantagenet line and began his own dynasty–the house of Lancaster. During Henry's reign, the Welsh tried to regain their freedom under the leadership of Owen Glendower. I won't tell you the ending. I'm finally keeping quiet...at least about one story!

You'll be hearing more about these Lancastrians in the next unit, for they were part of the famous War of the Roses. You may also have heard about two famous residents of England during Henry's reign–Dick Whittington and his cat!

And keep in mind that though the new king of France, Charles VI, had hoped to renew the war against Richard and England, and had even outfitted ships for the purpose, his insanity.... Well, I'll let you find out!

53a☙ General overview

An Island Story, by H.E. Marshall, Ch. L-LII	Gr. 3-8
Story of the Middle Ages, by Miller & Guerber, Ch. CXXVII-CXXXII	Gr. 4-8

Story of Britain, by R.J. Unstead, pp. 140-141	Gr. 5-12

Fiction/Historical Fiction

Men of Iron, by Howard Pyle (Troll Illustrated Classics)   Gr. 2-6
    This is a highly abridged version of the exciting classic cited below.

Bent is the Bow, by Geoffrey Trease   Gr. 3-7
    One of Trease's books for younger children; Welsh children meet Owen Glendower.

To See the Queen, by Katherine Gibson   Gr. 3-8
    I've not seen this, but it is supposedly about the very young queen of Richard II.

---

[186] Miller & Guerber 277-278.

The Door in the Wall, by Marguerite de Angeli   Gr. 3-10
  This is the don't-miss, long-beloved tale of a courageous crippled boy set during this era.

The Innocent Wayfaring, by Marchette Chute   Gr. 6-12
  An esteemed story of two travelling youths in England during the 1300s.

Men of Iron, by Howard Pyle   Gr. 6-12
  Boys especially love this story which takes place during Henry IV's reign.

Both Sides of the Border, by G.A. Henty   Gr. 7-12
  Henry IV and Owen Glendower do battle.

Gentle Falcon, by Hilda Lewis   Gr. 7-12
  Novel about Richard II's very young second wife, Isabella of France.

Katherine, by Anya Seton   Gr. 11-12
  This has been both recommended and *un*recommended to me; I'm not familiar with the contents myself. It is about John of Gaunt and his wife, but sounds like it includes some mature topics. This couple played a significant role in English history.

53b❀ Dick Whittington and his cat!

Dick Whittington and His Cat, by Marcia Brown   Gr. 1-4
  A popular children's picture book for many years simply because it's a good story!

Dick Whittington, by Catherine Storr (Raintree Stories)   Gr. 2-7

Cats of Destiny, by Fairfax Downey   Gr. 4-12
  One chapter in this book about famous historical cats is on Mr. Whittington's feline.

54❀ Moorish Spain

We've spent most of our time recently in France and England, with just brief mentions of Germany, Italy, and other nations. We've not visited Spain for a while, though, because it was 'on a different page' while under Moorish rule. The Moors' culture reached its height during the time of the Hundred Years' War[187] and the great Moorish palace, the Alhambra, was built then. If you'd like to take another peek at Moorish Spain, feel free. We'll also be visiting it more in the next guide, *TruthQuest History: Renaissance & Reformation*, when significant events occurred there.

---

[187] Bernard Grun, *Timetables of History* (New York: Simon & Schuster/Touchtone, 1991) 188.

54a⚜ General overview

The Moors, by Gerald Hawting   Gr. 5-12
> You've read parts of this already, so just check for pertinent sections.

Fiction/Historical Fiction

The Red Towers of Granada, by Geoffrey Trease   Gr. 5-12
> This was mentioned earlier, but fits here also because it shows much of medieval Moorish Spain.

Tales of the Alhambra, by Robert Goldston   Gr. 7-10
> An edited and adapted version of Washington Irving's *Alhambra*; see below.

*The Alhambra, by Washington Irving   Gr. 10-12
> This is a series of sketches and legends of Moorish Spain written mostly when Irving–a famous American writer of the 1800s–worked in an embassy there. It appears under various titles, such as *Legends of the Alhambra* or *Tales of the Alhambra*. You may find an abridged version. I believe some of these sketches include odd supernatural elements, so you may want to preview.

54b⚜ Alhambra

Child's History of Art, by Hilyer & Huey (*Architecture* section, Ch. 18)   Gr. 2-8
OR, *Young People's Story of Architecture: Gothic-Modern*, pp. 34-41

Amazing Buildings, by Philip Steele, pp. 14-15   Gr. 4-12

*Architecture, by Neil Stevenson, pp. 34-35 *(DK Annotated Guides)*   Gr. 7-12

55⚜ A Famous Book: Chaucer's *Canterbury Tales*

Do you remember? We found out earlier that John Wycliffe had not only a huge spiritual impact, but shaped the development of the English language too. Actually, there was a one-two punch on the language issue, for a great English writer–one of the earliest of significance and one of the most famous too–chose to write in the same English dialect as Wycliffe's Bible. Between the two of them, Middle English became the chief ancestor of our language today.

> While talking about famous authors, I should explain that Dante, a revered Italian poet, lived in the early 1300s. We could have discussed him in this guide, but Dante's writings relate to the thinking of the just-stirring Renaissance. We'll meet him, then, in *TruthQuest History: Renaissance & Reformation.*

Who was this writer? Geoffrey Chaucer! I bet you've heard of him! If not, you will! He wrote other books, but his most famous is *The Canterbury Tales*, written in the years just before 1400. This story follows several characters (and I mean *characters!*) on a pilgrimage to Becket's tomb.

Like Wycliffe, Chaucer's book had a spiritual impact too, though, ironically, by the opposite method and for different reasons. While Wycliffe's criticism of the church was scholarly, Chaucer's was humorous...and bawdy (be warned!) His *Canterbury* churchmen are far from perfect, and Chaucer poked fun at that. Believe it or not, this further opened the door for folks to begin honestly analyzing the situation in the church.

Chaucer also exposed human nature, in general. Leland Ryken, in *Invitation to the Classics*, makes suggestions for handling this when reading:

> *Good questions to ask are, What human failings does Chaucer present for our understanding? Following the hints laid down in the text, what does Chaucer offer as a corrective to these failings?*[188]

You'll be fascinated to know that Chaucer was intricately involved in all the things you've just been learning about: he fought in the Hundred Years' War, worked in the wool industry, traveled to Flanders, was under the patronage of John of Gaunt (who had also supported Wycliffe), and he even raised a son who was chief butler to King Richard II, Henry IV, Henry V, and Henry VI!

NOTE: If you decide to read or sample the original *Canterbury Tales*, be sure, parents, to preview for appropriateness!! Also, you must decide whether to tackle it in Middle English or an updated translation. There are children's adaptations which should be safer to read.

Middle Ages, by Dorothy Mills, Ch. XVI, Pt 1-2   Gr. 6-12
         These sections tell of pilgrimages and life on medieval highways; Chaucer is quoted once.
----

*Chanticleer and the Fox, by Barbara Cooney   Gr. 1-5
         One of the stories in *Canterbury Tales* retold for children; this is an esteemed book.

Looking at History, by R.J. Unstead, pp. 100-102a   Gr. 2-5

*The Canterbury Tales, edited by Barbara Cohen   Gr. 3-7
         Adapted version of Chaucer's stories, with illustrations by Trina Schart Hyman.

They Lived Like This in Chaucer's England, by Marie Neurath   Gr. 4-7

*Canterbury Tales, by Geoffrey Chaucer, adapted by Geraldine McCaughrean   Gr. 6-12
         This is the version Greenleaf likes and sells. They say it has been safely toned down.

---

[188] Cowan and Guinness 112.

Tales from Chaucer, by Eleanor Farjeon   Gr. 6-12
        Tales retold in narrative from lovely older author.

Chaucer and His World, by Ian Serraillier   Gr. 7-12

A Taste of Chaucer, edited by Anne Malcolmsen   Gr. 7-12
        Excerpts (in poetic form) and analysis.

Young Geoffrey Chaucer, by Regina Kelly   Gr. 7-12

*Invitation to the Classics, by Louise Cowan & Os Guinness, pp. 107-112   Gr. 9-12
        This book gives Christian analysis of famous works of literature.

*Canterbury Tales, by Geoffrey Chaucer   Various
        Remember, some of the tales are bawdy; use discernment!

Fiction/Historical Fiction

The Yellow Hat, by Nancy Faulkner   Gr. 7-12
        Fictional housemaid tells us of her master, Chaucer, in this novel.

56❧ The Hundred Years' War Winds Down...Thanks to a Teenage Girl!

I know this guide is supposed to end at the year 1400, but we can't leave in the middle of a war! We'll finish it, and then draw things to a close! So, back to France!

Do you remember? King Charles was insane, which didn't bode well for the country. His wicked wife and his uncles–the Dukes of This and the Dukes of That–had been, well, *duking it out!* (Hmm, I wonder if we can now guess the source of that idiom!) His son–the Dauphin–also tried to reign when he came of age, but he was weak, weak, weak!

Get the picture? France was a total mess! King Henry V of England (Henry IV had died) decided *he* was the man to clean it up! Alas, 100,000 people–who had already suffered so much–died as a result of that decision.[189] Henry invaded in 1415. I won't tell the story, but you should make note of one of history's most famous battles, fought later that year: the Battle of Agincourt. Why so famous? Because of the lop-sided odds and the oppositely lop-sided results! That's all I'm going to say on that topic!

---

[189] Miller & Guerber 297.

Henry V didn't live much longer after Agincourt, but his son, Henry VI, continued the fight. All seemed to be going his way...but he didn't plan on one little thing...or should I say, one little teenage girl–Joan of Arc!

The power of Henry VI in France weakened under Joan of Arc's rally. Skirmishes continued for several more years as the war sputtered to an inglorious end. The English troops finally pulled out. So, did the French leaders band together to rebuild? No. They did what they had done before and during the war: they ravaged the French countryside themselves, fighting for supremacy over the weak monarchy. How sad history is when peopled by ungodly men. It makes me realize again that without spiritual fire, life is cold, hard, and miserable. Don't ever let anyone tell you that Christianity is oppressive; instead, it's the only thing that frees us and our neighbors from our selfish, hurtful selves. You have a story to tell! People need to know this! People need to know that a vital relationship with God is not just nice, it's essential! Without it, the world lapses back into barbarian paganism. What a choice! But it's a choice we need to make clear! Let's get busy!!

56a❧ General overview

Story of the World: Volume 2, by Susan Wise Bauer, Ch. 26	Gr. 3-6
*Greenleaf's *Famous Men of the Middle Ages*, Ch. XXXI-XXXII	Gr. 3-7
An Island Story, by H.E. Marshall, Ch. LIII-LIV	Gr. 3-8
Story of the Middle Ages, by Miller & Guerber, Ch. CXXXIII-CXL (The remaining chapters will be cited in *TruthQuest History: Renaissance & Reformation* because they refer to events which took place well after the year 1400.)	Gr. 4-8
Middle Ages, by Dorothy Mills, Ch. XXI, Pt. 3-4	Gr. 6-12

Story of Henry V, by L. DuGarde Peach (Ladybird)	Gr. 3-8
The Story of Britain, by R.J. Unstead, pp. 142-150	Gr. 5-12
Long Bows of Agincourt, by Charles Norman	Gr. 6-12

Fiction/Historical Fiction

Gauntlet of Dunmore, by Hawthorne Daniel A boy tries to become a knight during the time of Agincourt.	Gr. 5-12
Sign of the Green Falcon, by Cynthia Harnett This esteemed British author of historical fiction tells of an apprentice of Dick Whittington's in a plot against Henry V! Many public libraries probably have this book.	Gr. 5-12

At Agincourt, by G.A. Henty   Gr. 7-12

Here Comes Harry, by Hilda Lewis   Gr. 7-12
    This novel–of interest to girls–is about the widow of Henry V (Catherine of Valois) and the childhood of her son, Henry VI.

Henry V, by William Shakespeare   Gr. 10-12
    For those who want to tackle Shakespeare, here is one of his historical plays.

56b❧ Joan of Arc (1412-1431)

You'll find oodles of books about Joan of Arc at your library. I'll just mention a sampling.

Joan of Arc: The Lily Maid, by Margaret Hodges   Gr. 1-4

Joan of Arc, by Shana Corey (Step Into Reading 4)   Gr. 2-3

Joan of Arc, by Josephine Poole   Gr. 2-6

Joan of Arc: Heroine of France, by Ann Tompert   Gr. 2-6

Beggars, Beasts and Easter Fire, by Carol Greene, Ch. 16   Gr. 2-8

A Book of Heroes, by Dorothy Heiderstadt, pp. 101-109   Gr. 3-6

Jeanne d'Arc, by Aileen Fisher   Gr. 3-7

Joan of Arc, by Johanna Johnston   Gr. 3-7

Joan of Arc, by Diane Stanley   Gr. 3-7
    As always, Stanley's illustrations are lush!

Joan of Arc, by Maurice Boutet de Monvel   Gr. 3-8

Joan of Arc, by Nancy Wilson Ross (Landmark)   Gr. 3-8

The Story of Joan of Arc, by Jeannette Covert Nolan (Signature) Gr. 3-8

St. Joan, the Girl Solider, by Louis de Wohl (Vision)   Gr. 4-12
    This is from a distinctively Catholic series.

The Girl in White Armor, by Albert Bigelow Paine   Gr. 7-12

| *Joan of Arc*, by Winston Churchill | Gr. 9-12 |

*Beyond the Myth: The Story of Joan of Arc, by Polly Brooks — Gr. 10-12
>This is a very recent book on Joan of Arc; I don't know its point of view.

*Joan of Arc and the Hundred Years' War in World History, by William Lace — Unknown

*Saint Joan of Arc: God's Soldier, by Susan Wallace (Encounter the Saints) — Unknown

Audio/Video

*Joan of Arc, starring Ingrid Bergman

Fiction/Historical Fiction

The Boy Knight of Reims, by Eloise Lownsberry — Gr. 6-12
>A (fictional) boy meets Joan of Arc.

*Personal Recollections of Joan of Arc, by Mark Twain — Gr. 9-12
>This, Twain felt, was his best book, and was the object of much research on his part. It is written from the point of view of one of Joan of Arc's (fictional) servants.

57 Tamerlane (Timur)

Lest you think all was going swimmingly for the people of Asia, be aware that Tamerlane–more exactly, Timur–was making war all over Asia Minor, India, Russia, and more! He descended from Genghis Khan–which is hardly surprising, given his career choice–and he lived from around 1336 to 1405. We haven't time to discuss it fully, but I did want to let you know.

**Greenleaf's *Famous Men of the Middle Ages*, Ch. XXX — Gr. 3-7

*Story of the Renaissance and Reformation, by C. Miller & H.A. Guerber, Ch. VIIb — Gr. 4-8

58 Drawing the Curtain on the Middle Ages

What can we say as we look back on almost 1,000 years of Europe's turbulent history?! Ah, we can speak one thing quickly and easily: *Wow! Does Christianity make a difference, or what?!* When you think of the degradation of the Roman Empire's last days, when you picture the depravity of the barbarian hordes rushing in, and then you see folks settling down to build farms, villages, cities, and nations, with magnificent cathedrals soaring over all...you begin to get a glimpse of the life-changing and world-changing power of God's truth! Actually, you see God Himself, for He doesn't just speak truth, He *is* truth.

I hope, after this study, you'll never fall for the lie that religion is only a private matter, and that public affairs are best left to those who claim 'spiritual neutrality.' There is no such thing! We've just seen that! If God is not acknowledged as the highest authority (*Big Belief #1*), humans are! And humanism is indeed a religion. It is worship of self. It is adoration and enjoyment of mankind's knowledge and power, limited and flawed as it is.

This is the choice each civilization faces, because it's the choice each individual *in* civilization faces. It's the choice faced even by members of the Christian church, for one can claim to be part of His body but then place self at the head. There is only One Head, in truth. Blessing, freedom, dignity, and creativity flow when the Lord and His man-loving laws are obeyed. On the other hand, humanists debase other humans (*Big Belief #2*), because to deny God's lordship is paganism, and paganism births barbarism—a deepening disrespect toward others as one seeks only his own pleasures and powers.

I hope these statements are no longer mere words or dry ideas. You've seen them paraded before you in full-color all during the roiling Middle Ages. You've seen the highs and the lows, the breakthroughs and the setbacks, the thrill of cultural victory and the agony of sinful defeat.

After all the great accomplishments of the church, it is sad to realize that by the late Middle Ages, the church had so long presented a remote, guilt-obsessed God—while indulging in its own corruption—that what had been widespread skepticism evolved into something much deeper. Spirituality became quite separate from God: either a mystical, meditative experience inside one's self, or a barren exercise of the intellect.[190] You'll notice *both* revolve around humanity, thus both leave a great void in the human heart, for we are not satisfied except in a living and loving relationship with our Creator. Many Europeans, however, felt Christianity offered no answers, and the church—the ancestral church of us all—was now too weak and too mired in its own sin to stop "the drift into total disbelief."[191]

But it was not Christianity which had come up empty. It had earlier made a profound impact! Indeed, it wasn't until humanism later *paraded* as Christianity that folks lost intimacy with God and lost dignity as individuals loved by Him. Likewise, it was humanism which had given unlimited power to human kings. King Henry V of England thought so much of his impulses that he brought about the death of 100,000 men in his personal pursuit of the French throne.[192] And he claimed to be a Christian all the while! Does not this mean something was terribly wrong?! Could not it be said he was putting himself above God's laws?! Was not this too much like his barbarian ancestors?! What does this say of his *Big 2 Beliefs?!* Yes, unlimited human

---

[190] Jackson 116.

[191] Jackson 125.

[192] Miller & Guerber 297.

power—whether in church or kingdom—is rarely a pretty sight. Humanism was turning back the clock.

Had God retired, though? No! His plan for mankind was still being worked. Just think: to the helpless peasants living in the 1300s, many things about life in Europe must have seemed unchangeable. Yet within just a handful of generations, things would change drastically! The power structures would not be the same, or would be gone altogether. Why? Because, ultimately, all authority is God's. When humans are not using it rightly, He does something about it. Yes, He works through flawed people. Yes, His human vessels were bundles of contradictions. Yes, they would, at times, badly implement their God-given ideas. But even then, God was not foiled. He understands that we are but dust and does not weary of shepherding us. That is *mighty* good news!

It's proof of the church's impact that there was both great good and a great void at the end of the Middle Ages, but *nature abhors a vacuum*. Where would folks seek to be filled? Would they turn more vehemently toward humanism and away from the Christianity, which had seemed to disappoint them? Or would they realize it was not God Who had failed, but people's understanding of and obedience to Him? You can bet the Lord was very active in leading people to His truth, and His actions along with human responses would determine the course of future history.

I hear the music! The curtain is lifting! The dramatic consequences of these very decisions are about to be revealed! We'll see the full drama in *TruthQuest History: Renaissance & Reformation*. See you there!

Don't forget!
It's time to finish up your
ThinkWrite 1–Investigation Supreme!

Appendix 1: *ThinkWrite* Responses

Below are sample responses to the ThinkWrite exercises in this guide. They help your students piece together the most important lessons of medieval history. You will also find they help you lead meaningful discussions and then analyze your children's responses.

ThinkWrite 1: Investigation Supreme!

> ### *ThinkWrite 1: Investigation Supreme!*
>
> Throughout your study of the Middle Ages you must carefully watch the *Big 2 Beliefs* of the secular rulers and the church leaders.
>
> That means you're looking for two things: Based on their actions, who do you think was their real authority? God or themselves? How did they treat others based on that view of authority?
>
> To help you sort this out, try to nail down the *Big 2 Beliefs* of a pagan, a barbarian, a humanist, and a Christian. How similar are these? Can one claim to be a Christian, and still be one of the above? Can people be pagans or barbarians now?
>
> At the end of this guide, please wrap up your insights. They'll be rich!

1) *Paganism* can be defined as a belief system **without** God at its center. Webster's *New Collegiate Dictionary* defines a pagan as "one who has little or no religion and who delights in sensual pleasures and material goods: an irreligious or hedonistic person." I think we can see something deeper in paganism, then. It is a desire to be one's own 'god,' to seek one's own pleasure, and to strive for one's own glory–especially glorifying characteristics in which one takes pride (*Big Belief #1*). There is little respect for other humans, since people have worth only if they give pleasure or glory to the pagan (*Big Belief #2*). The myths of the Teutonic pagans, for example, show bloodthirsty, conniving, and independent gods. Hmm. Sounds just like the Teutons' general behavior. Coincidence? I think not. They had created the gods and myths out of their own minds, so their spiritual beliefs show their deep-seated values.

What is the biblical truth?

> *Love the Lord your God with all your heart and with all your soul and with all your mind. This is the first and greatest commandment (Matthew 22:37-38).*
>
> *The fool says in his heart, 'There is no God.' They are corrupt, their deeds are vile... (Psalm 14:1).*

2) *Barbarism* has the connotation of acting on base, carnal desires, such as those for violence, cruelty, brutishness, bloodsport, domination, sensuality, destruction of things of value, lack of learning, etc. Barbarians usually have homemade gods of war which reflect–in reality–their own desires for war or violence. Thus, they usually make a god out of physical strength or military cunning and prowess (*Big Belief #1*). This first belief means that other people–especially weak people or folks who are useless in war–have no value; they are often treated violently to satiate the yearning for glorification of violence (*Big Belief #2*).

What is the biblical truth?

> *...whatever is true, whatever is noble, whatever is right, whatever is pure, whatever is lovely, whatever is admirable–if anything is excellent or praiseworthy–think about such things (Philippians 4:8).*

> *Love your enemies, do good to those who hate you... (Luke 6:27).*

3) A *humanist* is one who has put himself–not God–at the center of his own universe (*Big Belief #1*). Yes, like a pagan, he takes the role of God in his own life. Like a barbarian, he will seek his own pleasures, though they are usually more refined pleasures...at first anyway. Little respect is given to others–other than the surface respect which eases relationships–because self is on the throne (*Big Belief #2*).

4) The *Big 2 Beliefs* of a true Christian are utterly different. They acknowledge God's total supremacy, His act of creating the universe and mankind, and His right to make laws which govern all (*Big Belief #1*). Because God created mankind lovingly and sent His son to redeem them, humans are precious in His sight and are to be treated respectfully (*Big Belief #2*).

5) The students are asked to identify behaviors and thought patterns which would result from the aforementioned beliefs. These answers will vary widely, so no list is provided here. As a parent, you will be able to discern appropriate answers. This should result in excellent discussion with your students. The main point is that paganism always gives rise to barbarism, for when mankind is his own god, he places fluctuating and utilitarian value on others. Likewise, when God is denied as the creator and lawgiver, the intrinsic value of humans as the apple of His eye is lost. The sin nature in each human will lead him to selfishly hurt others when not restrained by God's good laws.

Yes, without God's supremacy and His laws about mankind, there is no absolute basis for right and wrong moral behavior. People do 'what is right in their own sight,' as God said about the backsliding Israelites in the Old Testament. When people do 'what is right in their own sight,' it is usually selfish and others are hurt. The decline continues until barbaric acts, such as devaluation of human life (abortion, euthanasia, lack of care for children and the elderly), sexual immorality, violence, bloodsport, etc., are commonplace.

We'll discuss the application of this general principle to the two great power structures of the Middle Ages further below.

6) Certainly, many folks have claimed to be Christians and members of the church, but hold non-Christian worldviews. You'll see that happen often in history...and in your neighborhood...and in yourself...for we are all insensitive to the degree to which secular thinking seeps into us from our surrounding culture.

7) Can people be pagans or barbarians now? The answer is most definitely *yes*. Our society has become quite committed to anti-God thinking (paganism) along with a mood of baseness and a destruction of cultural values (barbarism). Sin is still sin; it has the same roots. However, God loves pagans and barbarians, which we were before we accepted Christ. We should have a godly outlook when discussing paganism and barbarism, and should not pass on an attitude that would cause your students to alienate those who need the Lord, and to whom we are to be godly, humble, forgiving, and loving ambassadors.

The Church

The church, you see, is not peripheral to the world; the world is peripheral to the church. The church is Christ's own body, in which he speaks and acts, by which he fills everything with his presence (Eph. 1:22, *Message*[1]).

This is a theme verse in TruthQuest History, for we know that God is the great initiator of history, and He often works through His body, the church. Thus, the beliefs and actions of the church carry great weight in the world. In fact, it has been said that what the church is in one generation, the nation will become in the next.[2] I won't belabor that point here because it is discussed throughout this guide. It is the reason, though, that we must look both at the great accomplishments of the church and its flaws, for both affected Europe deeply.

In the first years after the fall of Rome, the church was the only source of order, learning, and ministry. This powerfully impacted the barbarian cultures, and virtually all the various tribes converted to Christianity over the centuries. The Viking conversion is a key example of this significance, for their horrendous raids ceased as Christianity changed their *Big 2 Beliefs*. There was in Europe a great and unifying Christian consensus, as Mr. Schaeffer puts it. For the common man, every part of medieval life felt imbued with His presence: the days, the months, the seasons, the years, the fields, the forests, etc.

For the sake of time, though, we must switch our focus to the growing humanism of the church. It has been discussed throughout this guide, as in the section on Medieval Learning; I will not delve heavily here. Please refer to the appropriate sections in the main guide, if you want clarification or explanation.

---

[1] I know the *Message* is a highly paraphrased rendition of the Bible so it only has certain merits, but the wording of this verse powerfully and effectively conveys an important truth to young people. Feel free to cross-reference literal translations as well.

[2] This was said by Peter Marshall during a homeschooling convention I attended.

Suffice it to say that the church had gradually *baptized* humanism[3] by placing higher emphasis on human authority than on God's authority (*Big Belief #1*). Examples of this thinking were: declaring new 'means' of salvation (such as going on crusade), new means of forgiveness (visiting Christ's tomb), and ignoring God's laws on the appropriate treatment of others (*Big Belief #2*). Many top church officials put more time into building their feudal empires than serving people. They were wildly wealthy (while the poor suffered terribly) and they maneuvered political power to their own benefit.

This is not the full story of the church, we know. Many church leaders and workers–from top to bottom–were sincere, devout, hard-working, and concerned about the decline in the church. We saw many heroes work for reform.

We must end our story quickly, though, so we must mention that as the church focused more on its own power, it began to position itself as the necessary professional in folks' relationship with God–in spite of its own obvious corruption. This was because God was increasingly portrayed as remote and guilt-obsessed. For example, important church areas were put behind screens, spiritual truths were labeled 'holy mysteries,' and in spite of the fact that few later medieval Europeans could understand Latin, the services continued in the language anyway. All this caused a tremendous loss of spiritual intimacy and a devaluing of each individual. Spirituality instead became quite separate from God: either a mystical, meditative experience inside one's self, or a barren exercise of the intellect.[4] You'll notice *both* revolve around humanity, thus both leave a great void in the human heart, for we are not satisfied except in a living and loving relationship with our Creator. Many Europeans soon felt Christianity offered no answers, and the church–the ancestral church of us all–was now too weak and too mired in its own sin to stop "the drift into total disbelief."[5] This opened the door to Europe becoming deeply skeptical of the church and looking for its empty heart to be filled elsewhere. That 'elsewhere' is the theme of our next guide: *TruthQuest History: Renaissance & Reformation*.

Remember, in saying this we are not pointing fingers at 'somebody else.' This church was the ancestral church of us all, which we've carefully explained in the guide. Please check in the main commentary for clarification. All cannot be repeated here.

The King

This drift toward humanism was turning back the clock of Europe's political development. At first the spread of Christianity had created wonderful leaders, such as Alfred the Great, who truly served their people. They defeated attacking enemies, protected the righteous, developed honest weights and measures, established markets, and boosted trade. Many also built schools, monasteries, and other important structures.

---

[3] Jackson 122.

[4] Jackson 116.

[5] Jackson 125.

Later, though, the humanism of the church would indeed be noticed by the kings. Again, this shows the authority of the church and also confirms that what the church is, the nations will become. The kings used church error as an excuse to indulge in their own selfish desire for unlimited power at the expense of others (*Big Belief #2*), thereby making themselves like God (*Big Belief #1*), rather than His deputy. For example, Henry V of England caused the death of 100,000 men in his personal pursuit of the French throne![6] Does that not show how much above God's laws he had elevated his own impulses?! He acted like his barbarian ancestors, but claimed to be a Christian all the while. Furthermore, you will see that political and economic structures, such as feudalism, were often demeaning and without opportunity or freedom. This would take Europe back toward its earlier roots in Greek and Roman times. Interestingly, independent cities began to grow as they built on Europe's strengths. These cities would be seedbeds for later change.

Final Thoughts

What is biblical truth regarding the role of the church, and the role of secular rulers?

> *...to prepare God's people for works of service, so that the body of Christ may be built up until we all reach unity in the faith and in the knowledge of the Son of God and become mature, attaining to the whole measure of the fullness of Christ (Ephesians 4:12,13).*

> *The kings of the Gentiles lord it over them; and those who exercise authority over them call themselves Benefactors. But you are not to be like that. Instead, the greatest among you should be like the youngest, and the one who rules like the one who serves....I am among you as one who serves (Luke 22:25-27).*

> *You know that the rulers of the Gentiles lord it over them, and their high officials exercise authority over them. Not so with you. Instead, whoever wants to become great among you must be your servant, and whoever wants to be first must be your slave--just as the Son of Man did not come to be served, but to serve, and to give his life as a ransom for many (Matthew 20:25-28).*

So, it was not Christianity which had come up empty. It had earlier made a profoundly positive impact! Indeed, it wasn't until humanism later *paraded* as Christianity that folks lost intimacy with God and lost dignity as individuals loved by Him. Likewise, it was humanism which had given unlimited power to human kings. And unlimited human power–whether in church or kingdom–is rarely a pretty sight. Yes, humanism was turning back the clock.

Let's remember, though, that our modern churches have *baptized* much secular thought as well, and we're barely aware of it! We, as members of the church, have the same profound effect on our world as did the medieval church. How are *we* handling this awesome mandate? Have we even done as much as the church of the Middle Ages? Look at what our nations have become? What does that say about *our* churches? About *us*?

---

[6] Miller & Guerber 297.

ThinkWrite 2

> ### ThinkWrite 2: "Shuffling the deck!"
>
> Begin a map showing the shuffling of the European people groups. There was a lot of movement! It shaped western history and the development of modern European nations, that's all!
>
> I'll be specific. Map the basic movements and/or locations of general groups (Celts and Teutons) and specific tribes (Britons, Picts, Scots, Franks, Vikings, Angles, Saxons, Jutes, Vandals, Visigoths, Ostrogoths, and Huns). You'll be working on this during the next several sections of this guide.

This project involves drawing a map portraying the location of the various barbarian tribes. This map can be added to your student's notebook, if one is being developed. For source information, there should be a map in whichever general resource(s) you are using. Or, libraries have historical atlases with this information. A good map is included in *The Barbarians*, by Richard Suskind, pp. 16-17.

ThinkWrite 3

> ### ThinkWrite 3: What'chya believe?"
>
> After you've gotten a taste of the Teutons' belief system, write a paragraph describing it. Be on the lookout for their beliefs about personal freedom. Give your hypothesis about what type of behavior you might see from people who held these beliefs. At the end, see if you're right!! You'll need this for your *Investigation Supreme* too.

Students could refer to the importance of brute strength, independence, and trickery in the Teutonic belief system. It seems these Germanic tribes selected their kings and that they included the warriors in public discussions, thus implying some political 'say-so' for the male members of the tribe. This report is based on a notation by the Roman historian, Tacitus. Its accuracy is being debated.

What behavior might be demonstrated by people holding the Teutonic beliefs? Two possible answers are that the people would be warlike and they would think 'might makes right'. Your students may have their own ideas.

ThinkWrite 4

> ### ThinkWrite 4: "Yeah, King Arthur!"
>
> What lessons can you learn from looking at the life of King Arthur?

These essays will be completely personal. No comment is needed here.

ThinkWrite 5

> ### ThinkWrite 5: "Charlemagne–how great was he?"
>
> What kind of man was Charlemagne? What about the contradictions in his life? What was the significance of the pope crowning him and his Roman title? What was his impact on history?

Charlemagne was one of the strongest and most beneficial leaders of the Dark Ages, but he also harbored the usual contradictions for kings of the era. He claimed to be a Christian, showed personal piousness, invested much into the church, was friends with the pope, tried to write better laws, pushed himself to learn reading, and showed a great respect for Christianity, but he could also be quite cruel and selfishly ambitious. These early kings didn't seem to grasp the difference between the barbarian *Big 2 Beliefs* they'd inherited and the great truths of Christianity. Yet, Charlemagne was much more advanced, civilized, and restrained than virtually all other kings before or long after him. The Dark Ages reached a cultural height under his reign. At the very least, we can say that what it meant to be a Christian was not fully understood then, for his conquest of the Saxons was bloody and he forced them to 'convert' to Christianity at swordpoint. His realm comprised much of western and central Germany by the time his war-making was done; this was quite large in a time so recently tribal.

The pope was involved in crowning Charlemagne as a Roman-style emperor. There were mixed motives for this. The pope was hoping to affirm his king-making power and reinforce the idea that Rome was the center of power. A contest of power would be played out on these issues over the next centuries. Yet, Charlemagne also seemed to crave the word 'Rome' in one of his titles. Richard Maybury points out in his *Ancient Rome: How it Affects You Today* that world leaders have long idolized, idealized, and imitated the power held by the Roman emperors.

In the end, Charlemagne did contribute to history. He helped shape the lands which would become France and Germany, and though done violently, he did introduce Christianity into new areas edging into eastern Europe as well as raising esteem for it throughout his realm. He brought a renaissance to Europe during a very dark time and tried to elevate education. These things all have effect.

ThinkWrite 6

> ### *ThinkWrite 6: "Feudalism"*
>
> Do some research on *feudalism*. Make sure you understand the concept and the terminology, such as *fief, vassal,* and *liege.*
>
> Don't stop there; you want more than just knowledge. You must dig deeper and use discernment, because the establishment of feudalism shows us the *Big 2 Beliefs* of the 'power brokers.' Who did they *really* think was 'God?' In other words, who had the ultimate authority to determine the principles which other people lived by? How did that first belief affect the quality of life for everyone else? Had the rulers' deep beliefs changed much from the time when their barbarian ancestors were in power?
>
> What does the Bible say about the treatment of employees in I Cor. 9:7-10 and I Tim. 5:18?
>
> Your conclusions here will probably contribute to your *Investigation Supreme!* Don't forget it!
>
> And while you're learning about knights, make sure you understand *chivalry.* It sounds like a big word, but it's especially important for boys to grasp. How does Scripture say men should treat women?

Feudalism is a political/economic system wherein individuals yield control of themselves and their lands to lords who protect them. They are then tied to the land and may not leave it. The serfs were required to give a certain amount of harvest to the lord; they could keep whatever–if any–was left. The peasant was obligated to submit, or give homage, to the lord, and they had to soldier when the lord gave the call to arms. Lords provided knights and fortifications (usually built by the serfs) for protection. These lords also gave homage and troops to higher lords. The highest lords could thus field relatively large armies. There were often confusing overlaps in the various layers. Lords were sometimes vassals to their own vassals for different estates.

Feudal Terminology:

Vassal...one who has given his land and service to a lord. A *serf* was the lowest vassal.

Liege...related to feudal lands and service, whether owing it or receiving it, as in *liege lord.*

Fief...the feudal estate owned by a lord.

Fee...the land owned by a lord that is being used by a vassal.

Knights...professional warriors supported by lords.

While there was sometimes pleasant aspects of agrarian and community life, feudalism was too often a type of political and economic bondage, because little respect was shown for the serfs at the bottom of the ladder. This shows that the *Big Belief #1* of many feudal lords was that they could be 'gods' and could thus ignore God's laws regarding treatment of others, instead making their own. Feudalism fed off the common people rather than providing them with safety so they could fulfill their unique life calling and be part of a free community.

It is my opinion that all of society suffered under feudalism, since it was so wrongly applied; slavery poisons the slaveholder as well as abusing the slave. The hearts of many nobles were hardened, and history sadly records that it was hundreds of years before this grim situation changed. I further believe that all suffered for another reason: European culture was not able to flourish when individual vassals were not free to pursue inventiveness, creativity, the arts, learning, etc. You won't see western Europe's growth until after there was more individual freedom. Feudalism didn't end in eastern Europe and Russia until roughly the 1800s. Those areas have hardly known freedom for they had communist *liege lords* shortly after feudalism ended.

Even though European society had become quite Christianized, there was not enough change in the *Big 2 Beliefs* held by the 'power brokers'. Like their earlier barbarian ancestors, too often 'might made right'. They may have become even more authoritarian than their ancestors, who seem to have had some representative councils, such as the Witan of the Saxons in England. Remember that the church had become much more authoritarian and centralized too, and civic government is affected by the nature of the body of Christ. Indeed, the church became one of the wealthiest feudal lords. Some estimates have the church owning 1/4 to 1/3 of all the land in Europe! It makes one wonder, then, how motivated the church was to work for change.

Scripture clearly states (in the verses cited in this *ThinkWrite* question) that employees are to be respected, receive pay for their work, and benefit from the increase produced by their labor. Communism always fails because, among other reasons, it violates this biblical principle of incentive.

Switching to the topic of knights, *chivalry* refers to "gracious courtesy and high-minded consideration especially to women" and "qualities (as bravery, honor, protection of the weak, and generous treatment of foes) of the ideal knight."[7] This was one of the great gifts of the medieval church to society--greater care for women--a quality almost never seen in non-Christian cultures.

The Bible tells husbands:

> *...be considerate as you live with your wives, and treat them with respect as the weaker partner and as heirs with you of the gracious gift of life, so that nothing will hinder your prayers.* I Pet 3:7

We did not discuss this more advanced topic in the guide, but you may want to know that chivalrous care for women began to deteriorate as the church presented a God who was more and more abstract and remote. Then the spiritual and practical aspects of life began to be

---

[7] *Webster's New Collegiate Dictionary* (Springfield, MA: G. & C. Merriam Co., 1977).

The Bible tells husbands:

...be considerate as you live with your wives, and treat them with respect as the weaker partner and as heirs with you of the gracious gift of life, so that nothing will hinder your prayers. I Pet 3:7

We did not discuss this more advanced topic in the guide, but you may want to know that chivalrous care for women began to deteriorate as the church presented a God who was more and more abstract and remote. Then the spiritual and practical aspects of life began to be separated. There was then less respect for 'real' women, who weren't seen as valuable compared to the abstract ideal of *woman*.[8] Isn't it wonderful that God's truths are real and practical?!

ThinkWrite 7

> ### ThinkWrite 7: "Leif turns over a new leaf!"
>
> What was the effect on Europe's history when the Vikings and other barbarians converted to Christianity?

Leif Ericson's conversion to Christianity exemplifies the enormous impact of the overall Viking conversion, slow as the changes were. Christianized Vikings had much less desire to plunder. Previously, society had been so thoroughly and repeatedly ravaged by the Vikings that building, trade, culture, art, literature, and even nations, could not develop. The Vikings burned and destroyed everything and everyone in their path. People were constantly engaged in battle with the Vikings or trying to 'pick up the pieces' after yet another ravage.

We've had to focus on the weaknesses of the church during the Dark Ages, because they had great bearing on the nature of the Dark Ages. However, the church was also the most positive aspect of the Dark Ages, as seen in the conversion of the Vikings. Let's not forget about the tremendous impact of the truth of Christ and the catholic church that promoted it!! The bottom line is that the Body of Christ has great influence on society, in both its strengths and weaknesses.

ThinkWrite 8

> ### ThinkWrite 8: "Darkness Lifts"
>
> What influences and factors brought about the end of the Dark Ages?

---

[8] Schaeffer 58.

In his book, *The Dark Ages*, Asimov points out that the development of the horse collar and a better plow made agriculture more efficient. Also, he says the pope's refunneling of the aggression of the militant factions of Europe into the later crusades against the Muslim conquerors of the Holy Land reduced the amount of war in Europe, but we haven't yet discussed the Crusades in this guide.

Lastly, stronger leaders such as Alfred the Great of England, Hugh Capet of France, Henry the Fowler, and Otto of Germany were establishing stronger nations. This strength was a blessing when it protected the residents from attack and from civil war, but it was a curse when it allowed the king to abuse the people. Knights such as El Cid of Spain were instrumental in supporting and toppling various kings. Anyway, it was a very contradictory time!

ThinkWrite 9

ThinkWrite 9: "Crusade!"

What were some of the results of the Crusades? How did they affect the crusaders, the Muslims, the Jews, and all of Europe, both then and now?

The Crusades resulted, first and foremost, in an enormous loss of life and property. Even children were promised salvation if they would get involved, but most of them died or were sold into slavery. In a different vein, the crusaders saw a different way of life: especially the Saracens' better cleanliness, food, fabrics, and scientific advancements. Some little bit of their knowledge was brought home. Trade was stimulated as the Europeans continued to desire eastern goods, especially spices which disguised the taste of their usually-spoiled meat or routine vegetables.

The spiritual differences between the Muslims and Christians were already enormous, but the atrocities of the Crusades created even deeper hostilities. As *Christ-bearers*, the Christians should have handled their disagreements differently, even if at war. Sadly, the Muslims saw little in the Christians to draw them to our faith.

ThinkWrite 10: "Division!

Yes, I hear you yelping at me, "This is history class, not math class! Why are we talking about division?" Well, do you understand the concept of *division of labor?* Do you know why it's important?

If you're old enough, think about the connection between economic and political freedom. Do they relate at all with spiritual freedom? Though we've talked about these ideas somewhat in earlier *TruthQuest History* guides, we'll further develop them in later guides, so don't worry if it is not clear now.

Information for this *ThinkWrite* is found in: **Whatever Happened to Penny Candy?* by Richard Maybury, for Gr. 5-12, or in other resources about simple economics.

Division of labor refers to individuals contributing their special gifts and abilities to society. The artistic people create art, the handy men build, the lovers of the soil grow food, the weavers make cloth, etc. This is a much more pleasant and productive way of life than when each person struggles to produce the same things. For example, it is difficult for each farmer to build or obtain blacksmithing tools, but one blacksmith can service many farmers with quality workmanship since there is economic incentive and provision for him to invest in good tools and supplies, and to develop his skills to a successfully marketable level. Just as with today's doctors, specialization leads to high levels of expertise.

We know the Romans believed their state was god (*Big Belief #1*) and that it had the right to completely control the citizens (*Big Belief #2*). This resulted in spiritual, political, and economic tyranny. Rather than respecting the rights and abilities of each individual to build his own life and care for his own family, the government manipulated economic policy to achieve the goals it perceived as important–namely, tax income. This tyrannical system resulted in economic dependence; the people could do nothing, create nothing, build nothing without the government. This philosophy was one of the seeds of feudalism as well.

Though we did not discuss this in the text, I would like to mention that it seems many modern western governments have become quite elitist. They see themselves as the rightful micro-controllers of the economy (revealing a god-like *Big Belief #1*). Rather than limiting their power to the proper role of protecting law-abiding citizens as they freely initiate their own enterprise (which would reveal correct *Big 2 Beliefs*), the governments seem to be usurping power and engendering dependency. Is this modern feudalism?

ThinkWrite 11

ThinkWrite 11: "What's up with Wycliffe?"

After studying the life of Wycliffe, please put into your own words the impact of his spiritual teachings, and if you can, discuss how they would make political changes as well. Don't worry, though. We'll cover this subject deeply in the next *TruthQuest History* guide.

The commentary in the Wycliffe section serves as the 'sample answers' for this *ThinkWrite*. The ideas were fully laid out there.

I'll just emphasize here that Wycliffe talked about strong ideas, such as we might now call freedom of conscience, where an individual is accountable to God for his beliefs and thoughts. This is why Wycliffe knew it was crucial that folks have direct access to God's Word in their own dialect. In other words, just as Roger Bacon said anyone should be able to see the truth of science and not have to merely memorize the pronouncements of human authorities, Wycliffe said the same in the spiritual realm: people reading the Bible have the opportunity to see key truths directly.

This was an enormous statement for its day; it gave great value and influence to common men and women. Western civilization is now based heavily on such ideas, for *the nature of political freedom rests on the nature of spiritual freedom.*

Appendix 2: Booklist

Below is a list of all the books/resources recommended (not required!) in this *TruthQuest History* guide. It is copyrighted, and is only for use by purchasers of this guide.

Important, Important, Important: *Opportunity,* not Obligation!

It is *not intended* that you purchase, find, or even read all the books cited in this guide! You can see how impossible that would be! *TruthQuest History* is completely different from curricula which depend on certain books, so users must think differently about it! Here, the goal is *not* to guide you through books, but through history...using books...whichever books are readily available! That's why so many are listed here–to give you the utmost opportunity to harness your public library without missing a gem!

When you (wisely!) decide to homeschool using real books, no matter what curriculum guide you choose, you're only able to use what's available. *Therefore,* this large booklist is *not* a burden, it's a benefit! It vastly increases the chances of finding the best available books on every topic! Relax! Enjoy!

*****

The asterisk (*) denotes a resource deemed in-print at the time of this writing. It does *not* denote a preferred book, as is often assumed. Series names appear in parentheses. Notes appear in brackets. Fuller information on all resources is in the main guide.

500 Hats of Bartholomew Cubbins, by Dr. Seuss	Gr. 1-5
Across a Dark & Wild Sea, by Don Brown	Gr. 3-6
Adam of the Road, by Elizabeth Janet Gray	Gr. 5-12
Adventures and Discoveries of Marco Polo, by Richard Walsh (Landmark)	Gr. 3-8
Adventures of Robin Hood, by Roger Lancelyn Green	Gr. 8-12
Adventures of Robin Hood, by Harry Ross (Bullseye Step Into Classics)	Gr. 1-4
Adventures with the Heroes, by Catharine Sellew	Gr. 4-9
Alfred, King of the English, by Carola Oman	Gr. 5-12
Alfred the Great, by Mary Fitt	Gr. 2-6
Alhambra, by Washington Irving [See note]	Gr. 10-12
All Men Tall, by Thomas Wheeler	Gr. 7-12
Amazing Buildings, by Philip Steele	Gr. 4-12
Ancient Arts: Stained Glass, by Sarah Brown [Activity kit]	Various
Anglo-Saxon Helmet (British Museum Cut-Out Model)	Various
Anglo-Saxons, by Peter Chrisp (Look into the Past)	Gr. 4-12
Anglo-Saxons, by Roger Coote (Look into the Past)	Unknown
Anna of Byzantium, by Tracy Barrett	Gr. 7-12
Apple and the Arrow, by Mary & Conrad Buff	Gr. 3-9
Arabian Nights [Select appropriate version]	Various
Arabs, by Harry Ellis	Gr. 4-10
Architecture, by Neil Stevenson (DK Annotated Guides)	Gr. 7-12
Armor Book, by Michael Berenstain	Gr. 2-7
Arrow Messenger, by D.R. Burleigh	Gr. 4-8

Art and Industry of Sand Castles, by Jan Adkins — Gr. 3-10

*Arthur, by Stephen Lawhead (Pendragon Cycle) — Gr. 9-12

*Arthur and the Sword, by Robert Sabuda — Gr. 2-6

*At Agincourt, by G.A. Henty — Gr. 7-12

*Atlas of Islam: People, Daily Life and Traditions, by Neil Morris — Gr. 3-12

Attila, by Stephen Vardy (World Leaders Past and Present) — Gr. 7-12

Attila the Hun, by Robert Webb (Masters of Infamy) — Gr. 7-12

*Augustine Came to Kent, by Barbara Willard — Gr. 4-12

Baghdad Mission, by Sidney Rosen — Gr. 3-9

*Ballad of the White Horse, by G.K. Chesteron — Gr. 10-12

Barbarians, by Odile Bombarde (Young Discovery Library) — Gr. 2-6

Barbarians, by Richard Suskind — Gr. 5-12

Baron's Booty, by Virginia Kahl — Gr. 1-3

Baron's Hostage, by Geoffrey Trease — Gr. 7-12

Battle of Hastings, by William Lace (Battles of the Middle Ages) — Gr. 6-12

Bayeux Tapestry, by Norman Denny — Gr. 3-12

*Be a Wolf! by Brad Strickland (Adventures of Wishbone) — Gr. 3-6

*Beautiful Stories from Shakespeare, by E. Nesbit [Various versions/titles] — Various

Beggars, Beasts and Easter Fire, by Carol Greene — Gr. 3-8

Beggar's Bible, by Louise Vernon — Gr. 4-8

Belisarius, by Glanville Downey — Gr. 8-12

Bent is the Bow, by Geoffrey Trease — Gr. 3-7

*Beorn the Proud, by Madeleine Polland — Gr. 6-12

*Beowulf, adapted by Rosemary Sutcliff — Gr. 9-12

*Beowulf — Gr. 10-12

*Beowulf the Warrior, adapted by Ian Serraillier — Gr. 6-12

*Beyond the Myth: The Story of Joan of Arc, by Polly Brooks — Gr. 10-12

Big John's Secret, by Eleanore Jewett — Gr. 6-12

*Bird's Nest, by Christoph Von Schmid (Lamplighter) — Gr. 3-10

*Birthdays of Freedom: Vol. 2, by Genevieve Foster — Gr. 2-6

Black Death, by James Day (Great Disasters) — Gr. 5-8

Black Fox of Lorne, by Marguerite de Angeli — Gr. 5-12

*Black Rood, by Stephen Lawhead (Celtic Crusade) — Gr. 8-12

Black Rose, by Thomas Costain — Gr. 11-12

Blood Feud, by Rosemary Sutcliff — Gr. 7-12

*Blood of the Moon, by George Grant — Gr. 11-12

Book of Heroes, by Dorothy Heiderstadt — Gr. 3-6

Book of Hugh Flower, by Lorna Beers — Gr. 5-12

Both Sides of the Border, by G.A. Henty — Gr. 7-12

Bowman of Crécy, by Ronald Welch — Gr. 7-12

Bows Against the Barons, by Geoffrey Trease — Gr. 7-12

Boy Knight, by G.A. Henty [Also titled *Winning His Spurs* and *Fighting the Sar...*] — Gr. 7-12

Boy Knight of Reims, by Eloise Lownsberry — Gr. 6-12

*Boy Named Giotto, by Paolo Guarnieri — Gr. 1-4

Boy of the Lost Crusade, by Agnes Danforth Hewes — Gr. 4-10

Boy's Froissart, by Sidney Lanier — Gr. 8-12

*Boy's King Arthur, edited by Sidney Lanier, illus. By N.C. Wyeth — Gr. 6-12

*Brendan the Navigator, by Jean Fritz — Gr. 3-7

Bright Hunter of the Skies, by Herbert Best	Gr. 7-12
Bright Thread, by Jack Steffan	Gr. 8-12
Brother Francis and the Friendly Beasts, by Margaret Hodges	Gr. 1-4
Brother Sun, Sister Moon: The Life and Story of St. Francis, by Margaret Mayo	Gr. 4-8
Brother to Galahad, by Gwendolyn Bowers	Gr. 7-12
Building Big, by David Macaulay	Gr. 5-12
Building the Book 'Cathedral', David Macaulay	Gr. 3-12
Buildings of Byzantium, by Helen & Richard Leacroft	Gr. 7-12
Buildings of Early Islam, by Helen & Richard Leacroft	Gr. 5-12
Byzantines, by Thomas Chubb	Gr. 4-12
Byzantium, by Stephen Lawhead	Gr. 9-12
Candle at Dusk, by E.M. Almedingen	Gr. 9-12
Canterbury Tales, by Geoffrey Chaucer	Various
Canterbury Tales, by Geoffrey Chaucer, adapted by Geraldine McCaughrean	Gr. 6-12
Canterbury Tales, edited by Barbara Cohen	Gr. 3-7
Cargo for a King, by J.S. Andrews	Gr. 7-12
Castle, by Mark Bergin	Gr. 3-9
Castle, by Christopher Gravett (Eyewitness)	Gr. 4-12
Castle, by Kathryn Hinds (Life in the Middle Ages)	Gr. 5-12
Castle, by David Macaulay	Gr. 4-12
Castle, by Struan Reid	Gr. 3-10
Castle, Abbey and Town, by Irma Black	Gr. 3-10
Castle at War, by Andrew Langley	Gr. 4-10
Castle Book, by Alfred Duggan	Gr. 2-8
Castle Diary: The Journal of Tobias Burgess, Page, by Richard Platt	Gr. 2-10
Castles, by Gillian Osband	Gr. 1-5
Castles, by Philip Steele (Kingfisher)	Gr. 4-10
Castles: Facts, Things to Make, Activities, by Rachel Wright	Various
Castles of the World Coloring Book (Dover)	Various
Cathedral, by David Macaulay	Gr. 3-12
Cathedral Builders, by Marie-Pierre Perdrizet	Unknown
Cathedral Stained Glass Coloring Book	Various
Cathedrals: Stone upon Stone, by Brigitte Gandiol-Coppin (Young Discovery)	Gr. 1-5
Cavalcade of Queens, by Eleanor Farjeon	Gr. 3-9
Celts of Northern Europe, by Kathryn Hinds	Gr. 7-12
Chanticleer and the Fox, by Barbara Cooney	Gr. 1-5
Charlemagne, by Susan Banfield (World Leaders Past and Present)	Gr. 8-12
Charlemagne, by Manuel Komroff (Messner)	Gr. 7-12
Charlemagne and the Early Middle Ages, by Miriam Greenblatt [See note]	Gr. 5-12
Charlemagne and the Twelve Peers of France, by Alfred J. Church	Gr. 5-10
Charlemagne: Monarch of the Middle Ages, by M. Stearns (Immortals of History)	Gr. 9-12
Chaucer and His World, by Ian Serraillier	Gr. 7-12
Children of Odin, by Padraic Colum [Is his *Nordic Gods and Heroes* a reissue?]	Gr. 5-12
Children's Shakespeare, by E. Nesbit [Various versions/titles]	Various
Child's History of Art, by V.M. Hillyer & E.G. Huey	Gr. 2-8

[Or portions reissued as *Young People's Story of ......*]

*Child's History of the World, by V.M. Hillyer	Gr. 1-4
[Or portion reissued as *Young People's Story of the Medieval World*]	
Chivalry and the Mailed Knight, by Walter Buehr	Gr. 4-12
*Chroncicles of Froissart, by Jean Froissart	Gr. 10-12
*Church, by Kathryn Hinds (Life in the Middle Ages) [See note]	Gr. 5-12
*Clothing, by Piero Ventura	Gr. 3-10
Coll and His White Pig, by Lloyd Alexander	Gr. 1-5
*Coloring Book of the Middle Ages (Bellerophon)	Various
*Connecticut Yankee in King Arthur's Court, by Mark Twain	Gr. 7-12
Constantinople: The Forgotten Empire, by Isaac Asimov	Unknown
*Cowardly Clyde, by Bill Peet	Gr. 1-3
*Crispin: The Cross of Lead, by Avi [See note]	Gr. 5-12
Cross and Crescent, by Richard Suskind	Gr. 6-12
*Cross-Sections: Castle, by Richard Platt and Stephen Biesty	Gr. 4-12
Crusader King: Richard the Lionhearted, by Richard Suskind	Gr. 4-8
Crusades, by Walter Buehr	Gr. 4-12
Crusades, by Chris Rice (DK Discoveries)	Gr. 3-8
Crusades, by Anthony West (Landmark)	Gr. 3-8
*Crusades: Failed Holy Wars, by Cherese Cartlidge	Gr. 8-12
Crusaders, by Joanne Jessop	Gr. 2-6
*Cut & Assemble a Crusader Castle: Krak des Chevaliers, by A.G. Smith	Various
*Cut & Assemble a Medieval Castle (Dover)	Various
*Cut and Make a Knight in Armor (Dover)	Various
*Cut and Make a Knight's Helmet (Dover)	Various
Dancing Bear, by Peter Dickinson	Gr. 5-12
Dark Age Warrior, by Ewart Oakeshott	Gr. 8-12
Dark Ages, by Isaac Asimov	Gr. 8-12
*Dark Side of Islam, by R.C. Sproul & Abdul Saleeb	Gr. 9-12
Dawn Wind, by Rosemary Sutcliff	Gr. 7-12
*Days of Knights and Damsels, by L. Carlson [Formerly *Huzzah Means Hooray*]	Various
*Days of the Knights: A Tale of Castles and Battles, by C. Maynard (DK Reader 4)	Gr. 3-6
*Design Your Own Coat of Arms (Dover)	Various
Devil's Brood, by Alfred Duggan	Unknown
Dick Whittington, by Catherine Storr (Raintree Stories)	Gr. 2-7
*Dick Whittington and His Cat, by Marcia Brown	Gr. 1-4
*Door in the Wall, by Marguerite deAngeli	Gr. 3-10
Door to the North, by Elizabeth Coatsworth (Land of the Free)	Gr. 4-12
*Dragon and the Raven, by G.A. Henty	Gr. 7-12
Dublin Crossing, by Sandy Dengler (Heroes of the Misty Isle)	Gr. 5-12
*Duchess Bakes a Cake, by Virginia Kahl	Gr. 1-3
*Duke and the Peasant: Life in the Middle Ages, by Sister Wendy Beckett	Various
*Early Middle Ages, by James Corrick	Unknown
*Early Middle Ages, published by Raintree Steck-Vaughn	Unknown
*Easy-to-Make Playtime Castle (Dover)	Various
*Ecclesiastical History of the English People, by Bede the Venerable	Gr. 12+

Gentle Falcon, by Hilda Lewis — Gr. 7-12
Gift for Genghis Khan, by Frances Alberts — Gr. 2-7
Gillespie and the Guards, by Benjamin Elkin — Gr. K-3
Giotto, by Mike Venezia (Getting to Know the World's Great....) — Gr. 1-4
Giotto and Medieval Art, by Lucia Corrain (Masters of Art) — Gr. 4-12
Giotto Tended the Sheep, by Sybil Deucher and Opal Wheeler — Gr. 2-8
Girl in White Armor, by Albert Bigelow Paine — Gr. 7-12
Glass, Stones, and Crown, by Anne Rockwell — Gr. 5-12
Glastonbury, by Donna Fletcher Crow — Gr. 8-12
Glorious Impossible, by Madeleine L'Engle — Gr. 5-12
Godiva, by Alfred, Lord Tennyson [See cautionary note] — Gr. 9-12
Gods and Goddesses of the Ancient Norse, by Leonard Everett Fisher — Gr. 2-6
God's Troubadour: St Francis of Assisi, by Sophie Jewett — Gr. 3-8
Going to War in Viking Times, by Christopher Gravett — Gr. 4-7
Golden Hawks of Genghis Khan, by Rita Ritchie — Gr. 7-12
Good King Wenceslas, by Mildred Luckhardt — Gr. 4-10
Good King Wenceslas, by Christopher Manson — Various
Golden Warrior, by Hope Muntz — Gr. 11-12
Grail, by Stephen Lawhead (Pendragon Cycle) — Gr. 9-12
Great Axe Bretwalda, by Philip Ketchum — Gr. 8-12
Great Invasion, by Clifford Alderman (Messner/Milestones) — Gr. 7-12
Green Blades Rising: The Anglo-Saxons, by Kevin Crossley-Holland — Gr. 9-12
Gregory the Great, by George Sanderlin (Vision) — Gr. 4-12
Growing Up in 13th Century England, by Alfred Duggan — Gr. 5-12
Growing Up with the Norman Conquest, by Alfred Duggan — Gr. 6-12
Growing Up in Viking Times, by Dominic Tweedle — Gr. 3-7
Gunpowder, by Richard Worth & Sandra Weber — Unknown
Hakon of Rogen's Saga, by Erik Christian Haugaard — Gr. 3-12
Hammer of Gaul, by Shane Miller (Credo) — Gr. 6-12
Hamster History of Britain, by Janis Mitchell — Gr. 2-8
Harald and the Giant Knight, by Donald Carrick [and others in series] — Gr. 1-3
Hastings, by Samuel Crompton — Unknown
Hastings, by Philip Sauvain (Great Battles and Sieges) — Gr. 4-7
Havelok the Dane, by Kevin Crossley-Holland — Gr. 7-12
Havelok the Dane, by Ian Serraillier — Gr. 7-12
Hawk and the Dove, by Penelope Wilcock — Gr. 9-12
He Went with Marco Polo, by Louise Kent — Gr. 5-12
Heart of the Wood, by Victor Sharoff (Break-of-Day) — Gr. 1-3
Heart's Conquest, by Gladys Malvern — Gr. 7-12
Hengest's Tale, by Gillian Paton Walsh — Gr. 6-12
Henry V, by William Shakespeare — Gr. 11-12
Heraldry: The Story of Armorial Bearing, by Walter Buehr — Gr. 4-12
Here Comes Harry, by Hilda Lewis — Gr. 7-12
Hereward the Wake, by Charles Kingsley — Gr. 11-12
Hero Tales from the Age of Chivalry, by Jean Froissart — Gr. 8-12
    [Abridged version of *Chronicles of Froissart*.]

Heroes and Saints, by R.J. Unstead	Gr. 3-9
Heroic Deeds of Beowulf, by Gladys Schmitt (Legacy)	Gr. 4-8
Hidden Treasure of Glaston, by Eleanore Jewett	Gr. 6-12
High Courage, by Rosemary Weir	Gr. 5-12
High King's Daughter, by Theodora DuBois	Gr. 7-12
History of the Sword Coloring Book (Dover)	Various
Holy Roman Empire and Charlemagne in World History, by Jeff Sypeck	Gr. 10-12
Holy Twins, by Kathleen Norris	Gr. 2-4
Horn of Roland, by Jay Williams	Gr. 3-10
Houses, by Piero Ventura	Gr. 3-10
How Should We Then Live? by Francis Schaeffer [Book or video format]	Gr. 8-12
How Would You Survive the Middle Ages? by Fiona Macdonald	Gr. 3-7
Hundred Years' War, by William Lace	Gr. 7-12
Huzzah Means Hooray! by Laurie Carlson [Now titled *Days of Knights and D..*]	Various
I Wonder Why Castles Had Moats, by Philip Steele	Gr. 1-4
Ice Falcon, by Rita Ritchie	Gr. 6-12
Idylls of the King, by Alfred, Lord Tennyson	Gr. 11-12
If All the Swords in England, by Barbara Willard	Gr. 4-12
If You Lived in the Days of the Knights, by Ann McGovern	Gr. 2-5
Illuminated Alphabet Coloring Book	Various
Illuminations, by Jonathan Hunt	Gr. 1-5
Illustrated Book of Knights, by Jack Coggins	Gr. 3-7
Illustrated Encyclopedia of Costume and Fashion from 1066 to the Present by Jack Cassin-Scott [Some low-cut necklines]	Various
Importance of Charlemagne, by Timothy Biel	Gr. 6-12
In Freedom's Cause, by G.A. Henty	Gr. 7-12
In the Time of Knights, by Shelley Tanaka	Gr. 4-10
Incredible Explosions, by Richard Platt & Stephen Biesty	Gr. 4-12
Innocent Wayfaring, by Marchette Chute	Gr. 6-12
Invaders of Rome, by Bern Keating	Gr. 5-12
Invitation to the Classics, by Louise Cowan & Os Guinness	Gr. 8-12
Iron Charm, by Joanne Williamson	Gr. 6-12
Iron Lance, by Stephen Lawhead (Celtic Crusade)	Gr. 8-12
Islam, by Philip Wilkinson & Batul Salazar (Eyewitness)	Gr. 5-12
Island Story, by H.A. Marshall	Gr. 3-8
Isle of Glory, by Jane Oliver	Gr. 10-12
Ivanhoe, by Sir Walter Scott [Many versions/editions]	Various
Ivory Horn, by Ian Serraillier	Gr. 5-12
Jackaroo, by Cynthia Voight [See note]	Gr. 7-12
Jeanne d'Arc, by Aileen Fisher	Gr. 3-7
Joan of Arc, by Maurice Boutet de Monvel	Gr. 3-8
Joan of Arc, by Winston Churchill	Gr. 9-12
Joan of Arc, by Shana Corey (Step Into Reading 4)	Gr. 2-3
Joan of Arc, by Johanna Johnston	Gr. 3-7

Land Beyond, by Ruth Knight	Gr. 5-10
Lantern Bearers, by Rosemary Sutcliff	Gr. 7-12
Le Morte D'Arthur, by Sir Thomas Malory	Gr. 11-12
Lebek: A City of Northern Europe Through the Ages, by Xavier Hernandez	Gr. 4-12
Legend of the Cid, by Robert Goldston	Gr. 7-12
Legend of William Tell, by Terry Small	Gr. 1-8
Legends of the North, by Olivia Coolidge	Gr. 5-12
Leif Ericson: Explorer, by Ruth Weir (Makers of America)	Gr. 2-6
Leif Erikson the Lucky, by Frederic Kummer	Gr. 5-12
Leif the Lucky, by Ingri & Edgar Parin d'Aulaire	Gr. K-3
Leif the Lucky: Discoverer of America, by Erick Berry (Garrard Discovery)	Gr. 1-5
Leif's Saga, by Jonathan Hunt	Gr. K-3
Leonard of Pisa and the New Math of the Middle Ages, by Joseph & Frances Gies	Gr. 7-12
Leopards and Lilies, by Alfred Duggan [See note]	Gr. 8-12
Life in a Medieval Abbey, by Tony McAleavy	Unknown
Life in a Medieval Castle, by Tony McAleavy	Unknown
Life in a Medieval Castle and Village Coloring Book (Dover)	Various
Life in Celtic Times, by A.G. Smith & William Kaufman (Dover Coloring Bk)	Various
Life in the Middle Ages, by Jay Williams (Giant Landmark)	Gr. 6-12
Life in the Time of Harald Hardrada and the Vikings, by Peter Speed	Gr. 4-8
Life of Charlemagne, by Einhard	Gr. 11-12
Light Beyond the Forest, by Rosemary Sutcliff	Gr. 7-12
Light in the Shadow, by Ravi Zacharias	Gr. 10-12
Lion of St. Mark, by G.A. Henty	Gr. 7-12
Lionheart: Richard Coeur-de-Lion, by George Baker	Gr. 9-12
Lionhearted, by Charles Reznikoff	Gr. 9-12
Little Duke, by Charlotte Yonge	Gr. 5-12
Little Dusty Foot, by Marian Magoon	Gr. 4-10
Long Bows of Agincourt, by C. Norman	Gr. 6-12
Long Fall, by Penelope Wilcock	Gr. 9-12
Looking at History, by R.J. Unstead	Gr. 2-5
Lost Baron, by Allen French	Gr. 6-12
Lost Ruby, by Christoph Von Schmid (Lamplighter)	Gr. 3-10
Luttrell Village, by Sheila Sancha	Gr. 3-10
Macbeth, adapted by Leon Garfield [See note]	
Made in the Middle Ages, by Christine Price	Gr. 5-12
Magician's Apprentice, by Sidney Rosen [Not really about magic]	Gr. 4-12
Magna Carta, by C.W. Hodges	Gr. 4-9
Magna Charta, by James Daugherty (Landmark)	Gr. 5-12
Maid at King Alfred's Court, by Lucy Foster Madison	Gr. 4-12
Make This Model Castle (Usborne)	Various
Make This Model Town (Usborne)	Various
Make This Viking Settlement Cut Out Model (Usborne)	Various
Making of a Knight, by Patrick O'Brien	Gr. 1-4
Man Who Loved Books, by Jean Fritz	Gr. 1-6

Man with a Sword, by Henry Treece	Gr. 6-12
March on London, by G.A. Henty	Gr. 7-12
Marching to Jerusalem, by Ruth Holberg	Gr. 7-12
Marco Polo, by Gian Paolo Ceserani	Gr. 3-6
Marco Polo, by Charles Graves (Garrard World Explorer)	Gr. 1-5
Marco Polo, by Manuel Komroff (Messner)	Gr. 7-12
Marco Polo, by Kathleen McFarren (FactFinders)	Unknown
Marco Polo, by Struan Reid	Unknown
Marco Polo, by Robert Strathloch	Unknown
Marco Polo: A Journey through China, by Fiona Macdonald	Gr. 3-7
Marco Polo for Kids, by Janis Herbert [See note]	Various
Marco Polo: His Notebook, by Susan Roth	Gr. 3-12
Marguerite Makes a Book, by Bruce Robertson	Gr. 3-7
Marsh King, by C. Walter Hodges	Gr. 7-12
Marvellous Blue Mouse, by Christopher Manson	Gr. 1-4
Marvelous Misadventures of Sebastian, by Lloyd Alexander	Gr. 4-10
Mathematicians are People, Too: Vol. 2, by Luetta & Wilber Reimer	Gr. 3-8
Medieval Castle, by Harold Foster [Or any of the original *Prince Valiant* tales]	Gr. 1-6
Medieval Alphabet to Illuminate (Bellerophon)	Various
Medieval Castle, by Fiona Macdonald (Inside Story)	Gr. 3-10
Medieval Castle, by Don Nardo	Gr. 6-12
Medieval Cathedral, by Fiona Macdonald (Inside Story)	Gr. 3-10
Medieval Cats, by Susan Herbert	All ages
Medieval Cookbook, by Maggie Black	Various
Medieval Costumes Paper Dolls (Dover)	Various
Medieval Fashion (Dover)	Various
Medieval Feast, by Aliki	Gr. 1-4
Medieval Jousts and Tournaments Coloring Book (Dover)	Various
Medieval Knights, by David Nicolle (See Through History)	Gr. 4-9
Medieval Knights Paper Soldiers (Dover)	Various
Medieval Life, by Andrew Langley (DorlingKindersley)	Gr. 6-12
Medieval Monastery, by Fiona Macdonald (Inside Story)	Gr. 4-12
Medieval Town, by Daisy Kerr (Worldwise)	Gr. 3-7
Melor: King Arthur's Page, by Catherine Owens Peare	Gr. 5-12
Men in Armor, by Richard Suskind	Gr. 6-12
Men of Iron, by Howard Pyle	Gr. 6-12
Men of Iron, by Howard Pyle (Troll Illustrated Classics)	Gr. 2-6
Merlin, by Stephen Lawhead (Pendragon Cycle)	Gr. 9-12
Merry Adventures of Robin Hood, by Howard Pyle	Gr. 8-12
Merry Ever After, by Joe Lasker	Gr. 2-6
Message of St. Francis, edited by Sister Nan	Gr. 6-12
Messenger from K'itai, by D.R. Burleigh	Gr. 4-8

*Raising a Modern-Day Knight, by Robert Lewis	Parents
*Rare Benedictine, by Ellis Peters (Brother Cadfael Mysteries) [See note]	Gr. 9-12
Red Cape, by Rachel Varble	Gr. 5-12
Red Falcons of Tremoine, by Hendry Peart	Gr. 5-12
*Red Keep, by Allen French	Gr. 6-12
Red Towers of Granada, by Geoffrey Trease	Gr. 5-12
*Reluctant Dragon, by Kenneth Grahame	Gr. 2-6
Richard the Lionhearted, by W.N. Pittenger (Immortals of History)	Gr. 8-12
Ride into Danger, by Henry Treece	Gr. 9-12
Right Line of Cerdic, by Alfred Duggan	Gr. 9-12
Rival Cities, by M. Gregg Robinson	Gr. 9-12
*Road to Camlann, by Rosemary Sutcliff	Gr. 7-12
*Road to Damietta, by Scott O'Dell	Gr. 7-12
Road to Miklagard, by Henry Treece	Gr. 8-12
Robert Bruce: King of Scots, by Nina Brown Baker	Gr. 6-12
*Robin Hood, by Paul Creswick	Gr. 7-12
*Robin Hood, by J.W. McSpadden	Gr. 7-12
*Robin Hood and Little John, by Barbara Cohen	Gr. K-3
*Robin Hood of Sherwood Forest, by Ann McGovern	Gr. 3-10
Robin Hood Stories, by Edward Dolch	Gr. 1-3
Robin Hood's Arrow, by Eugenia Stone	Gr. 3-8
*Romanesque Art and Architecture, by Ana Martin	Gr. 4-12
*Rosa of Linden Castle, by Christoph Von Schmid (Lamplighter)	Gr. 3-10
Sailor Who Captured the Sea, by Deborah Lattimore	Gr. 1-4
Saint... [See also: St.]	
*Saint Francis, by Brian Wildsmith	Gr. K-3
*Saint Francis Celebrates Christmas, by Mary Walsh	Gr. 1-5
*Saint Francis of Assisi, by Mary Alves (Encounter the Saints)	Unknown
*Saint George and the Dragon, by Margaret Hodges	Gr. 2-6
*Saint Joan of Arc: God's Soldier, by Susan Wallace (Encounter the Saints)	Unknown
*Saint Julian, by Walter Wangerin, Jr.	Gr. 10-12
Saint Thomas Aquinas and the Preaching Beggars, by Brendan Larnen (Vision)	Gr. 7-12
*Saladin and the Kingdom of Jerusalem, by Lee Hancock	Unknown
*Saladin: Noble Prince of Islam, by Diane Stanley	Gr. 2-8
Saxon Britain, by Tony Triggs	Gr. 4-12
Saxon Villages, by Robin Place (Beginning History)	Gr. 2-5
*Scottish Chiefs, by Jane Porter, illus. by N.C. Wyeth	Gr. 8-12
Secret Beyond the Mountains, by Rita Ritchie	Gr. 7-12
Secret Fiord, by Geoffrey Trease	Gr. 7-12
Seven Kings of England, by Geoffrey Trease	Gr. 4-10
*Shakespeare's Stories, Vol. 1, by Leon Garfield	Parental decision
Shield Ring, by Rosemary Sutcliff	Gr. 8-12
Shuttle and Sword, by Hawthorne Daniel	Gr. 5-12
Sign of the Green Falcon, by Cynthia Harnett	Gr. 5-12
Sigurd & His Brave Companions, by Sigrid Undset	Gr. 4-12

Silk Route, by John Major	Gr. 2-8
Simple Prince, by Jane Yolen	Gr. K-3
Singing Windows, by Mary Young	Gr. 3-12
Sir Dana: A Knight, by Dana Fradon	Gr. 3-9
**Sir Gawain and the Green Knight*, by J.R.R. Tolkien	Gr. 7-12
Sir Kevin of Devon, by Adelaide Holl	Gr. 1-4
So Young a Queen, by Lois Mills	Gr. 8-12
Son of Charlemagne, by Barbara Willard	Gr. 4-10
Son of the Land, by Ivy Bolton	Gr. 5-12
Song of Roland, by Eleanor Clark (Legacy)	Gr. 2-8
Song of Roland, by Robert & Marguerite Goldston	Gr. 9-12
**Song of Roland*, by Dorothy Sayers	Gr. 9-12
Sons of the Steppe, by Hans Baumann	Gr. 8-12
Snorri and the Strangers, by Nathaniel Benchley (History I Can Read)	Gr. 1-3
Squire for King Arthur, by Eugenia Stone	Gr. 2-7
St. Benedict, by Mary Fabyan Windeatt (Vision)	Gr. 4-12
St. Catherine of Siena, by Mary Fabyan Windeatt	Gr. 5-12
St. Francis, by Pelagie Doane	Gr. 3-8
**St. Francis of Assisi*, by G.K. Chesterton	Gr. 10-12
**St. Francis of Assisi: The Happiest Man Who Ever Lived*, by Robert Kennedy	Unknown
**St. George for England*, by G.A. Henty	Gr. 7-12
St. Joan, the Girl Solider, by Louis de Wohl (Vision)	Gr. 4-12
St. Louis and the Last Crusade, by Margaret Hubbard (Vision)	Gr. 4-12
**St. Thomas Aquinas*, by G.K. Chesterton	Gr. 10-12
St. Thomas Aquinas: The Story of the Dumb Ox, by Mary Fabyan Windeatt	Gr. 5-12
Star and the Sword, by Pam Melnikoff	Gr. 4-12
**Step Into the Celtic World*, by Fiona Macdonald	Gr. 6-10
**Stories from Shakespeare*, by Marchette Chute	Gr. 6-12
**Stories of Charlemagne*, by Jennifer Westwood	Gr. 7-12
Stories of Famous Sea Fights, by Frank Knight	Gr. 4-12
Stories of the Norsemen, by Johanna Johnston	Gr. 2-7
Story of a Castle, by John S. Goodall	Gr. PreK-2
Story of Britain, by R.J. Unstead	Gr. 5-12
Story of Elswyth, by Eileen Meyler	Gr. 8-12
Story of Henry V, by L. DuGarde Peach (Ladybird)	Gr. 3-8
Story of Joan of Arc, by Jeannette Covert Nolan (Signature)	Gr. 3-8
**Story of King Arthur and His Knights*, by Howard Pyle	Gr. 9-12
Story of Knights and Armor, by Ernest Tucker	Gr. 4-12
Story of Leif Ericson, by William O. Steele (Signature)	Gr. 3-9
**Story of Liberty*, by Charles Coffin	Gr. 5-12
Story of Marco Polo, by Olive Price (Signature)	G. 3-8
**Story of Roland*, by James Baldwin	Gr. 6-12
Story of Rolf and the Viking Bow, by Allen French	Gr. 5-12
Story of Siegfried, by James Baldwin	Gr. 8-12

Treasure Chest: Knights	Various
Treasure of Siegfried, by E.M. Almedingen	Gr. 5-12
Trial and Triumph: Stories from Church History, by Richard Hannula	Gr. 5-12
Troubadour, by René Guillot	Gr. 4-12
True Book of Knights, by John Lewellen (True Books)	Gr. K-2
True Princess, by Angela Hunt	Gr. K-4
Truth about Castles, by Gillian Clements	Gr. 1-5
Truthful Harp, by Lloyd Alexander	Gr. 2-6
Turn in the Road, by Cateau DeLeeuw	Gr. 6-12
Twelve Bright Trumpets, by Margaret Leighton	Gr. 4-12
Twelve Great Philosophers, by Howard Ozman	Gr. 3-8
Two Travelers, by Christopher Manson	Gr. 1-4
Under the Influence, by Alvin Schmidt	Gr. 9-12
Unveiling Islam, by Ergun & Emir Caner	Gr. 11-12
(Usborne) Time Traveller Book of Viking Raiders, by Civardi/Graham-Campbell	Gr. 3-7
(Usborne) Time Traveller Knights & Castles, by Judy Hindley	Gr. 4-8
Venetians: Merchant Princes, by Thomas Chubb	Gr. 9-12
Venice: Birth of a City, by Piero Ventura	Gr. 3-9
Viking, by Susan Margeson (Eyewitness)	Gr. 5-12
Viking Adventure, by Clyde Robert Bulla	Gr. 1-5
Viking Explorers, by Walter Buehr	Gr. 3-10
Viking Explorers, by Luigi Pruneti	Gr. 3-7
Viking Explorers, by Rupert Mathews (Beginning History)	Gr. 2-6
Viking Longboats, by Margaret Mulvihill	Gr. 3-7
Viking Longship, by Lynda Trent	Unknown
Viking Ships to Cut Out & Put Together (Bellerophon)	Various
Viking Times, by Antony Mason (If You Were There)	Gr. 4-7
Viking Town, by Jacqueline Morley (Metropolis)	Gr. 4-7
Vikings Treasure Chest	Various
Viking Warriors, by Tony Triggs	Gr. 4-10
Viking World, by Julie Ferris (Sightseers)	Gr. 4-9
Vikings, by Gillian Chapman (Crafts from the Past)	Various
Vikings, edited by John D. Clare (Living History)	Gr. 4-12
Vikings, by Elizabeth Janeway (Landmark)	Gr. 4-10
Vikings, by Kate Petty	Gr. K-2
Viking's Dawn, by Henry Treece	Gr. 8-12
Viking's Sunset, by Henry Treece	Gr. 8-12
Voyage to Coromandel, by Margaret Leighton	Gr. 6-12
Voyagers West, by Margaret Johansen	Gr. 6-12
Walter Dragun's Town, by Sheila Sancha	Gr. 4-10
Ward of King Canute, by Ottilie Liljencrantz	Gr. 8-12
We Were There with Richard the Lionheart at the Crusades, by Robert Webb	Gr. 3-8

*What Will You See Inside a Mosque, by Aisha Khan	Gr. 3-6
*Whatever Happened to Penny Candy? by Richard Maybury	Gr. 5-12
When Knights Were Bold, by Eva March Tappan	Gr. 6-12
Where Valor Lies, by Adele & Cateau DeLeeuw	Gr. 5-12
*Whipping Boy, by Sid Fleischman	Gr. 2-8
*White Company, by Sir Arthur Conan Doyle	Gr. 5-12
*White Dove, by Christoph Von Schmid (Lamplighter)	Gr. 3-10
*White Stag, by Kate Seredy	Gr. 4-10
William Tell, by Margaret Early	Gr. 1-6
*William Tell, by Leonard Everett Fisher	Gr. 2-7
William Tell, by Katharine Scherman (Legacy Books)	Gr. 3-8
*William the Conqueror, by Hilaire Belloc	Gr. 8-12
William the Conqueror, by Thomas Costain (Landmark)	Gr. 3-8
William the Conqueror, by Elizabeth Luckock	Gr. 6-12
William the Conqueror, by L. DuGarde Peach (Ladybird)	Gr. 2-6
Winning His Spurs, by G.A. Henty [Also titled Boy Knight and Fighting the Sar...]	Gr. 7-12
*Wolf of Gubbio, by Michael Bedard	Gr. 3-6
*Wonder Clock, by Howard Pyle	Gr. 4-12
Work of St. Francis, by MacKinlay Kantor	Gr. 4-8
*World in the Time of Charlemagne, by Fiona Macdonald	Gr. 6-12
*World of the Medieval Knight, by Christopher Gravett	Gr. 6-12
World of Marco Polo, by Walter Buehr	Gr. 3-8
*Wounds of God, by Penelope Wilcock	Gr. 9-12
*Wulf the Saxon, by G.A. Henty	Gr. 7-12
Year of the Horse, by Rita Ritchie	Gr. 7-12
Yellow Hat, by Nancy Faulkner	Gr. 7-12
*Yo, Vikings! by Judith Schachner [See note]	Gr. 1-3
*You Wouldn't Want to Be a Medieval Knight, by Fiona Macdonald	Unknown
Young Alfred the Great, by Naomi Mitchison	Gr. 7-12
Young Geoffrey Chaucer, by Regina Kelly	Gr. 7-12
Young Man with a Sword, by Jane Oliver	Gr. 9-12
Young People's Story of Architecture: 3,000BC-Gothic, by Hillyer & Huey	Gr. 2-8
Young People's Story of Fine Art: 15,000BC-1,800AD, by Hillyer & Huey	Gr. 2-8
Young People's Story of Sculpture, by Hillyer & Huey	Gr. 2-8
Young Robert Bruce, by Jane Oliver	Gr. 7-12

General Resources, cited frequently, but not required:

*Birthdays of Freedom: Vol. 2, by Genevieve Foster	Gr. 2-5
Child's History of Art, by V.M. Hillyer & E.G. Huey	Gr. 2-8
(Or, reissues titled Young People's Story of....)	
*Child's History of the World, by V.M. Hillyer	Gr. 1-4
Dark Ages, by Isaac Asimov	Gr. 8-12
*Famous Men of the Middle Ages, by Greenleaf	Gr. 3-7
*Famous Men of the Renaissance & Reformation (Greenleaf)	Gr. 3-7
Fire Upon the Earth, by Norman Langford	Gr. 4-10

How Should We Then Live? by Francis Schaeffer [Book or video format]	Gr. 8-12
**Island Story*, by H.E. Marshall	Gr. 3-8
Looking at History, by R.J. Unstead	Gr. 2-5
Middle Ages, by Dorothy Mills	Gr. 6-12
**Middle Ages: Cultural Atlas for Young People*, by Mike Corbishley	Gr. 3-10
No Other Foundation: The Church Through Twenty Centuries, by Jeremy Jackson	Gr. 11-12
Story of Britain, by R.J. Unstead	Gr. 5-12
**Story of Liberty*, by Charles Coffin	Gr. 5-12
**Story of the Middle Ages*, by Christine Miller & H.A. Guerber	Gr. 4-8
**Story of the World: Volume 2*, by Susan Wise Bauer	Gr. 3-6
**Trial and Triumph: Stories from Church History*, by Richard Hannula	Gr. 5-12

Audio/Video:

**Adventures of Robin Hood*, starring Errol Flynn

**Brother Sun, Sister Moon*, about the life of St. Francis [See note]

**Castle*, by David Macaulay

**Cathedral*, by David Macaulay

**Crusades*, old classic produced by Cecil B. DeMille

**El Cid*, starring Charlton Heston

**Inspector General*, a very funny film starring Danny Kaye

**Ivanhoe*, starring James Mason

**Ivanhoe*, starring Robert Taylor & Elizabeth Taylor

**Joan of Arc*, older version starring Ingrid Bergman

**John Wycliffe: The Morning Star*

**King Arthur and His Knights*, told by Jim Weiss, esteemed storyteller

**Lady Godiva*, starring Maureen O'Hara is appropriately done [not like photo on cover]

**Robin Hood*, animated version [in one scene, Robin poses as fortune-teller as a plot device]

**Story of Robin Hood*, nice, older Disney film, starring Richard Todd

This booklist is only for those persons who have already purchased the companion *TruthQuest History* guide.

Bibliography

Asimov, Isaac. *The Dark Ages*. Boston: Houghton Mifflin, 1968.

Coffin, Charles. *The Story of Liberty*. Gainesville, FL: Maranatha Publications, 1987.

Cowan, Louise and Os Guinness. *Invitation to the Classics*. Grand Rapids, MI: Baker Books, 1998.

Foster, Genevieve. *Birthdays of Freedom: Volume 2*. New York: Charles Scribner's Sons, 1952.

Greene, Carol. *Beggars, Beasts and Easter Fire: Stories of Early Saints*. Batavia, IL: Lion Publishing, 1993.

Grun, Bernard. *The Timetables of History*. New York: Touchstone Book, published by Simon & Schuster, 1991.

Haaren, John and A.B. Poland; edited by Cynthia & Robert Shearer. *Famous Men of the Middle Ages*. Lebanon, TN: Greenleaf Press, 1992.

Hannula, Richard. *Trial and Triumph: Stories from Church History*. Moscow, ID: Canon Press, 1999.

Hotchkiss, Jeanette. *European Historical Fiction for Children and Young People*. Metuchen, NJ: Scarecrow Press, 1967.

Houghton, S.M. *Sketches from Church History*. Carlisle, PA: Banner of Truth Trust, 1980.

Jackson, Jeremy. *No Other Foundation: The Church Through Twenty Centuries*. Westchester, Illinois: Cornerstone Books, 1980.

Langford, Norman. *Fire Upon the Earth*. Philadelphia: Westminster Press, 1950. (Ignore last chapter.)

Marshall, H.E. *An Island Story*. New York: Frederick A. Stokes, 1920.

Metzner, Seymour. *World History in Juvenile Books*. New York: H.W. Wilson, 1973.

Miller, Christine and H.A. Guerber. *The Story of the Middle Ages*. Fort Collins, CO: Nothing New Press, 2002.

Moffett, Samuel Hugh. *A History of Christianity in Asia: Volume 1*. San Francisco: HarperCollins, 1992.

Ridenour, Fritz. *So What's the Difference?* Glendale, CA: GL Regal Books, 1979.

Schaeffer, Francis. *How Should We Then Live?* Old Tappan, New Jersey: Fleming H. Revell, 1976.

Seward, Desmond. *The Hundred Years War.* New York: Atheneum, 1978.

Shippen, Katharine B. *Leif Eriksson: First Voyager to America.* New York: Harper and Brothers, 1951.

Syme, Ronald. *Invaders and Invasions.* New York: W.W. Norton, 1964.

Unstead, R.J. *The Story of Britain.* Camden, New Jersey: Thomas Nelson, 1969.

_____. *Heroes and Saints.* London: Carousel Books, 1964.

Webster's Biographical Dictionary. Springfield, Massachusetts: G. & C. Merriam, 1943.

Webster's New Collegiate Dictionary. Springfield, Massachusetts: G. & C. Merriam, 1977.

Westwood, Jennifer. *Stories of Charlemagne.* New York: S.G. Phillips, 1972.